READING STEPHEN SONDHEIM

STUDIES IN MODERN DRAMA
VOLUME 10
GARLAND REFERENCE LIBRARY OF THE HUMANITIES
VOLUME 2065

STUDIES IN MODERN DRAMA
KIMBALL KING, *Series Editor*

Reading Stephen Sondheim

A Collection of Critical Essays

Edited and with an introduction by
Sandor Goodhart

Garland Publishing, Inc.
a member of the Taylor & Francis Group
New York & London
2000

Published in 2000 by
Garland Publishing, Inc.
A member of the Taylor & Francis Group
19 Union Square West
New York, NY 10003

Copyright © 2000 by Sandor Goodhart

10 9 8 7 6 5 4 3 2 1

Library of Congress Cataloging-in-Publication Data
Reading Stephen Sondheim : a collection of critical essays / edited by
　　Sandor Goodhart.
　　　　　p.　　cm. — (Garland reference library of the humanities ; vol.
　　2065. Studies in ethnic art ; vol. 10)
　　　ISBN 0-8153-2832-X (alk. paper)
　　　1. Sondheim, Stephen—Criticism and interpretation. 2. Musicals—
United States—History and criticism. I. Goodhart, Sandor.
II. Series: Garland reference library of the humanities : vol.
2065. III. Series: Garland reference library of the humanities.
Studies in modern drama ; v. 10.
ML410.S6872R4　　1998
782.1'4'092—dc21　　　　　　　　　　　　　　　　98-44434
　　　　　　　　　　　　　　　　　　　　　　　　　　CIP
　　　　　　　　　　　　　　　　　　　　　　　　　　MN

Cover photograph of Stephen Sondheim by Michael Le Poer Trench.

Printed on acid-free, 250-year-life paper
Manufactured in the United States of America

READING STEPHEN SONDHEIM

To my mother
Evelyn Love Goodhart,
who introduced me to
the pleasures of musical comedy

Somebody let me come through.
—Stephen Sondheim, *Company*

I'm the fragment underneath!
—Stephen Sondheim, *Pacific Overtures*

Contents

PART 2: PLAYS

General Editor's Note

Several times Garland Publishing, Inc., has experienced such an overwhelmingly positive response to a Casebook on a particular author that readers have requested another volume covering different aspects of the same work. Hence Lois Gordon's *Harold Pinter: A Casebook* (1990) was followed by Penelope Prentice's *The Pinter Ethic: The Erotic Perspective* (1994), and Leslie Kane's *David Mamet: A Casebook* (1992) was complemented by Kane's single-volume study of a major Mamet play, *Glengarry Glen Ross: A Casebook* (1996). Soon there will be new books on August Wilson and John Osborne, which will supplement our previous Casebook Studies.

It is not surprising that a playwright/musician as accomplished as Stephen Sondheim would cause our readers to demand additional coverage of his *oeuvre.* Joanne Gordon's *Stephen Sondheim: A Casebook* (1977) stimulated interest in a second Sondheim volume. Hence, Sandor Goodhart's *Reading Stephen Sondheim: The End of Ever After* will present fresh essays on literary issues raised by Sondheim's contributions. A dozen distinguished critics have explored Sondheim's "musicals" in relation to other more traditional works in that theater genre. The modernist and postmodern aspects of the author's plays are explored, as are a variety of approaches to his work, including deconstruction, Lacanian theory, Freudian and Jungian interpretations, gay and lesbian accounts of gender relations, Marxism, and more traditional formalist and thematic methodologies used by Americanists, Comparatists, and students of dramatic literature in general. The individual essays respond to a growing need for in-depth analysis of one of the twentieth century's more important artists.

Sandor Goodhart, perhaps best known for his distinguished Johns Hopkins University Press volume, *Sacrificing Commentary: Reading the End of Literature* (1996), is Professor of English and Director of Jewish Studies at

Purdue University. He offers new and exciting approaches to Sondheim's musical dramas and reveals the ways in which they illuminate contemporary American culture.

Kimball King

Preface and Acknowledgments

SANDOR GOODHART

This book is an attempt to treat Stephen Sondheim's work seriously within the academy. My claim is that his work warrants being read with as much care as we read that of Arthur Miller, Eugene O'Neill, Tennessee Williams, Edward Albee, and other writers of dramatic literature we prize as "first-rate." Musical theater is an American invention. Sondheim's lyrical work in this field is the best there is. It is intellectual, analytic, funny, cynical, moving, adult, and above all, deeply thoughtful. It constitutes a sustained critical commentary on how we live our lives in America and especially how we make musical theater. One would think that attention would be paid.

Other books on Sondheim have been written. Craig Zadan, Joanne Gordon, Martin Gottfried, and Stephen Banfield, have all written fine and important volumes.[1] But none of these volumes have inspired the kind of full-fledged literary critical assessment afforded our other great writers. Two new books have appeared within the last two years—a biography by Meryle Secrest and a casebook on Sondheim edited by Joanne Gordon.[2] Perhaps the current volume along with these others will help to inaugurate a change in attitude toward his work and gain a new serious critical consideration for it long overdue.

Completing this book is completing a debt to myself made some time before my academic career. My mother used to take me in the 1950s to the Schubert Theater in Philadelphia to see the tryouts of new musical comedies before they made their way to Boston and ultimately to Broadway. Rodgers and Hammerstein musicals were the major attraction, but we also saw the works of Meredith Willson, Frank Loesser, Lerner and Loewe and many others. We devoured these shows. We saw whatever came through—in the original New York production, or early touring companies. We bought the original cast recordings, saw the movie versions (often in disappointing adaptations), bought (and played and sang) the vocal selections, and eagerly awaited the coming season.

I was hooked. The peculiar combination of acting, singing, and dancing before elaborate sets, intricate lighting and sound arrangements, and a live orchestra—in modes that ranged from tragedy to comedy to melodrama (sometimes in the same scene)—was mesmerizing. The pleasure was not an intellectual one but something else. Looking back upon it, I think it was probably akin to the pleasure we derive from myths. We were part of the baby-boomer generation. Television was in its early stages. The movies employed much more realistic treatments. But on the musical stage, imagination was given free reign and we were able to enjoy the stories of romantic love and happy endings—boy meets girl, boy loses girl, boy gets girl—in an endless variety of settings and registers. While straight plays were bringing us the theater of the absurd—Sartre, Camus, Anouilh, Beckett, Albee, Pinter, etc.— musical comedies were assuring us that everything would work out.

Was it escapist? Is *No Exit* or *Endgame* a more appropriate response to Nazism and the threat of nuclear annihilation? Perhaps. Rodgers and Hammerstein probably dealt with issues like slavery, regionalism, racism, Nazism, and gender relations in as forthright a manner as these other plays, although they always allowed the resolutions (and especially romantic love) to overtake the difficulties they raised. Probably because of these resolutions it has been fashionable to be disdainful of these plays and their probings as less than serious endeavors. But if we are interested in cultural studies, and interested in particular in understanding America at a certain moment of its history, we can probably do little better than turn to these stylized productions that for twenty years solved all our problems.

In any event, it was a nurturing experience and I indulged while it lasted. When I got to the university in 1964, I put it away with all other such "childish things."

Then along came Stephen Sondheim. I had been aware of Sondheim's name through its association with *West Side Story*, *Gypsy*, and *A Funny Thing Happened on the Way to the Forum*. But in the 1970s, *Company*, *Follies*, and *A Little Night Music* introduced something entirely new to the Broadway stage. I realized that what he was up to was nothing less than a full-blown critique of musical comedy as a genre. Here was our first intellectual practitioner of the craft. *Company* specifically challenged all of the myths of marriage and happy endings Rodgers and Hammerstein's plays endorsed. *Follies* continued the challenge into the genre itself. The entire history of the American musical stage—from Sigmund Romberg and Victor Herbert to George Gershwin and Cole Porter to Sondheim's immediate mentors and predecessors—was brought into focus in what was in essence a staged funeral. *A Little Night Music* continued the foray into established genres—drawing upon Ingmar Bergman's highly literary film, *Smiles of a Summer Night*, as a touchstone.

And then he was off and running. *Pacific Overtures* musicalized an invasion of a Japanese island in the nineteenth century by a US naval commander.

Sweeney Todd set to music the grand guignol story of a serial killer. *Sunday in the Park with George* constituted itself as a talking and singing painting. *Merrily We Roll Along* put personal friendships and the kinds of business and social interactions that surround the mounting of a Broadway production onto center stage within a framework that moved backward in time. *Into the Woods* reread children's fairy tales from distinctly adult and more cynical perspectives. *Assassins* sang the praises one could muster to those who have attempted to murder our political leaders. And *Passion* registered the opportunities for unconditional love relations available between a handsome man and an unattractive woman who has been stalking him.

Not on the surface your customary musical comedy themes! These works challenged the myths of romantic love and its happy endings in virtually every context in which it had earlier been conceived. But they did more than that. They brought into question the contexts in which these myths were invoked: their origins, their strategies, their costs. They allowed us, in short, to "read" these myths where earlier productions had really only allowed us to enact them. They opened us to the possibility of interpreting this material in ways that connected it with the most thoughtful writing of our time. That Sondheim has continued in these plays (and numerous contributions to other cinematic and vocal projects) to reinvent himself, and to reinvent the genre in which he has worked, remains a tribute to one of the most extraordinary artistic itineraries of our era.

The introduction and twelve essays collected all submit Sondheim's work to the scrutiny of literary criticism. All of the contributors are academicians. All teach in English or other literature departments, although some also work in theater arts and other humanities departments. I have encouraged the use of a critical apparatus and of theoretical methodologies (psychoanalytic, Marxist, formalist, deconstructionist, etc.), and I have designed the book with classroom use in mind. The first six essays concentrate on themes, sources, and institutions that are important to Sondheim's plays, and the second six concentrate on specific plays.

I have encouraged interest within the profession in Sondheim's writing for a number of years, and I invite others to do the same. I convened the first session of the Modern Language Association Convention on Stephen Sondheim's work in December 1993.[3] Versions of the papers from that session were printed soon after in an issue of *Ars Lyrica*.[4] I taught a course on Sondheim's work at the Cornell Adult University in the summer of 1993, and worked the following spring on the first issue of *The Sondheim Review* as its Associate Editor.[5] I moderated a second academic meeting on Sondheim, a special session of the Modern Language Association Convention December 1995, and printed an abbreviated version of my paper in the Atlanta-based periodical, *Jezebel Magazine*.[6] Courses should continue to be taught in literature (as well as music and theater arts) departments on Sondheim's work.

Conferences should continue to be held. And Sondheim should continue to be invited to participate. If we don't read his commentary seriously now, to mix and match some statements attributed to an ancient Jewish sage, when shall we do so?

A number of individuals have played a role in bringing this book to fruition, and I would like to thank them and to acknowledge gratefully their contribution. Kimball King, the general editor for Casebooks on Modern Dramatists at Garland, encouraged me in this project from the outset. He assisted in innumerable ways at times when it seemed as if the project might not happen. Phyllis Korper, the editor at Garland when my contract was signed, was equally kind and supportive. Kristi Long (and her assistant, Becca Mac-Laren) guided the project along when Garland became part of the Taylor and Francis Group. More recently, James Morgan (senior editor), Mia Zamora (his assistant editor), and Alexis Skinner (the production editor)—who joined the staff when Garland merged with Routledge—have encouraged me and been exceedingly generous with their time and effort. Finally, Tom Adler, a professor and head of the English Department at Purdue University, a teacher of dramatic literature himself, and a kindred spirit with regard to Sondheim's work, has taken every opportunity to support me in this project. He generously offered his own fine essay for inclusion, and assisted me in innumerable small ways at every stage. The book is a significantly better one for his participation in it.

I would also like to thank especially Stephen Sondheim, in the first instance for suggesting Michael Le Poer Trench's wonderful photograph of him (which now adorns the book's cover), but more generally for his interest in the project, for taking the time from his busy schedule to read the manuscript in its entirely, for offering helpful comments about technical and factual issues, and for sharing his reflections upon matters of interpretation and production history. I hope the book does him honor.

My greatest debt, however, is to Suzanne McAuliffe. I met Suzanne as my student in the course I taught on Sondheim's musicals at the Cornell Adult University in the summer of 1993, and we remained friends and co-Sondheim *aficionados* ever since. When the plans for doing this book were finalized, I immediately asked her to assist me with the editorial process and she has done a magnificent job. She has guided me through the tricky waters of a project such as this one in more ways than one. She has attended to endless details and spent countless hours in the library, at the computer, and going over the text with me in ways that stretched her family's hospitality to the limit. To Suzanne and to her family—Kevin, Claire, and Will—my debt of gratitude is profound.

The following individuals and organizations have granted me permission to reproduce portions of the work to which they hold the rights, and that permission is hereby gratefully acknowledged. I thank Michael Le Poer Trench for permission to use the cover photograph of Stephen Sondheim. For the use of extended quotations from *Anyone Can Whistle,* music and lyrics by Stephen Sondheim. © 1964 (renewed 1992) by Stephen Sondheim. Burthen Music Company, Inc., owner of publication and allied rights for the World. Chappell and Co., sole selling agent. Used by permission. For the use of extended quotations from *Assassins,* music and lyrics by Stephen Sondheim. © 1988 by Rilting Music, Inc., all rights administered by WB Music Corp. Used by permission. For the use of extended quotations from *Company,* music and lyrics by Stephen Sondheim. © 1970 by Rilting Music, Inc. and Herald Square Music. All rights on behalf of Rilting Music, Inc. administered by WB Music Corp. Used by permission. For the use of extended quotations from *Follies,* music and lyrics by Stephen Sondheim. © 1971 by Rilting Music, Inc., Burthen Music Company, Inc., and Herald Square Music. All rights on behalf of Rilting Music, Inc. administered by WB Music Corp. Used by permission. For the use of extended quotations from *A Funny Thing Happened on the Way to the Forum,* music and lyrics by Stephen Sondheim. © 1962 (renewed 1990) by Stephen Sondheim. Burthen Music Company, Inc., owner of publication and allied rights for the World. Chappell & Co., sole selling agent. Used by permission. For the use of extended quotations from *Into the Woods,* music and lyrics by Stephen Sondheim. ©1987. Rilting Music, Inc., all rights administered by WB Music Corp. Used by permission. For the use of extended quotations from *A Little Night Music,* music and lyrics by Stephen Sondheim. © 1973 by Rilting Music, Inc., all rights administered by WB Music Corp. Used by permission. For the use of extended quotations from *Merrily We Roll Along,* music and lyrics by Stephen Sondheim. © 1981 by Rilting Music, Inc., all rights administered by WB Music Corp. Used by permission. For the use of extended quotations from *Pacific Overtures,* music and lyrics by Stephen Sondheim. © 1981 by Rilting Music, Inc., all rights administered by WB Music Corp. Used by permission. For the use of extended quotations from *Passion,* music and lyrics by Stephen Sondheim. © 1994 by Rilting Music, Inc., all rights administered by WB Music Corp. Used by permission. For the use of extended quotations from *Sunday in the Park with George,* music and lyrics by Stephen Sondheim. © 1984, 1985. Rilting Music, Inc., all rights administered by WB Music Corp. Used by permission. For the use of extended quotations from *Sweeney Todd,* music and lyrics by Stephen Sondheim. © 1979. Rilting Music, Inc., all rights administered by WB Music Corp. Used by permission.

NOTES

[1] See Zadan 1994, Gordon 1992, Gottfried 1993, and Banfield 1993.

[2] See Secrest 1998 and Gordon 1997.

[3] The meeting, "'Happily Ever After': The Criticism of Stephen Sondheim," was convened as a Special Session of the Modern Language Association Convention in Toronto, in December, 1993. Ann Marie McEntee, Kay Young and Allen Menton read

Contributors

THOMAS P. ADLER is Professor and Head of English at Purdue University, where he teaches modern dramatic literature. Among his several books are *Mirror on the Stage: the Pulitzer Plays as an Approach to American Drama* (West Lafayette, IN: Purdue University Press, 1987), *"A Streetcar Named Desire": The Moth and the Lantern* (Boston: Twayne Publishers, 1990), and *American Drama 1940–1960: A Critical History* (New York: Twayne; Toronto, Canada: Maxwell Macmillan International, 1994). He has also written numerous articles and book chapters, including, most recently, essays in the Cambridge Companion volumes on Miller, Williams, and American Women Playwrights.

SANDOR GOODHART is an Associate Professor of English and the Director of the Jewish Studies Program at Purdue University. He is the author of *Sacrificing Commentary: Reading the End of Literature* (Baltimore: Johns Hopkins University Press, 1996), and numerous essays on dramatic literature, literary theory and criticism, the Hebrew Bible, and modern Jewish philosophy. He has been fascinated with musical comedy since childhood.

SHOSHANA MILGRAM KNAPP is an Associate Professor of English at Virginia Tech and the author of numerous articles on nineteenth- and twentieth-century figures, including Dostoyevsky, Hugo, Ayn Rand, George Eliot, Tolstoy, George Sand, E. L. Voynich, Victoria Cross, and Napoleon.

JOSEPH MARCHESANI is an Assistant Professor of Integrative Arts for The Penn State University at McKeesport. He has published essays on gender identity in science fiction and the uses of science fiction in teaching technological literacy. His interest in Sondheim has developed through a class that he teaches on the popular arts, which includes musical theater.

ANN MARIE MCENTEE is an Assistant Professor of Communication Arts at Allegheny College. She has published several articles and reviews about Stephen Sondheim and early twentieth-century American theatre. Her interest in the Ziegfeld Follies led her to explore Sondheim's treatment of that theatrical art form.

ALLEN MENTON, Ph.D., is a composer living and working in the Los Angeles area. His works have been performed on both the East and West coasts, and he is currently working on a musical adaptation of Henry James' novel *The Ambassadors.* In the summer of 1993, he taught a course on Stephen Sondheim for Cornell University's summer Adult University Program, together with Professor Sandor Goodhart.

FRANCIS R. OLLEY is a Professor of English and Performing Arts at St. Joseph's University in Philadelphia, Pennsylvania, where he teaches in the Department of English and the Department of Fine and Performing Arts. He is also the Director of the University Theatre. He has published *Romantic Elements in the Plays of Thomas Middleton* (University Microfilms, 1965) and numerous articles on Renaissance drama and modern theatre. He has always found Stephen Sondheim, whether working alone or in collaboration, as most reminiscent of the greatness of early seventeenth-century threatre.

PAUL M. PUCCIO is an Assistant Professor of English and Humanities at York College of Pennsylvania. His interests include Victorian literature and culture, film and literature, and narratives of school and college experience. He has published in *Modern Language Studies, Dickens Quarterly, Family Matters in the British and American Novel* (Popular Press, 1997), and *The Sondheim Review.*

SCOTT F. STODDART is an Associate Professor of Liberal Arts and Humanities at Nova Southeastern University. He is the author of *Prescriptive Lens: The "Spectacle" of the Gay Male Image in Hollywood Cinema* (soon to be released from University of Illinois, 1999) and editor of *Telling Tales: Fictive Visions and Filmic Revisions,* a two-volume anthology of essays on film adaptations of fiction (no publisher signed yet). He has published numerous essays on the work of Henry James, F. Scott Fitzgerald, E. M. Forster, Stephen Crane, the plays of Stephen Sondheim, and the films of Martin Scorsese, Jane Campion, Anthony Minghella.

KAY YOUNG is Assistant Professor of English at the University of California, Santa Barbara. She has written essays on Hollywood romantic comedy, the male/female team comedy, Kierkegaard, and is completing a manuscript on couples, conversation, and comedy in fiction and film. Kay was raised on the music of Sondheim, and finds it "easy" to hum (something like whistling).

INTRODUCTION

READING SONDHEIM:
THE END OF EVER AFTER

INTRODUCTION

Reading Sondheim
The End of Ever After
Sandor Goodhart

In 1978, Thomas Adler wrote that Stephen Sondheim is "the single most important force in the American musical theater" today.[1] The ten major productions to which he has contributed are "among those works for the American stage that can be said to have not only artistic merit but a literary value as well."[2] The "American musical theater has him to thank today for 'being alive,' and what is more, for being *adult*."[3]

Adler's judgements were rendered six years before Sondheim had written with James Lapine the play for which he won a Pulitzer Prize, and in a context in which Sondheim's work was underappreciated.[4] Earlier in the decade, audiences had left his plays before they were half through. His tunes were considered unhummable. Theater critics were divided over his work (some embraced his innovations, others lamented the lack of more traditional forms), but among the theater-going public his writing was generally considered clever and intelligent but cold.[5] And it had become an adage among Broadway and off Broadway investors that a Sondheim play never made money.[6] Writing at the end of the 1970s, Adler was among the first to defend the literary value of Sondheim's work and suggest that he be regarded among writers like Eugene O'Neill, Arthur Miller, Edward Albee, Tennessee Williams, and others who make up the modern and postmodern American dramatic tradition.[7]

Twenty years later, little if anything has changed. Sondheim has now some sixteen projects to his credit (not counting the numerous musical anthologies that have been produced from his work or the many movies he has scored). He has won an unprecedented number of awards and accolades. He is regarded as a lyricist's lyricist on Broadway (to whom new young artists routinely turn for advice).[8] His musical dramas are performed more than those of any other lyricist or composer in the field. His group of admirers has grown to a cult following. And yet the appearance of a new Sondheim musi-

3

cal on Broadway is still capable of drawing venom from major critics, a Sondheim project still breaks even at best, and within the academy his work still remains largely unnoticed.[9]

What is going on? Why has Sondheim's work eluded serious academic treatment? One reason, no doubt, that his work has not proved as viable commercially as that of other less talented artists concerns the way in which American culture (and Broadway as it is part of that culture) works. As a rule, repetition is the order of the day. If a movie named *Rocky* or *Beverly Hills Cop* proves successful, it is assumed that multiple versions with the same cinematic formula will be similarly successful, and investors are interested. Once *Oklahoma!* was acknowledged as a hit, *Carousel* was quick to follow with many of the same elements—although Rodgers and Hammerstein had the peculiar genius to deepen that material. Even Lerner and Loewe were subject to the rule, and as successful as *My Fair Lady* was, *Camelot* saw fit to match *My Fair Lady* with the same headliner—Julie Andrews.

So long as Sondheim participated in projects dominated by established talents or proven patterns, in other words, his own work was validated. *West Side Story* was innovative, but Leonard Bernstein's reputation going into it was impeccable, and after all this was Shakespeare. *A Funny Thing Happened on the Way to the Forum* was a departure, but the play showcased some of the major comic talents of the moment—Zero Mostel, Phil Silvers, Jack Gilford. The music of Jule Styne, the book of Arthur Laurents (who had worked on *West Side Story*) and the vocal talents of Ethel Merman guaranteed that *Gypsy* would be a success. Only when he ventured into something untried (as he did in *Anyone Can Whistle*) or was assigned and accepted the impossible task of filling Oscar Hammerstein's shoes with Richard Rodgers (as he was in *Do I Hear a Waltz?* after the former's death) did his success waver.

Yet as his work since the 1970s has become increasingly well known (again in part as a result of combining forces with a respected production team including, among others, Harold Prince, Michael Bennett, Boris Aronson, and James Goldman), Sondheim has continually eschewed such repetition, continually sought to remake himself, to reinvent his style. Just when we think we know what he does, he does something else. He does *Company* and *Follies* which the critics define as "concept musicals" (ie., without overarching plot), then he does *A Little Night Music* where the plot is paramount. We notice that the first three shows of the 1970s all have love interests in a Westernized setting, and then he does *Pacific Overtures* which has no major love interests, which is set in a non-Western environment, and which is centrally concerned with international politics and trade economics. We observe that Sondheim has written musicals in the early 1970s in which the proportion of song to libretto is roughly equivalent to what it was in the days of Rodgers and Hammerstein or Lerner and Loewe, and that his themes are usually humanistic and uplifting. And then he writes *Sweeney Todd* which is almost entirely sung, which features as its hero a serial murderer (whose big first act finale is a song extolling cannibalism), and which explores as its central concern violent revenge. Perhaps it is not entirely bizarre that financial backers—whose investments depend upon stable economic returns—have been wary of supporting projects that from their perspective at least can vary so unexpectedly.

Another factor impacting the acceptance (or nonacceptance) of Sondheim's work may be what has been happening to the academy in the last fifty years—at least within the humanities. Within departments of English, American, comparative, and foreign literatures, for example, a major shift has been underway. Immediately after the war, the "new criticism" ruled. John Crowe Ransom, Allen Tate, Cleanth Brooks, Robert Penn Warren, William Wimsatt, and others defined a methodology of close critical reading derived from Matthew Arnold that freed literary analysis from the ideological and theological battles of former times by regarding the literary work as autotelic—as organically constituted, but separable finally from the influences of origin or surroundings.

In the 1960s, however, a new intellectual current emerged. Imported largely from France, and quickly dubbed "structuralism" and then "poststructuralism," this movement was language based (rather than subject or object based), and attempted to open the consideration of literature to anthropology, linguistics, psychoanalysis, philosophy, historical study, and other fields in which a structuralist approach was conceivable. A battle ensued. The old guard (which was largely Anglo-German in orientation) vigorously resisted this "Gallic incursion" which seemed to challenge its ability to talk critically and authoritatively about the classical (and not so classical) works of the Western canon. Claude Lévi-Strauss, Roland Barthes, Jacques Lacan, Jacques Derrida, and Michel Foucault came to replace in prominence older more strictly literary icons and new interpretations of Emile Durkheim, Ferdinand de Saussure, Freud, Martin Heidegger, and Nietzsche supplanted older views that had been guided by positivist and moralist perspectives now considered too parochial.

The welcome reception of Sondheim's work within the academy amidst this raging battle had little chance for success. Music and theater arts departments were primarily (and remain primarily) production oriented, and chose to deal with these struggles in neighboring humanities departments by excluding them. Sondheim's plays could be performed but not discussed either at home or in print.[10] English and American literature departments on the other hand, where discussion of Sondheim's postmodernist inventions might have been welcomed, were besieged by other demands, and relegated all such "outside" proposals as aberrant, second in line at best to the claims for attention of contemporary fiction or poetry, claims which were from their point of view more compelling and the demands of which were themselves already exceedingly high. An article with a sexy title like "Deconstructing Sond-heim" could appear in the *New Yorker*.[11] A course or two could be taught at Cornell University in the summer to alumni and other interested adults.[12] A session or two devoted to Sondheim's work could be run at the annual Mod-ern Language Association Convention to accommodate member interest or in conjunction with the interests of private organizations.[13] But the sustained and serious consideration of such work would have to wait for a more propi-tious moment, and interest in promoting such study came to be regarded, if not as eccentric, then as idiosyncratic—something of an irony for a pro-fession engaged in dismantling the distinction between the center and the margins.

Thus, it has only been very recently that it has been even possible to con-template such a serious treatment in the academy at all. As the dust begins to settle in the late 1990s, and instructors trained in the 1970s and after assume tenured positions, the study of Stephen Sondheim's work may yet find a place among the variety of feminisms, gay and lesbian perspectives, new histori-cisms, Lacanian psychoanalytic views, Foucauldian archeological ap-proaches, Derridean deconstructive interpretations, and old time formalist methodologies now competing for critical attention in an increasingly rar-efied academic atmosphere. But the outcome is by no means certain.

And then there is the question of popular culture. From the point of view of the academy, "musical comedy" as it was called in the 1950s and 1960s, while a uniquely American invention, was to be regarded as largely unsophis-ticated and lacking in high seriousness, the equivalent, say, of a play by Noel Coward rather than one by Bertolt Brecht. If Sondheim had long before ac-quired the reputation within the field of Broadway and off-Broadway com-posers of being too brainy, clever, witty, or intellectual—in short, too highbrow, he was still concomitantly regarded among academics as not high-brow enough, as too closely linked to the sources of popular entertainment to be treated as more than a passing curiosity.

In a sense, of course, that particular story is an old one. The names of Robert Frost, T. S. Eliot, Henry James, Ezra Pound, and Henry Miller are suf-ficient to remind us that we have rarely in this country prized our native tal-ents first. It is as if there is something about the American psyche that requires our cultural products to be validated abroad before they can be taken seri-ously at home. Frost was dismissed as a naive nature poet until he was ac-cepted in England. The intellectualism of Eliot, James, or Pound himself found a foreign audience before it found a domestic one. And the prurience of Henry Miller—although the secret delight of adolescent baby boomers in this country—piqued the native Puritanical strain to issue a ban on his works from which the writer's reputation has not yet fully recovered. Sondheim's intel-lectualism, his New York Jewishness, his roots in the Rodgers and Hammer-stein musical comedy and Tin Pan Alley tradition ruffle the sensibilities of white Anglo-Saxon Protestant academics. It is not without interest that we are willing to hire Sondheim to teach a course in the university in this country only after he has given one at Oxford, or that we support a newsletter devoted to his work only after one has already appeared in England.[14]

If Sondheim were working in the medium of film like Woody Allen, or the medium of fiction like Philip Roth, Saul Bellow, or Bernard Malamud, or the medium of nonmusical drama like Arthur Miller, or at least doubled in the field of serious musical composition like George Gershwin, perhaps his work might have found a hearing. Certainly he has worked on the fringes of all of these fields. But musical drama is the "road not taken" of the "road not taken" in these matters, and laboring as he does primarily in musical drama, Sondheim's work seems to have been limited over the last thirty years to the destiny of all "popular" artists—however richly deserving of serious attention on its own merits.

Whatever the reasons for its exclusion, the fact of that exclusion remains, and the book that follows is in the first instance an attempt to remedy that situation, to take up Adler's suggestion, to break through the academic silence and read Sondheim's work with the seriousness it deserves.

But there is a second agenda, one that is somewhat more difficult to specify although it may be more critical than the first. The reasons for excluding the work of Sondheim in particular may exceed those we have cited—the economics of popular American culture, the polemical makeup of the humanities from the sixties to the nineties, the elitism of the academy. Sondheim is a thinker, a philosopher, a commentator. His work embodies what, again, Adler noted early on as "the glow of thought." We may be afraid of Sondheim, afraid of what he has to tell us about ourselves—about our loves, our relations with our parents and children, our fairy tales, our violence. If we have excluded his work, perhaps it is because at some level we do not want to hear what he has to say, and do not want to hear precisely because in some manner we have *already* heard, and do not like the result. To grant Sondheim's work the same intellectual rigor he grants his subject matter is to bring Sondheim's thinking into the open and that gesture may feel to us at root dangerous since it threatens to upset the structure of denial we have studiously maintained for so long. To take seriously what he tells us about our marriages in *Company* or *Follies* or *Night Music*, or what he tells us about our politics in *Pacific Overtures* or *Assassins*, or what he tells us about our support for the arts (or about the nature of the creative process) in *Sunday in the Park with George*, or about the real status and afterlife of our fairy tales in *Into the Woods*, or about obsessional behavior in *Sweeney Todd* or *Passion*, may make it hard to get on with our day.

Let a full-fledged consideration of the history of musical comedy (and of Sondheim's place within that history) begin, we may be prepared to say to ourselves. Let the academy get over its elitism and its debilitating polemics as commercial interests have begun to get over the stigma of "a Sondheim musical." The reading of Sondheim's work may still terrify. Moreover, the gravest threat to understanding Sondheim may be yet to come. If his work has been excluded by not talking about it, it may be even more thoroughly excluded by talking about it. Academic history is rife with examples of writers whose troublesome implications are silenced as much by the domestication attendant upon academic exaltation as they are by academic oblivion. What guarantee do we have that a resistance to understanding cannot organize itself even where the articulation of Sondheim's commentary is the most explicit? If we undertake to read Sondheim, we must do so with the full awareness of the threat involved and the terrors (and their consequences) that may ensue. That is not of course a reason for not undertaking such a project, for letting things remain as they are. But it is perhaps a reason for continued vigilance.

I

What would it mean, then, to read Sondheim seriously? Sondheim is a songwriter. He writes music and lyrics. If we are not suggesting that we confine our examination to Sondheim's nonmusical work (and we are not), then it seems at least curious to found an analysis upon a reading of Sondheim, an examination of what has been set down on a page as opposed to what is beheld in performance or heard on recordings (and even then, upon only a portion of what is set down, since for the most part in this study we will not discuss the music).

To read Sondheim in this context is to consider everything he has done as part of a coherent body of work, which is to say, as the product of systematic choice, effort, selection. Whether the songs are heard, read, or experienced in performance, whether we examine the music and the lyrics or just the lyrics alone, *some* set of choices, *some* selection, has been made to constitute that work and it is the separability of those conditions from that result that is analyzable. The examination of the performance of a symphony is certainly not the examination of a symphony. But neither is the examination of one or another of its extant manuscripts. It is the relation of what we might be tempted to call the "symphony itself" to one or another of its multifarious manifestations that is here in question.

The problem is not unlike that faced by linguists and semiologists when the execution of a particular phonological unit differs from context to context, even overlapping at times with other phonological constructions to which it is necessarily opposed, and the solution may be borrowed. What we examine is the *langue* not the *parole*, the set of differences not the manner in which such differences are executed, expressed, or become concretely manifest. To read Sondheim is to isolate what is distinctive about his work in whatever context that distinctiveness happens to be encountered.

But how are we to do that? How are we to isolate that distinctiveness? In part at least, to read within an academic context is like reading anywhere. To read Sondheim is like reading Shakespeare, Arthur Miller, James Joyce, William Blake, or *The New York Times* for that matter. It is also like reading a nontextual event, the use of a particular kinship system in anthropology, for example, or the laughter of a particular individual in psychology.

In its broadest sense, to read is to interpret, to find whatever is being read (a thing, a word, a person) to be the result of a set of happenings that are other than arbitrary, to be governed by a design of some kind rather than being the product of random chance. If we name what is determined to be so governed as the "text," then we may say that all reading is necessarily "textual" reading, and all texts are necessarily able to be read.

But reading within an academic context also has a particular history, one which is now nearly two centuries old. Literary criticism as we currently understand it was formed as part of the so-called historical critical method in philosophy at the turn of the nineteenth century whereby the subject of consciousness could be imagined before an object of knowledge. Whatever the origins of this new epistemology, M. H. Abrams has noted that the appearance in European letters of such a subject poised before such a "contemplation object" (and of the "art for art's sake" movement of which it is a part) aligns itself with the development in cultural life of the lecture hall, the concert hall, and the art museum, institutions which all displace the homes of the wealthy as the locus in which within an older system of patronage a lecturer, a musician, or an artist could display the results of his or her efforts for others to encounter.[15]

What was pleasurable in this object of contemplation was clearly separable from what was knowable, as much so as aesthetics was from epistemology, or *dulce* from *utile* in a much older cultural order. And the two standard modes of apprehension of a given work or text were taken to be formalization and interpretation, which is to say, the examination of the formal generic considerations of a work, or the development of an isomorphism between that work and the set of historical, cultural, or religious ideas in whose context it was produced and whose circulation it continued.[16] Borrowed from religious contexts, such an activity was part of a process of sacralization and the hallmark of such a larger process was (and remains) differentiation. The great literary text was modeled on that of sacred scripture. From Wordsworth and Coleridge, through Matthew Arnold, T. S. Eliot, I. A. Richards, and the denizens of the New Criticism, such an understanding was maintained. The sacred trappings of such critical activity could certainly be removed, so much so in fact that the movement could be introduced in America (as noted above) ironically to counter raging ideological or theological battles. But the sacrificial structure of this movement itself, the exaltation of literary writing and its "miraculous" powers, conceived within this "natural supernaturalism" or "covert theology," remained fundamentally intact.[17]

Thus to read from within such an academic context is primordially to make distinctions, and the New Criticism about which we have spoken above is a criticism built upon such limit-taking, upon a separation that is to say of the product from the process, the work from the labor which produces it, whether that labor or effort is understood to derive from an "author" or a cultural-historical context in which the individuals assigned such a designation lived and worked. What is authoritative in Shakespeare's plays from this perspective is not the man (about whom we know very little) nor even the Elizabethan era (about which we know a great deal) but the "plays themselves," and the ways in which both the writer and Elizabethan culture may be said to derive from (or be implied by) such internal dramatic discussions. The work of Wayne Booth in *Rhetoric of Fiction* on the "implied author" in fiction, and of Wellek and Warren in *Theory of Literature* on the distinction between "internal" and "external" considerations in literary study reflect these postulates.

To read seriously an author like Shakespeare in accord with this Arnoldian poetics would be to read what his texts have to offer us independently of whatever that author has to say about them, whatever impressions his readers may have of them, and whatever theatrical traditions, production histories, or biographical details a scholar is able gather with regard to them. Such engendering agencies may, of course, be studied and the results may confirm or rebut our reading of the plays. But they can never substitute, in this view, for that more primary reading. To engage in such a fatal substitution is to proceed fallaciously, and the list of "fallacies" one is capable of committing in this domain (and therefore should avoid)—authorial, affective, biographical, romantic or pathetic, and others—was touted as defining the mainstay of responsible critical reading. It is easy to see why such a methodology fared better with dead writers than living ones who could intervene at any moment to challenge the views of overzealous critics.

At the same time, determining what the plays of Shakespeare (or the texts of any writer) are up to independently of all such external considerations may be no easy task, and in fact may curiously depend upon those very considerations from which such criticism would like to keep them separate. For if we turn to examine the "plays themselves," by what criteria shall we understand them? The plays themselves, the work, the text, we may all agree, are indisputably made up of language. But if we are not to read philology alone, then we would seem to have necessarily to pass through mechanisms of social construction by which ideas like the author or readers or the historical, religious, and cultural background—and in general all such functions in which we situate conscious and knowing subjects and objects—would be permeated.

Thus arose in the 1960s a language based criticism that challenged the new critical postulates of an earlier generation by challenging the presuppositions upon which they were formed, and specifically the independence they claimed was possible between internal and external critical considerations. It is not that the author's intention *really does* matter after all, they argued, but that there is no way of separating finally that intention from its own textuality. The statement by an author or a reader or a scholar about a text or context is no more (or less) than any other text a text to be read, and one moreover to be read with the same seriousness and integrity as the first. And in fact, the very possibility of distinguishing a first from a second, primary from secondary texts in such circumstances quickly becomes less a matter of knowledge or inquiry than an exercise in critical hegemony.

Thus to read Sondheim's work in the 1990s, to read what is distinctive about Sondheim, is to read Sondheim's language wherever it occurs, whether it be within the lyrics or the music or his own comments about the work, or the responses of his readers (or auditors or audience) to the work, or aspects of production to which he has distinctively contributed. And each of the contributors to the volume that follows read one or more aspect of Sondheim's work in such a manner.

But what then does it mean to read Sondheim's "language?" How, for example, can we be sure that we are reading Sondheim's language as opposed to something else? And what guarantee do we have that even the close reading of such language gives us access to what is distinctive about Sondheim any more than older appeals to Sondheim's conscious intention or the impressions of readers or audiences? Is it not possible that disclosing the intertextual relation between any text and all other texts is another way to obscure that significance (as much so, in fact, as claiming that texts are separable from contexts)?[18]

To read Sondheim's texts closely as language, then, in my view (and here is what is distinctive about my own perspective), is to read them as commentary, and, in particular, commentary that functions as an extension or extremity or trace or witness of its subject matter.

This final point with regard to reading Sondheim is perhaps the most difficult one. In *Sacrificing Commentary. Reading the End of Literature*, I argued at length for the understanding of literature as commentary and commentary as witness. The great works of our literary tradition, I proposed, are in fact a form of commentary about that tradition, and by sequestering such commentary as "literature" we deny ourselves the finest critical perspective our culture has to offer us.

And what are such "inner" literary commentaries? Precisely, the prophetic reading of myths that our culture would read representationally; the staging of the limits of any act of mythic appropriation—whether that act occurs within a play by Sophocles or Shakespeare, within a passage of Hebrew scripture, or even within the reflections of a Jewish writer about the Holocaust. To read prophetically is to give up illustrating the "content" of the myth for a demonstration of its origins, its strategies, and its consequences, a demonstration, moreover, which is coextensive or continuous with (and thereby a reenactment of) its own subject matter.

The work of Stephen Sondheim, I would like to suggest, offers in the contemporary setting something of the same fundamentally critical spirit, a prophetic reading of the myths by which we conduct our lives. More precisely, I would suggest that Sondheim stages in full a critique of the one myth that has dominated the musical stage in America and our lives as we live them in accord with that myth—namely, the myth of a happy ending. In the second half of this introduction, I will turn to an extended example of such a critique.

To read Sondheim's work as commentary is thus in short to read Sondheim as reading—in both the nominative and verbal sense. It is to read his text as smart, as intelligent about such matters of interest to us as we pride ourselves as being (if not more so), and to read that intelligence as evidenced by its very presentation. Put another way, we may say that to read Sondheim's distinctiveness is to read his disclosure of a crisis, of a breakdown ironically of distinction itself, of the collapse of the differences by which we would maintain in fantasy a difference where it is no longer efficacious and its limits begin to appear. Whether it is question of our relationships with others (our parents, our children, our spouses, our lovers, our friends), our politics at home or abroad (and their relation to mythic thinking), the process of our aging (and its relation to memory and infirmity), our fairy tales (and what follows them in the real world), our obsessions for passion or revenge (and *their* real life consequences), our artistic representations and theatricalizations (on stage, on paper, in art), or our breakdowns in all of the above domains, what Sondheim shows us is the inadequacy of our responses, the difficulties attendant upon our responses (and our assertion of privilege all the more fervently for those difficulties), and in general, our projection of responsibility for such behavior—such distance, desire, and violence—outside the reach of our everyday decision-making capacities.

To read Sondheim seriously is to encounter, to come face to face with, those crises and those responses, an encounter we would—understandably— rather not undertake.

II

The individuals whom I have invited to contribute to this volume share certain characteristics. They are for the most part all members of English literature departments in colleges or universities. They all love Sondheim's work. And they all find in that work, in one manner or another, a reading or commentary worthy of being taken seriously.

I have divided the twelve essays into two groups. In the first group I have included all those that for the most part deal with multiple themes or plays or contexts. In the second, I have included all those that focus largely upon a single play.

Thus, Thomas Adler's opening essay surveys the entire range of Sondheim's contribution to the musical stage. He locates Sondheim's dramatic output in particular within the tradition of other major writers for the American stage—principally, Eugene O'Neill, Edward Albee, Harold Pinter, and Arthur Miller—and registers the drift of his work against changing stylistic trends in theater from realism to postmodernism.

Allen Menton identifies the figure of the mother that occurs repeatedly in Sondheim (often in relationship with a child—for example, in *Gypsy*, *Whistle*, *Night Music*, *Sweeney Todd*, *Pacific Overtures*, *Sunday*, and *Woods*), the numerous moments of breakdown or madness in his plays (that he finds often linked to such relationships), and ways in which art comes to function at times as a mediator of the tensions between the two.

Kay Young observes that the happy ending and the institution of marriage that sustains it has been a staple of the American musical stage for its entire history. A part of the radical quality of Sondheim, in plays like *Company*, *Follies*, *A Little Night Music*, *Sunday*, or *Into the Woods*, she argues, is their undoing of the happy ending that earlier productions would promise.

Ann McEntee takes seriously Frank Rich's pronouncement that *Follies* is a "postmodern" play and explores the efforts by the team of artists (of which Sondheim is one)—which included Harold Prince, Michael Bennett, Boris Aronson, and James Goldman among others—to explode more realistic treatments of its themes, and the misunderstandings of those efforts by contemporary critics. Sondheim's "Loveland" sequence in particular, she observes, both celebrates and challenges the kind of theatrical extravaganzas that Ziegfeld's Follies in the 1930s repeatedly staged.

Shoshana Knapp focuses upon the Rousseauistic belief that Fosca and Giorgio share in *Passion* regarding the uniqueness or singularity of their affection, and sets it against the very different treatment of their love relationship presented respectively by Scola and Tarchetti.

Paul Puccio and Scott Stoddart follow the variety of ways in which Sondheim employs duets throughout his writing, both as a way of paying homage to the duet tradition of the American musical stage, but also as an accompaniment to his more philosophically critical deconstructive positions with regard to that tradition, an accompaniment that is itself, they argue, both secondary to that critique and its very center.

Paul Puccio's essay on *Night Music* opens the second grouping. In it, he argues that more important even than Bergman's *Smiles of a Summer Night* as a source for Sondheim and Wheeler's play is Shakespeare's *A Midsummer Night's Dream*, a play which like Sondheim and Wheeler's explores the magical "green world" of myth and ritual.

Joseph Marchesani's essay on *Sweeney Todd* draws our attention to the ways in which Sondheim and Wheeler present their hero in three successive psychological stages which he identifies, along with contemporary French psychoanalytic practitioner Jacques Lacan, as imaginary, symbolic, and real. When read in terms of these registers, he argues, the play charts systematically both the mind's deepest ordering principles, and the movement of one mind in particular—Sweeney's—from naiveté, to a sense of injustice, to psychotic break.

In his essay on *Merrily We Roll Along,* Scott Stoddart argues that our understanding of the play (and perhaps as well Broadway's rejection of it after all sixteen performances) is complicated by the fact that the play reproduces an earlier play with the same name by George S. Kaufman and Moss Hart from 1934; that like its predecessor it proceeds in reverse chronological order; and that it was revived and revised in 1985 in significant ways. The revisions, Stoddart argues, make clear that for Sondheim it was the friendship between Franklin Shepard and Charlie Kringas that was primary, and not Franklin's marriages as the critics routinely assume; a fact that we overlook, Stoddart suggests, at the peril of our own indictment by the play before us.

Frank Olley's essay compares the work of Sondheim and Lapine to the Jacobean theater of 1606 to 1610 of which Shakespeare was certainly a part. *Sunday,* for example, in his view, is not unlike *Winter's Tale* or *Tempest* in its presentation initially of a chronological time which turns out, in fact, in a later moment to be the stuff of artistic illusion.

Scott Stoddart argues that *Into the Woods* deconstructs our normative understanding of gender relations, challenging in act 2 in fundamental ways the "happy ending" promised in act 1. At quite a remove from the self-centeredness of the fairy tales with which the musical opens, the play concludes in a much deeper appreciation of aloneness and the need for working together toward a common goal.

And finally, in my own essay on *Passion,* I suggest that the peculiar plot turn at its center may find its analogue in an epistolary fictional mode that was certainly part of the source material (Tarchetti's nineteenth-century Italian novella) from which first the film and then the play is drawn, but that also appears to structure the anecdotal narrative by which Sondheim—in at least one published interview—takes account of his own experience, an experience that turns out to reflect most of the themes raised in these twelve essays.

These twelve essays offer a variety of critical approaches. Informed by deconstruction, Lacanian psychoanalytic theories, Freudian and Jungian psychological interpretations, gay and lesbian accounts of gender relations, Marxism, as well as more traditional formalist and thematic methodologies used by Americanists, comparatists, theater studies specialists, and students of dramatic literature, these essays are nothing if not multifarious. Nor do they necessarily agree with my own perspective, or with each other. The only requirement for inclusion—apart from the ones mentioned above—was an informed, serious, responsible, critical reading of Sondheim's work. My hope is that their plenitude will inspire students to develop their own contributions.

III

To say as I have that my hope for this book is that it inaugurates a serious critical reading of Sondheim is not to say that there have not been full-length

considerations of his work before this moment, or that they have not been serious. To the contrary, Craig Zadan, Joanne Gordon, Martin Gottfried, and
Stephen Banfield have all completed book length projects on Sondheim and
their efforts among others are exceedingly important ones.[19] Zadan, who is a
Hollywood producer, was the pioneer in this field with *Sondheim and Co.* in
1974, and for a long time the only individual who had undertaken any sustained treatment of Sondheim. He did the spadework from which all else has
followed. He gathered the anecdotes and the statistics. He knew and interviewed the participants. He examined and collated the first reviews. His book
remains in its revised and updated edition of 1994 the starting point of any
serious critical account of Sondheim's work.

Gordon heads the directing program of the Theater Department of the
University of California at Long Beach and has done equally fine work. She
has the merit of having written the first book within an academic context. Her
volume, *Art Isn't Easy. The Achievement of Stephen Sondheim*, which was
first published in 1990 (and revised in 1994 with an additional chapter on *Assassins* and a change of subtitle to *The Theater of Stephen Sondheim*) and includes a full critical apparatus (with endnotes and bibliography of primary
and secondary materials), judiciously presents the themes of all the major
plays, and in general gathers for the student of Sondheim all the primary research materials necessary for further study.

Likewise, Martin Gottfried's book *Sondheim*, which was first published
in 1993, attempts an assessment of the full range of Sondheim's career.[20] For
a long time Gottfried wrote reviews of Sondheim's plays for their New York
theater openings, and to this body of theater criticism and evaluations he has
added numerous photos, material from interviews he has conducted with
teachers and friends of Sondheim, and a chapter on Sondheim's life.

And finally Banfield, who is a musicologist, and head of the music
school at the University of Birmingham examines in his book *Stephen Sondheim's Broadway Musicals* the totality of Sondheim's output from a musicological perspective.[21] Banfield points out that Sondheim's use of music in his
plays has been almost totally ignored and undertakes to fill in that gap. His
book, which is massive, includes a comprehensive list of Sondheim's songs,
and will undoubtedly prove the reference book to all future musicological
studies of the plays.

Yet four books in forty years on Sondheim does not constitute a field and
for the most part these books are not works of literary criticism. Banfield
himself notes that all books in this domain will be either journalistic, schol-
arly, or theoretical. Zadan's book, comprehensive as it is in 1974 (and in its
revised format later) regarding the details and anecdotes surrounding the production of Sondheim's plays, is founded almost entirely on interviews and
personal knowledge. Gottfried adds to his theater criticism some important
photos and biographical information. Gordon is the scholar of the group,

giving full citations for the material Zadan and Gottfried often cite only in passing and quoting others at length. And Banfield undertakes first full length practical and theoretical treatment of the music.

But no one has done the same as he has for the lyrics, or for their relation with music to the dramatic context in which both function, or for the relation of such dramatically situated musical numbers to the larger body of writing which each successive productive endeavor of Sondheim's rebuilds, or for the relation of Sondheim's writing to other writing in the same period. A theoretical book on Sondheim, one that marshals the full resources of the extraordinary and subtle advances that have been made in literary theory over the last thirty-five years and undertakes to think in these terms the entirety of his deconstructive project (let alone its relation to other projects), has, in Banfield's understated pronouncement, "not been forthcoming."[22]

The four books and assorted other materials that have been written, in short, are indispensable to a critical reading of Sondheim. But they are not substitutes for one. Excellent as they are, none presents a coherent systematic analytic approach to Sondheim's writing that is attentive to the full range and implications of his singular evolving enterprise, nor takes as its primary goal the disclosing of the project or itinerary of his thought.

The goal of the present book, then, is to open the door a little wider to the Sondheim industry that, in my view, is undoubtedly on its way. In the attempt to inspire students to read Sondheim more closely, more carefully, more thoughtfully, more systematically (and teachers to teach Sondheim in the same open spirit), the collection will work to make available to a wider reading public the extraordinary riches which have for too long been the exclusive property of a private though faithful audience, and expand appreciation of the "finest lyricist the American theater has ever produced."[23]

IV

By way of conclusion to this introduction, and as a way of getting started, let me turn in the second half of this essay to two plays to which Sondheim contributes music and lyrics at the beginning of the 1970s in which the theme I would argue that will concern him in one manner or another throughout his career is announced. "Happily Ever After" is the title to a song Sondheim wrote in the late 1960s, to be sung by the protagonist at the culminating moment in *Company*, when his views on marriage are finally expressed.[24] The title reflects the three words of a phrase repeated several times in the song. In their full lyric, dramatic, and historical productive context, the words—and the emotional explosion they suggest—may offer us a way of thinking about some of the issues we have been raising.

> Someone to hold you too close,
> Someone to hurt you too deep,

> Someone to love you too hard,
> Happily ever after.
> Someone to need you too much,
> Someone to read you too well,
> Someone to bleed you of all
> The things you don't want to tell—
> That's happily ever after.
> Ever, ever, ever after
> In hell.

The song makes clear in no uncertain terms Robert's view of marriage as he has seen it at close range interacting as he did with five couples of the play. What you get is invasion. What's more, you get it forever, without end. Perhaps Sondheim is thinking of Sartre who has one of his characters in *Huis Clos (No Exit)* say "L'enfers, c'est les Autres" ("hell is other people"), or perhaps of the postmodernist commonplace in the late 1960s that sometimes hell is attaining the object of your desire.[25] But whatever its source, Robert's rejection of the "happy ending" promised by marriage is unmitigated.

Harold Prince was uneasy with the ending and the song was dropped from the Boston opening of the musical because Prince deemed it too "negative," too "bitter." Sondheim replaced it with the more familiar "Being Alive," which starts similarly, but softens the singer's declaration by embedding it within the verse and intermittent dialogue, and within a rhythm that is considerably less driving.[26]

> Someone to hold you too close,
> Someone to hurt you too deep,
> Someone to sit in your chair,
> To ruin your sleep . . .
> . . . .
> Someone to need you too much,
> Someone to know you too well,
> Someone to pull you up short
> And put you through hell . . .

> DAVID: You see what you look for, you know.
> JOANNE: You're not a kid anymore, Robby, and I don't think you'll ever be a kid again, kiddo.
> PETER: Hey, buddy, don't be afraid it won't be perfect . . . The only thing to be afraid of really is that it won't *be*! (113-14)

"Being Alive" *is* probably the better song, finally, not because it is less bitter (it is only slightly so) but because it is more comprehensive. In addition to Robert's cynical perspective on the prospect of marriage, it presents an avowal of his vulnerability. From "Someone to hold you too close" the song moves to "Somebody hold me too close," a change in grammatical person that reflects a change in emotional tone from the anger of accusation to the pain of a plea for help. In the dramatic context, the change is motivated by a request from Amy (the one individual to whom Robert has proposed) to make a commitment.

> AMY: Blow out the candles, Robert, and make a wish. *Want* something! Want
>   *something!*
> ROBERT:
>   Somebody hold me too close,
>   Somebody hurt me too deep,
>   Somebody sit in my chair
>   And ruin my sleep and make me aware
>   Of being alive, being alive.
>   Somebody need me too much,
>   Somebody know me too well,
>   Somebody pull me up short
>   And put me through hell and give me support
>   For being alive. (115-16)

The new ending also offers Robert insight. By contrast with the conclusion of the earlier song which had simply justified its initial position (". . . sure, feel a little lonely, / But fly, / . . . / That's happily ever after, / Ever, ever, ever after, / For now!"), Robert is now able to view things from a wider angle—that of existential survival.[27]

> . . . alone is alone, not alive.
> Somebody crowd me with love,
> Somebody force me to care,
> Somebody let me come through.
> I'll always be there, as frightened as you,
> To help us survive
> Being alive, being alive, being alive. (116)

Sondheim could of course argue that Robert is not ready to display such vulnerability or such insight, and that such emotional exposure remains a "cop-out" on the character development to that point, although one could reply that the current version does not necessarily lead to marriage either, that it is still possible for Robert to disappear from his party of friends.[28]

But it seems to me that whether we adopt the first or the second version as most appropriate to the play we have witnessed, the exclusion of the first is instructive and reflects something of the difficulty about which we have been speaking in this introductory essay: namely, the difficulty of Robert speaking among his friends, and the difficulty of hearing Robert speak so forthrightly about those themes—both within the play and without.

The problem is not a minor one. All of *Company* may be said to be in some sense about the impossibility of speaking and Sondheim's lyrics describe little else. Beyond the superficial politenesses, marriages in *Company* appear to survive (if we take Sondheim's lyrics seriously) not by sharing thoughts and fears about ultimate concerns or the future but by moving in short order from the marriage contract ("I do") to accusation ("You don't"), to denial ("Nobody said that"), to scapegoating ("Who brought the subject up first?"), a pattern which generates, in the words of one observer, a "city of strangers" (55).[29]

And so when Robert does speak and express either his anger or his pain (and either song expresses both, although in different ways), something decisive has taken place—a kind of breakthrough in the play's pattern to that point, and perhaps as well in that of musical comedy. To soften that movement, to ameliorate the difficulties it raises (whether we do so in our productions, our reviews, our scholarship, or our literary criticism) is to do more than miss what the play has to show us. It is to participate within it, to partake in the impoverished lives of the individuals that Robert's speaking and the play at large so brilliantly exposes.

The final scene, in which we come to understand that the entirety of the play's action may have taken place inside Robert's head—just before he entered the darkened room (while standing *center stage, listening*), or just after (perhaps while making a wish)—assumes its most powerfully deconstructive potential in this light. The play is not plotless, as most critics routinely say. It is rather overburdened with plots. And each of them constitutes a wish or desire for a happy ending by which the fires within each of the characters, like the candles atop Robert's birthday cake, may continue to burn. To live within any one of those plots exclusively, as to live within any one of the five marriages Robert observes, is to extinguish all the rest, to obliterate the richness of the insight to which he has just come and which the play at large has just shared with us. To make a wish is also to blow out all the other candles. It is a choice, Sondheim tells us, that many make, but one that may also come with unexpected consequences.

On the other hand, if "two is dreary," "one's impossible." To live outside of all such happy endings, as Robert seems to have managed to do for a long time, is to gain that insight at the expense of getting close to someone. The emptiness of Robert's relations to Marta, Kathy, and April seems little compensation. If there is a closeness to someone Robert has been able to develop independently of marriage, the play doesn't reveal that relationship to us. The play offers no clear solution to the dilemma, to what we might call the problem of "counting" in the play, and we are left at the end only to contemplate Robert's enigmatic smile. But even posing the problem is a quantum leap ahead of earlier musical comedy efforts.

The second example with which I would like to conclude this introductory essay comes from *Follies*. The 1971 production of *Follies* was conceived before *Company* (as a play entitled *The Girls Upstairs*) and so, although its opening follows the latter play chronologically, *Follies* in a sense also precedes *Company*. The importance of this production of *Follies* within the corpus of Sondheim's work before and since, in my view, is hard to overestimate.[30] In it, the speaking that could not be articulated during most of *Company*—the hell that turns out to condition the happily ever after of marriage—is made explicit. It is as if two of the couples from *Company* could be interviewed after thirty years of marriage and queried about the happiness and contentment their relationship has brought them. The answer is not a pretty one.

The show assumes the form of a party, a reunion given by a character whose name is Dmitri Weismann but who is clearly a stand-in for an individual like Flo Ziegfeld. The party, we are told, is given for his former *Follies* participants, a final opportunity before his theater comes down, "to glamorize the old days, stumble through a song or two, and lie about ourselves a little" (7).

The party follows the normal patterns such an event may be expected to follow—up to a point. People greet each other with some surprise and anxiety. They chat about the past, about changes that have taken place over the years. A few of the musical numbers in which the group formerly participated are restaged and the distance between then and now becomes clear. And in general nostalgia and the pleasures of nostalgic memory rule.

But very quickly as the party proceeds, the food, wine, and music continue to flow, the contemporary anxieties are alleviated, another pattern begins to emerge. The old flames begin to be rekindled. From "do you remember who loved who" begins to appear "do you know who still loves who." And in this context, the title word of the show quickly assumes a second meaning. The Ziegfeld extravaganzas, the Follies of the 1920s and 1930s which the participants formerly only dimly remembered, now give way to the follies of love and romantic passion, the tangled set of secret longings within which the characters have continued to identify themselves.

The play focuses principally upon four characters: Ben, Phyllis, Buddy, and Sally. Benjamin Stone is a well-to-do former United Nations diplomat who said the wrong thing to the wrong person one day and now heads a foundation. He is not growing old gracefully and has come to the party seeking to restore his endangered youth. Phyllis Stone is his stylish and sophisticated wife who has stood by him all these years and now begins to fear that she has lost herself in the process. Sally Durant Plummer is Phyllis's former roommate and, like Phyllis, was once herself a Follies showgirl (which is why both have been invited to this party). The freshness and innocence she cultivated thirty years ago has been fading of late into a chronic depression, as she realizes she may never attain the sophistication she craves. Buddy Plummer is her traveling salesman husband whom she married because she could not marry Ben (who would not have her), and with whom she has had two children. Like Phyllis with her own spouse, Buddy has had to make do over the years in one fashion or another, but has generally stuck by his partner and her impossible longings.

Thrown together again after all these years, the foursome quickly begin to reminisce. The men recall their days of courtship as stagedoor Johnnies, waiting for "the girls upstairs," and as they do so, the ghosts of former years—physical embodiments of Ben, Phyllis, Sally, and Buddy in their younger days who at first are a shadowy presence on the stage—begin increasingly to assume realistic and kinetic stature, and to enact their parts along with them.

As the evening progresses, options that at first appeared a fantasy escape from contemporary angst begin to be contemplated as a serious possibility. What began the evening as an offshoot of love-longing (the follies or foolishness of bygone romantic love) becomes now the ardor of mature and agonizing passionate possibility. What if Ben were really to leave his wife Phyllis (for whom he professes a profound dissatisfaction) and marry Sally (about whom he once dreamed)? What if Sally Durant Plummer of Phoenix, Arizona were really to leave her salesman husband, Buddy, to marry the famous and successful Benjamin Stone, who has been her secret love all these long years?

These plans will of course crumble under the weight of their own problematic constitution ("Facts never interest me," says another character at one point, "What matters is the song"). And with their crumbling the meaning of the title word begins to assume its third and most ominous investment. As the past becomes increasingly inseparable from the present, and fantasy progressively indistinguishable from reality, the older medieval sense of folly as madness—preserved in French as *la folie*—comes to dominate and the characters sequentially project their internal boundary crises and breakdowns onto the social arenas in which they continue (with mounting difficulty) to function.

The crisis builds slowly. Buddy overhears Sally's proposal to Ben (although not Ben's rejection of it), and sings to himself of his desire for the "right girl"—neither Sally at home, nor his mistress, Margie, on the road. He confronts Sally, who is unable to face Ben's rejection and so converts it into an acceptance. Meanwhile, Ben relates to Phyllis his desire for a divorce, not because of Sally (whom he admits he has "never" loved), but because "There's no one in my life; there's nothing. That's what's killing me" (75). Buddy, who is now "steaming," confronts Ben, who promptly tells Sally (who has followed Buddy to Ben's presence, ready to elope with her secret love), "But I never said I loved you, did I?" (79), and all hell breaks loose.

As the breakdown of communications reaches its paroxysm, each of the characters begins simultaneously and noisily denouncing their younger selves (who have now become visceral presences as well), accusing them of having destroyed their lives, and vowing to get even with them for it, all the while promising their partner a renewed faithfulness and love. And in the midst of the confusion that results (which the stage directions describe as "senseless now, completely unintelligible and rather frightening" [82]), the entire stage suddenly reverts to an eighteenth-century indoor theater replete with Dresden dolls, cavaliers, and extravagantly costumed Follies showgirls.

> . . . *drums start to roll, trumpeters in Medieval costumes emerge from the shadows, heavenly music is heard, drop after drop comes flying down, all valentines and lace, and as the lights rise to bright gold, dancers, young and beautiful, all dressed like* Dresden Dolls *and* Cavaliers, *appear.* Ben, Phyllis, Buddy, *and* Sally, *eyes wild, and half-demented, stand in the midst of it all taking their first look at "Loveland."* (83)

The sequence that follows will occupy most of the rest of the play. The Chorus enters and sings first.

> Time stops, hearts are young,
> Only serenades are sung
> In Loveland,
> Where everybody lives to love. (83)

The Choral singing is punctuated by the appearance successively of six showgirls in "vast hoop skirt" with "naked midriff, a modest bodice and, on top, a soaring headdress" representing six attributes of love relationships: music, flowers, rapture, secrets, devotion, and jewels. The four younger versions of the lovers, no longer memories or ghosts now, take the stage to sing of their hopes for the future.

Young Ben:
> You're gonna love tomorrow.

Young Phyllis:
> Mm-hm.

Young Ben:
> You're gonna be with me.

Young Phyllis:
> Mm-hm.

YOUNG BEN:
You're gonna love tomorrow,
I'm giving you my personal guarantee. (88)

The young lovers are followed by the four principal characters, each of whom now takes the stage and sings of their lives in a Follies act of their own: Buddy, of the vicious circle of desire in which he finds himself caught; Sally, of her obsession with Ben; Phyllis, of her inability to free herself from the two competing images of herself or of herself and Sally; and Ben, of his inability to give up control.

A curtain drops and suddenly Buddy appears. No longer precisely sure who "the right girl" is but certain he has not married her, he has become now a vaudeville clown, in *plaid baggy pants, bright blue jacket, and derby hat*, touting his toy automobile which is *suspended from his waist*, and driven insatiably from one female haven to another. Two showgirls assist him in the roles of "Margie" and "Sally," and with them he sings "I've got those / 'God-why-don't-you-love-me-oh-you-do-I'll-see-you-later' / Blues" (95).

The three scoot off. The curtain parts slightly, and Sally is revealed. In *clinging, beaded silver* nightclub dress, with microphone in hand, cute little Sally Durant from Phoenix has now become a languid torch song singer à la Helen Morgan, whose musical lines begin to repeat themselves and consequently to reflect the paralysis about which she sings. A variant of the phrase "It's like I'm losing my mind" occurs no less than six times in the song's short verses.

The lights fade to a facial spot. The spot dims and goes out. A *jazzy* trumpet theme starts up and now suddenly Phyllis Stone appears, *wearing a short, fringe-skirted bright red dress*, accompanied by a chorus line of young male admirers, and sporting *long and shapely legs* and a *knowing grin*. In a number out of a forties screen musical, she breaks into a show-stopping and highly charged song and dance routine telling the story of "juicy Lucy" and "dressy Jessie" who are "itching to be switching roles" (103), two figures who are at once herself in younger and contemporary versions, and the roles in which she and Sally have been endlessly caught.

The stage empties and finally Ben Stone, complete with top hat, tails, and cane, makes his entrance. Leading a chorus line of dancing leg-kicking show-boys and showgirls à la Fred Astaire, he has become a carefree hoofing dandy, offering advice to the lovelorn and woe-ridden about carefree living: "Learn how to laugh, / Learn how to love, / Learn how to live," (104-05). "Do I lose my grip?" he asks at one moment in his song (106), and begins suddenly to forget his words. By the time he reaches "One day they're diplomats" his lyrics have begun looping together and instead of singing "Me, I like to live, / Me, I like to laugh, / Me, I like to love" as he did previously (105-06), he sings "Me, I like to love, / Me, I . . ." (107) and loses hold of the script entirely.

Amidst this bevy of beautiful young men and women he can no longer remember his lines, and now begins darting frenetically among them (as they continue to dance) searching for a sympathetic ear into which he may pour the vagaries of his own self-hate. The Follies drops suddenly fly up and we are back in the Weismann theater, although we are also, the stage direction tells us, "inside Ben's mind." And as Ben continues to collapse in a barrage of fragmentary outbursts from past entanglements, and the stage erupts into a chaos (in which "the cacophony . . . is terrible" and "everything we've seen and heard all evening is going on at once, as if the night's experience were being vomited" [108]), the mad theatricalization of the innermost desires and incapacities of each of the principal characters would seem complete.

What has happened? On the one hand, these musical numbers have expressed for these characters their deepest desires. In exaggerated and highly stylized form, they have staged the personas and conflicts with which each has been struggling throughout the play, the set of oppositions by which each has constructed his/her own identity. But the characters have also assumed these parts in the midst of a *crise*. The Follies curtains and costumes have arrived in the middle of a madness which is in high gear, "just as there seems to be no possible way out" (83) the stage directions tell us. Acting in reality as if you are in the privacy of your own mind is the textbook instance of the word. Neurotics believe in ghosts, psychoanalysts are fond of saying, but psychotics believe ghosts. At the moment of the peak intensity in their exchange with their younger selves, all communication with the "outside world" has vanished.

The Follies extravaganza before us, in other words, is thus both happening and in a curious way, not happening at all, and both this happening and this nonhappening are taking place before us in the theater and within the play itself. *We* see it as theatrical, as a mini-Follies, as reminiscent of the Ziegfeld extravaganzas of earlier years, from which some of the performers have in fact come. But if we were to ask what has been realistically occurring for the characters while this theatrical event has been in progress, we would be hard put to answer, and not only because this event is a fiction.

This gala event is not a series of musical numbers like others in the play. It is not a series of dramatic songs, for example, the bubbling up of an emotional expression which *we* understand as song but which the characters understand as a kind of conversation. Nor is it a diegetic song of which this play is also full, in which an awareness of the song being performed is also a part of the dramatic action. What we *can* say is that at the moment of the break what is substituted is a narrative, a set of musical stories in which the scripts for the conflicts are enacted and which stands in the place of what can only be described as a gap or hole in the dramatic action.

There is a similar narrative break in Jerzy Kosinski's *The Painted Bird* that may help us to think about the problem.[31] The narrator is a young boy (of six or seven) who has been wandering the countryside in Poland during the

Holocaust, having been dislocated from his parents. He has been witness to atrocities in the villages in which he has lived, and has been subject to them. In one village he comes to stay with an elderly woman who is regarded respectfully by the villagers as something of a witch or shaman.

On one particular occasion he contracts a fever, and the old woman, Olga, decides to "plant" him. She takes him to a field, digs a hole, puts him in it, fills it in with dirt up to the boy's head, and leaves him there. "Like an abandoned head of cabbage," he says, "I became part of the great field" (21). During the night he is awakened by the noise of a flock of ravens who are circling overhead. They begin to land, and although at first they are wary of the boy, gradually they move closer. The boy begins to scream, and for a time that gesture wards them off. But that strategy finally fails and they surround him and begin to peck at his head.

> I turned my head from side to side, loosening the earth around my neck. But my movements only made the birds more curious. They surrounded me and pecked at me wherever they could. I called loudly, but my voice was too weak to rise above the earth and only seeped back into the soil without reaching the hut where Olga lay.
>
> The birds played with me freely. The more furiously I swiveled my head to and fro, the more excited and bold they became. Seeming to avoid my face, they attacked the back of my head.
>
> My strength ebbed. To move my head each time seemed like shifting a huge sack of grain from one place to another. I was crazed and saw everything as through a miasmal fog.
>
> I gave up. I was myself now a bird. I was trying to free my chilled wings from the earth. Stretching my limbs, I joined the flock of ravens. Borne abruptly up on a gust of fresh, reviving wind, I soared straight into a ray of sunshine that lay taut on the horizon like a drawn bowstring, and my joyous cawing was mimicked by my winged companions.
>
> Olga found me in the midst of the swarming flock of ravens. I was nearly frozen and my head was deeply lacerated by the birds. She quickly dug me out. (23-4)

How are we to read such a passage? The words are clear. But in the context in which they appear they constitute a narrative break. The scene cannot have happened the way it is described. We are in a world where indeed horrible things can happen, but not one in which people can fly, or at will become birds and "[soar] straight into a ray of sunshine."

What is "happening," we may say, is a traumatic event, one too powerful for words, one that overwhelms the human registry system so that the only ways to describe it are by means of fragments or shards which emerge from it. The narrative is not entirely arbitrary. It describes after all, a mode of escape from a threatening situation. But neither is it representational. Its connection to the reality it offers us is metonymic rather than metaphoric. It is continuous with that reality rather than analogous to it. It literalizes in the text a bit of language that is itself derivative from and thus an extension of the situation.

> I was myself now a bird. . . . Stretching my limbs, I joined the flock of ravens. Borne abruptly up on a gust of fresh, reviving wind, I soared straight into a ray of sunshine . . . .

The bizarre inappropriateness of the language to the event is itself the evidence for the taking of flight.

In a similar way, it seems to me, we may understand the mini-Follies of the present production. The mini-Follies is a narrative break. But it is not one that occurs out of context (as it does for example in the *Follies in Concert* version where none of this explanation applies). The ghosts of the younger versions of all the characters have been haunting the stage all evening, and we have had no difficulty describing them as "living memories," the literalizations of the older characters' thoughts about what occurred in the past. Even the intense interaction of the characters with the younger selves may be described as the literalization of the act of giving body to their past to the extent that they can audibly be heard doing so and not themselves be able to tell the difference between the ghosts and real others, between those whom they can see right through and saying (as for example Ben does) "you see straight through me" (110).

To some extent then the Follies may be described as a continuation and intensification of that literalization process. They are wearing their emotions on their sleeves, we may say. They think they are Helen Morgan or Fred Astaire, that they are leading around a chorus of beautiful young men or that they have women waiting for them in every port. But unlike the earlier scene in which they yelled at younger versions of themselves (which can be translated as the enactment of their memories), this series of events cannot have happened at will. We can speak to an earlier version of ourselves, but we cannot become Helen Morgan or Fred Astaire. When such events do occur, and we witness it on stage as the Follies, we have entered their minds entirely. But we are at the same time entirely outside their minds because in fact historical events like the ones we are witnessing did occur. They were also called the Follies and those characters that we see before us performed in them.

It is precisely that quality of being at once absolutely within their minds and absolutely outside their minds within memory of the historical event known as the Follies that breaks the boundaries of what can be spoken. Sally could and perhaps did enact roles that resembled Helen Morgan in her Follies years, but she did not become Helen Morgan. The suspension of disbelief never extended to that point, and if she ever imagined that it did she would quickly have been removed from the show.

Take, for example, Mama Rose in *Gypsy*. Like Sally she also has theatrical aspirations. She has never been herself a performer as Sally has, but she has been deeply involved with the theater. And when her second daughter and husband leave her, she loses it. In "Rose's Turn," she takes to the stage and acts as if she is the star, as if she is the one they came to see, a dramatic confusion that seems to derive—at least in the way Ethel Merman delivers the lines in the original production—from her relationship to her own mother.[32] But never for a moment do we think that she is really the star of the diegetic song she is performing. We regard her action as simply the form her breakdown takes, one which for another individual might have assumed another form. For us to believe that she is really the star, the world would suddenly have to alter and she would suddenly have to be projected into the starring routine in front of us.

Which is exactly what happens in Follies. It is as if each of the characters is suddenly projected into the starring role in a number by which they would clearly define their struggle but the numbers for each have somehow been co-ordinated (so that they are not happening all at once) and nothing but the numbers is happening (so that we don't see others gaping on curiously while all this is taking place, and there is no "outside world" to be observed or observing). From the point of view of the characters it makes no difference. They have lost communication with the outside world for the moment, and they perform their numbers whether they are doing it on a Follies stage or, like Mama Rose, on a vacant stage observed only by her daughter.

But for us it makes a difference and in fact makes all the difference. For while for them it is private fantasy (albeit private fantasy which has subsumed the social and real worlds), for us it's the Follies. It's what we came to the theater expecting to see. Watching a mini-version of the Follies which happens to coincide line for line and point for point with their madnesses, *we* are suddenly drawn into their drama.

And that participation on our part is decisive. For suddenly there is no way to tell whether what we are watching is one or the other. We cannot deny it is the Follies since in all regards it reproduces the Follies sequence in miniature. But neither can we deny it is the madnesses of the characters since in all regards it is also the culmination of their emotional lives as we have seen them develop. As these numbers are at once their madness and also routines within a familiar, historically datable, theatrical extravaganza, a new identification becomes possible. At this moment of the most intense repetition, of the transference of the old upon the new, and the projection of the inner upon the outer, madness, *la folie*, has also become once again, precisely, theater.

Or to put it the other way around, theater and madness at this moment in the play are one and the same. Theater we may say in this context is madness coordinated, stylized, organized. Madness, by the same token, we may say is theater that has escaped the confines of the stage and now plays to anyone who will listen. Subtracting the presence of the outside world from madness, and choosing theater that concerns the themes that have animated the emotional lives of the characters, we produce a result in which the two are indistinguishable—the Follies sequence by which the play concludes.

There is only a "hole" in the dramatic action, in other words, if we think representationally or metaphorically. If we think metonymically there is nothing "behind" what we see, not because it is empty, but because there is no foreground and background to speak of, only two parallel series of associations which happen to have converged at this present point: one at a party where there is also a theater (the Weismann theater), another at the theater where there is also a party (the show *Follies*); one at which a madness assumes the form of a presentation of a bit of theater, another at which a theatrical event assumes the form of the presentation of a bit of madness. The madness for which the Follies substitutes cannot be represented on stage not because words are inadequate but because there are no words, because what we mean by representation (among other things) is the ability to distinguish words from worlds (or saying from being) and it is that distinction that has collapsed. The fragmentary substitutions of theatrical bits from the past—ours or those of the characters—allows us to witness what the characters cannot: namely, that absence of words, that collapse of distinction, that impossibility of representation.

But as soon as we make this identification, as soon as we recognize that what now is madness once was theater (and conversely that what now is theater once was madness), something else becomes clear, something I would suggest that may be the key to the whole show. For suddenly we come to understand in a way that was not apparent before that the entire play has been a circle. The very theatricalizations with which the play opened, numbers which recalled musical events thirty years earlier and whose originals are now—in the minds of the party-goers (and perhaps the audience as well)—dim recollections, were already themselves (we also now come to understand) the *same* projections into which the play has just a moment ago climactically erupted, the same madness writ large, so to speak, by which those on stage and those off chose (and continue to choose) to disavow themselves of their own responsibility for the breakdown of boundaries they are currently experiencing.

The experience that the characters thought at the beginning of the evening was behind them, in other words, was in fact before them. Their enactments have succeeded beyond their wildest expectations. The future upon which they have counted has turned out only a future anterior, a modality of what "will have happened" as they continue to enact a drama that has already occurred. In the beginning of the evening was memory, the nostalgic recollection of what was past. Then memory gave way to enactment, the reappropriation of the dramas of the past acted out in the present. Then that enactment in turn gave way to a kind of interruption of the reality principle as the characters pursued their chosen or imagined parts independently, finally, of the social obstacles—the consensual symbolic universe—around them. But finally that interruption, that madness itself, assumed the form in their present which coincided identically with (and thus was inseparable from) the theatrical forms the characters initially remembered, as if in the future of *this* present they would once again look back upon this madness as simply theater.

Theater, in other words, in this play, in this context, has become for Sondheim and Goldman neither more nor less than the projections of the scripts by which we live our lives in the face of their own incapacities. The famous Shakespearean adage "All the world's a stage" becomes in Sondheim's music and lyrics and Goldman's libretto—as undoubtedly it was already in Shakespeare's plays—not a truism but the expression of a crisis. All the world should not be a stage. We should be able to tell the difference between the stage and the world. And when those boundaries go, whether they go within our romantic relationships, our marriages, our fairy tales, or more dangerously and more publicly within our political commitments, the result may well prove devastating.

And in the face of *this* doubling, of the superimposition of madness upon theater that *Follies* offers us (with the infernal and vicious repetition which is its signature), the only characters who survive are those who can pick up the pieces—the fragments—and move on. Sally Durant, for example, seems unable to do so. "We're gonna go and get some rest," her husband Buddy tells her. "And then we're gonna make plans for tomorrow" (110). Looking up at the "ruined theater" around her, hardly able to move, and perhaps thinking of the future about which the younger versions of the four lovers sang, she remarks: "Oh dear God, it *is* tomorrow." Ben Stone, on the other hand, seems curiously able to continue. Ben, who has prided himself on sophistication and self-control, and consequently whose collapse on stage has been the most spectacular, is able to confront his wife, Phyllis (who has curiously and courageously stayed by him all these years, and is able to pick up the pieces, even amidst this shattering). He is able to say to her, "I've always been afraid of you. You see straight through me and I've always thought, 'It isn't possible; it can't be me she loves'" (110). The ghost of his former self, this "thing of darkness," this empty transparency that has been following him around the stage all evening, he is able to acknowledge his own.

From memory, to enactment, to madness, to theatricalization, to sober reality, to the possibility of new recollection. One more turn of the spiral has occurred. But in the process, for those of us who have witnessed it, and perhaps as well for those of us who have gone through it (if indeed the two are separable), something decisive has taken place. Some new awareness has become possible. The refrain sung repeatedly by the younger lovers, "You're gonna love tomorrow," is indeed no longer a viable option, either as a strategy of delay ("tomorrow" as an adverb), or as the identification of a future love object ("tomorrow" as a noun). The fact of the matter, as Sally notes, is that "it *is* tomorrow." The life you have led while you were waiting for your life to begin has been your life. But in place of that future, that "tomorrow," something else has become available: a new opening to experience, a new honesty about responsibility and obligation, a new maturity and adulthood.

Follies has, in short, completed the itinerary opened in *Company*, and the two plays form in this fashion a complementarity, what we might call the "before" and "after" of the happy ending. The problem has been posed in these plays in its entirety, and turns out not to be limited to marriage, or love, or even the musical comedy tradition. It concerns our being in the world at large: being in all the contexts in which it has traditionally been posed—in our imaginary lives (in which we construct images of ourselves), in our symbolic or social lives (in which we answer to the law and to language), and in the real lives in which we age and die. The spell has not yet been broken. That will come later in *Into the Woods*, when the Witch will be able to sing "Careful the tale you tell. / *That* is the spell."[33] Until that moment, Sondheim, along with the various librettists with whom he works, will continue to map out the various ways in which the happy ending fails us, and what as a result we take it upon ourselves to do about it.

Happy endings have been with us for a long time, perhaps as long as there have been stories. In the Western world, the happy ending as we understand it has its origins not in American theater, of course, but in comedy itself as a genre, as we inherit it from the Romans and Greeks, from playwrights like Plautus to whom Sondheim turned when he wrote *Forum*, or like Aristophanes to whom he will turn shortly when he scores *The Frogs*. And a critique of the happy ending was already a part of Shakespeare's theater from which Sondheim would also learn so much in *A Little Night Music*. One could argue that the entire history of Shakespearean tragedy emerges from the collapse of the happy ending, and the registry of the consequences of its failure—for Hamlet, Othello, Lear, Macbeth, Anthony, and Coriolanus.

But the criticism Sondheim lodges against that happy ending is more specific and concerns in part at least the use made of it by the culture supporting musicals like those of Rodgers and Hammerstein or the traditions preceding them, a use which is deeply bound up in the American psyche with its European origin as "declaration of independence," and a bill of rights or entitlements, among which are declared to be "life, liberty, and the pursuit of happiness," a use which can in fact also include murder. "Everybody's / Got the right / To their dreams" (7), sing the chorus of assassins in the play of the same name. The monstrous truth in this regard is not that the happy ending is an impossible dream but to the contrary that as sustained by marriage and by a political, legal, and industrial economy, it is an eminently possible end to accomplish, although life within it—in certain conditions—may be unbearable. What Sondheim makes clear, in any event, is its price tag. Fairy tales, Sondheim will have his characters sing in *Into the Woods*, "come true, / Not free" (136). Unless we take stock of the inordinate danger that attends living our fairy tales, we are bound to suffer the consequences of their success and impose those consequences—in an egregious and often bloody fashion— upon others: in political, economic, psychological, social, marital, aesthetic experience, and generally all the ways in which we continue to relate to others and to ourselves.

To begin to uncover this disclosure on Sondheim's part, to trace this price—this loss, this "little death"—in all his lyrical, musical, and dramatic gestures (as he traces it in all aspects of our lives), is the task I envision for the book that follows. It is one that I suspect will continue to concern us for some time to come, those of us who love Sondheim's work, who continue to find enduring literary and critical value in what he does, and who look forward to his recognition within the academy and general populace as the most original and thoughtful and serious writer the American musical stage has ever produced.

NOTES

[1] Adler 1978, 513-25.

[2] Adler 1978, 513.

[3] Adler 1978, 524.

[4] For a discussion of the Pulitzer prize winners and Sondheim in that context, see Adler 1987.

[5] For a sample of the kinds of reviews Sondheim was getting in the early years of the 1970s, see Barnes 1970 and 1971, Clurman 1971, Gill 1970, Gottfried April 27, 1970, April 5, 1971, April 25, 1971, and February 26, 1973, Gussow 1970 and April 1971, Harris 1970, 1971, and 1973, Hewes 1970 and 1971, Kalem 1971 and 1973, Kaufmann 1970, Kelly 1970, Kerr 1970 and 1971, Kroll 1971 and 1973, Lahr 1970, Newman 1970, O'Conner 1970, Popkin 1971, Probst 1971 and 1973, Schubeck 1971, Simon 1971, Tolliver 1973, Watt 1970, 1971, and 1973, Watts 1970, 1971, and 1973, and Wilson 1973.

[6] Zadan and Gordon make these points repeatedly. See Zadan 1994 and Gordon 1992.

[7] See Adler 1978. Frank Rich had also done so. See Prince 1974, 169-70.

[8] It is reported, for example, that the makers of *Rent* turned to Sondheim when the show seemed in some difficulty.

[9] In a review of *Passion*, John Lahr writes that Sondheim's "perverse brilliance" and "intellectual ambition" has "brought the American musical" to a "dead-end." See Lahr 1994, 89.

[10] Marvin Carlson's work is a notable exception. See Carlson 1993. Bigsby's book, which claims to treat the entirety of modern American drama, mentions Sondheim as one of three names responsible for *Forum*. See Bigsby 1992.

[11] Schiff 1993.

[12] I proposed such a course for the Cornell Adult University program in the summer of 1994 which I taught with Allen Menton. I described it in the first issue of *The Sondheim Review*. See Goodhart June 1994.

[13] I proposed and moderated a "Special Session" on Stephen Sondheim at the annual convention of the Modern Language Association in December of 1993. I proposed, moderated, and read a paper at a meeting of the Ars Lyrica Society as an "Associated Meeting" of the annual convention of the Modern Language Association in December of 1995.

[14] Sondheim also taught a course at Southern Methodist University in the fall of 1994.

[15] See Abrams, "Art-As-Such" (1985), and *Doing Things with Texts* (1989), among other writings.

[16] See Foucault on these two modes at the conclusion of *The Order of Things* (1970).

[17] Abrams calls this "covert theology" within a context of "natural supernaturalism." See Abrams 1971.

[18] There is another problem. We speak in this essay as if the idea that Sondheim has written all of this work is without complication—comparable, for example, to saying that Arthur Miller wrote all of his work. Yet it is very clear from what has been written about the making of shows like *Follies* or *Company* that a great many talents went into the effort—those of Harold Prince, Michael Bennett, Boris Aronson, not to mention the efforts of orchestrators, costume designers, and librettists who clearly contributed significant portions. By what right may we call this work Sondheim's? The simple (and perhaps unexpected) answer in this case is that we do not have any right and that, indeed, is a problem. Were we to consider, say, *Follies*, or *Company* alone, we could probably not clearly identify what is peculiarly Sondheim's as opposed to Prince's or Bennett's—albeit, neither could we identify what is uniquely another's. But as the body of Sondheim's work begins to accumulate, and as we begin to see what remains constant from work to work and collaborator to collaborator, the task gets easier, and that becomes another argument for considering not just an individual work, but the whole range of Sondheim's output, everything for which he has been given the credit.

There is another issue. In what sense can we speak of a text in this domain in the way that we can of a novel by Salmon Rushdie or a poem by Carolyn Forché? If Forché or Rushdie publish a text, and we read it, we can point to the page on which the verbal effect occurs. If we want to make a point about a painting we can point to a spot where that effect is generated. If we want to talk about a film, we have the technology now to stop the film and point to the very frames in which the event occurs. But "where" is musical comedy? Where is the text to be analyzed? The event combines dance, music, acting, and compounds the textualization problem of all of these. In this regard the problem is not unique to musical comedy, of course. It is one that is faced by opera and to different extents by dance and other types of theatrical performances. Musical comedy is only a new combination of proportions allotted to spoken language, dance, singing, and visual effects. At its most typical it combines the dance of a dance recital, the acting of straight theater, the singing of opera, and the visual effects of other visually oriented entertainment spectacles. As before, we offer no clear solution to this difficulty, which needs to be addressed further, although this kind of textualization and authorship question may offer another reason for the delay of a full and serious consideration of Sondheim within the academy (as Banfield notes). See Banfield 1993, 3.

[19] See Zadan 1994, Gordon 1992, Gottfried 1993, and Banfield 1993.

[20] For an assessment of Gottfried's book, see McMillin 1994.

[21] For a review of Banfield's book, see Menton 1994.

[22] Banfield 1993, 4.

[23] Banfield 1993, 1.

[24] Sondheim, "Theater Lyrics", 95. The last song of *Company* was particularly troublesome for Prince. No fewer than four songs were tried. "Marry Me, A Little" in which Robert proposes to Amy (who has not married at the end of act 1) was the first. His proposal was thought to be "too knowing" for the character and so "Multitudes of Amys" was written to make it more believable. "Happily Ever After" was inserted in the Boston opening. Prince thought that song too "negative" and "bitter" (although Sondheim describes it as a "scream of agony") and so "Being Alive" was substituted. See "Theater Lyrics," 92-7.

[25] Sartre 1962, 91.

[26] Furth and Sondheim 1970.

[27] Sondheim, "Theater Lyrics," 92-7.

[28] See Gordon 1990 for her discussion of the issue.

[29] For comments by Sondheim, Prince, and Furth that Manhattan is "the perfect metaphor for their work [in *Company*]," see Gordon 1992, 39-41.

[30] Goldman and Sondheim 1971.

[31] Kosinski 1978.

[32] Sondheim comments [in taped remarks to Sandor Goodhart] that it is a "mistake that many people make" to think that Rose is invoking her relationship to her own mother. "It's a common [mistake] because of Ethel Merman's performance of 'Rose's Turn.' When she is saying 'M-M-M-Momma,' she's not referring to her own mother. She is stuttering on the repeated use of the word 'Momma,' as in 'Momma's talkin' loud,' which refers, of course, to herself, [and] because she has reached the phrase 'Momma's lettin' go—,' which causes her mind to sort of hit a blank wall (because that's the thing that Gypsy told her in the blowout in the dressing room scene). 'M-M-M-Momma' is a stuttering because her mind has stopped, and not a call for help from her mother. Ethel never quite understood how to do it so it always sounded as if she were calling for her mother.

[33] Lapine and Sondheim 1992, 136.

PART 1

SOURCES, INSTITUTIONS, THEMES

CHAPTER 1

The Sung and the Said
Literary Value in the Musical Dramas
of Stephen Sondheim
Thomas P. Adler

In 1974, Stephen Sondheim and Burt Shevelove collaborated on a musical adaptation of *The Frogs*, which does for Aristophanes pretty much what they had done for Plautus eight years earlier in *A Funny Thing Happened on the Way to the Forum*.[1] In the later play, Dionysos, who believes that we "lack passion" in our lives, journeys to Hades to bring Bernard Shaw back to earth.[2] After hearing a lively competition between Shaw and Shakespeare, however, Dionysos decides that instead of Shaw (who "stand[s] for the great abstractions: conscience, virtue, integrity" [116]) what the world and theater most need is "a *poet* . . . to lift [them] out of their seats" (120) so that they will be actively inspired to do something about salvaging the earth they have abused. In lyrics to a song entitled "The Sound of Poets" that might well express their writer's own artistic credo, the Chorus charges the poet to attempt the following:

> Bring a sense of purpose,
> Bring the taste of words,
> Bring the sound of wit,
> Bring the feel of passion,
> Bring the glow of thought
> To the darkening earth. (124)

These are all achievements that Sondheim, the single most important creative force in the American musical theater from the 1960s through the 1990s, has accomplished since that night now almost forty years ago when New York audiences first heard his lyrics in the revolutionary dance musical *West Side Story*. And if the myopic critics did not even mention his name the next morning in their notices, they have had numerous occasions since then to remedy their oversight in reviewing the fifteen other shows in which

Sondheim has been creatively involved either as lyricist or as lyricist–composer—including *Company*, *Follies*, and *A Little Night Music*, for which he won an unprecedented three successive Tony Awards, and *Sunday in the Park with George*, for which he won, with librettist James Lapine, a Pulitzer Prize.

In this essay, I will test out a number of critical approaches to Sondheim's work—generic, formalist, thematic—in an attempt to assess his contribution to the musical as a form. In the first part, I will focus in particular on those shows (usually done in collaboration with producer–director Harold Prince) that depart most markedly from the integrated book musical epitomized by Rodgers and Hammerstein's *Oklahoma!* and *South Pacific*. And in the second part, I will center on those works since the beginning of the 1980s (in collaboration with George Furth, John Weidman, and James Lapine) in which Sondheim has explored somewhat darker, more modernist, themes, ones that have also interested other dramatists like Eugene O'Neill and Edward Albee. I will argue, ultimately, that Sondheim is distinct among writers for the American musical stage in that he has a philosophy, an ideology that he continually expresses and deepens throughout his musicals and that raises them above the realm of popular entertainment—though they are, happily, still that—and places them among those works for the American stage that can be said to have not only artistic merit but a literary value as well.

To say as much is not to suggest, of course, that there were no "serious" musicals before Sondheim—for we can go back as far as Kern, Hammerstein, and Ferber's *Showboat*, or the Gershwins' *Porgy and Bess*, or Blitzstein's *The Cradle Will Rock* for these. Nor is it to say that no composer–lyricist had ever before developed a distinctive style—for the urbane sophistication tinged with skepticism that Cole Porter displayed to the nth degree is that. Nor, finally, is it to imply that no team had ever before expressed a recurring outlook on life through a number of shows—for we can point to the optimistic faith in man found in such Rodgers and Hammerstein songs as "You'll Never Walk Alone" from *Carousel*, and "Climb Every Mountain" from *The Sound of Music* for that. But all these earlier efforts attempt something quite different from what Sondheim undertakes—which is to consistently embody and refine several themes into that rarest of all achievements in this popular context—a body of thought.

I

The integrated book musical which, in theory anyway, ideally permits only those songs that either advance the plot or reveal character, is an extension or outgrowth of the representational, illusion-of-reality drama that dominated the American stage at least until the beginning of World War II (and is still a potent force today). Yet when we acknowledge that no matter how realistic a play is in its trappings we, as audience, are still tacitly aware that we are in a theater watching only an imitation of reality, pretending that we are *not* pretending, then it becomes clear that the *total* illusion of reality is, strictly speaking, an artificial goal—though its very artificiality opens up the possibility of its becoming art. How much more true this claim must necessarily be of the musical, where the suspension of disbelief is even more complete, since most people do not go singing and dancing through life.

The aesthetic principle governing the occurrence of song in the organic book musical is analogous to that governing the use of poetry in drama. Just as poetry, according to T. S. Eliot, is appropriate in the drama only when prose is no longer capable of containing and conveying the emotion, so, too, one can justifiably break into song only when dialogue can no longer adequately express feeling or, in Sondheim's own words, "the climaxes of emotion and action erupt into music because they can't go further without it."[3]

This eruption is perhaps nowhere better evident in the musicals with which Sondheim has been associated than at the end of *Gypsy* (1959, with book by Arthur Laurents and music by Jule Styne), which Sondheim calls—and I concur—"one of the two or three best shows ever written . . . the last good one in the Rodgers and Hammerstein form."[4] In "Rose's Turn," the boundary between the sung and the said becomes virtually indistinguishable as Mama Rose, while admitting that she pushed her daughters into show business so that they could achieve in reality what she had dreamed of accomplishing for herself, desperately pleads for her own belated chance at stardom. Her knowledge that the talent, drive, and ego essential for success really did exist—and still are there—must now be emotionally supported and nurtured by her daughter, Gypsy Rose, in what Sondheim views as an imperative reversal of roles: "You outgrow your parents and then eventually they become your responsibility . . . they become your children."[5]

Developments in the nonmusical drama in the 1940s and 1950s in the direction of nonrepresentational, nonillusionistic staging helped alter audience expectations about the musical theater as well, and their demand for the integrated book musical began to wane, opening the way for an acceptance of freer forms. So, by the 1960s, we have Jones and Schmidt's *The Fantasticks* and *Celebration*, Littlewood's *Oh, What a Lovely War!*, Leigh, Darion, and Wasserman's *Man of La Mancha*, and, especially, Kander, Ebb, and Masteroff's *Cabaret*, all of which, in their own way, are technically the equivalents of Wilder's *Our Town* and *The Skin of Our Teeth*, Williams' *The Glass Menagerie* and Miller's *Death of a Salesman*. All turn a seeming liability into a definite asset, deliberately emphasizing that we are in a theater, glorying in the theatrical form *as* form. Readily accepting nonrealistic devices of staging and structure in even our serious drama, we now no longer demand that every song lyric develop the plot line or enhance character motivation. Song can become commentative (or editorial, if you like), illustrative, connective, a punctuation device, or a device to be employed for exposition. It can also be used contrapuntally, or even serve—and this would ordinarily be anathema in the dramatic form—as a breather.

In short, when song can once again exist for itself and still, instead of detracting from the aesthetic design and integrity of the whole, complement it, the uses of song within the musical drama become almost boundless. Martin Gottfried and others have termed this new type of musical the "concept musical."[6] We might also, despite Sondheim's disparagement of the too exclusively didactic Brecht as "humorless" ("his points," Sondheim writes, "[are] so obvious in the text itself that the songs have no surprise or wit"), call this new freer kind of musical the "epic musical," if by epic we understand what Brecht did, namely, a play which narrates or relates rather than exclusively dramatizes or incarnates events.[7] Some critics, including Emanuel Azenberg, who finds shows like *Company* and *Follies* "soulless," would go so far as to attribute a dose of Brechtian alienation or estrangement to Sondheim's musicals.[8] It seems to me, however, that Sondheim avoids this distancing precisely because his music is, by its very nature, emotional in its appeal, and also because there almost always is, with the exception of *Pacific Overtures* (which the scenic designer Boris Aronson says flatly is "about issues and not about people and moods"), a central figure(s) with whom we empathize (as there often is, too, in Brecht, his theory notwithstanding).[9]

Pacific Overtures (1976, with book by John Weidman) is the most unconventional of Sondheim's musical plays and, because it is political in its thrust, also the most overtly Brechtian. Musically, it blends a vaguely Oriental style throughout with, here and there, touches of the pulsating urban rhythms one finds in the Leonard Bernstein of *On the Town* and *West Side Story*, and even a splash of John Philip Sousa and a dash of the French cancan and a measure of Gilbert and Sullivan recitative for added flavor. Stylistically, it owes several debts to the Kabuki theater: first, for its Reciter, who is alternately observer, narrator, storyteller, ironic and/or moral commentator, and bridge between action and audience; second, for its black-clad stagehands who shift scenery; and finally, for its use of a *hanamichi* or runway.

Telling the story of the Westernization of Japan, the show takes its title directly from the journals of Commodore Perry who arrives there in 1853, in appearance "a lionlike figure of terror from a child's dream, complete with flowing white mane," anxious to impose civilization—by barbarous force if necessary.[10] (This achievement in itself would seem to qualify it for honors as the first Broadway musical directly spawned by our involvement in Vietnam.) As presented in the opening song, "The Advantages of Floating in the Middle of the Sea," Japan is deliberately insular and isolated, a nation for whom "beauty is truth" (Keats's words) and the most valued activities are the painting of screens and the ritualized taking of bows. In general, scenes without music alternate with those with music; some of them, such as the

"Chrysanthemum Tea," are entirely sung. There are even times when we have lyric-as-poem, as in "Poems," with its haiku-like and tanka-like forms, or the enchanting "Someone in a Tree," which, built on the Berkeleyan notion that nothing exists but what is seen or observed, stresses the importance of the least individual, or of the lesser phenomenon over the greater:

> I'm a fragment of the day.
> If I weren't, who's to say
> Things would happen here the way
> That they happened here?
> . . . .
> It's the fragment, not the day.
> It's the pebble, not the stream.
> It's the ripple, not the sea,
> Not the building but the beam. (59-60)

Except for a minor thread, *Pacific Overtures* lacks what most musicals consider indispensable, a love interest—which may partially account for its limited popularity. (Indeed, even when there is a love plot in his shows, Sondheim until *Passion* ordinarily tends to eschew the love duet that has become a staple of the musical comedy form.) But the probable reason for its failure with audiences—and Weidman's book is more at fault here—quite likely resides in the inability to keep interest from waning in act 2, which is essentially no more than a series of separate scenes illustrating the thesis that capitalism and industrialization bring dehumanization in their wake, that the hallowed idea of progress has its sour notes as a culture and its beauty are destroyed, that the distorted values which we introduced to Japan have ironically come back to haunt us. The pupil has learned the master's lesson only too well and now beats the West at its own game. At the end, time is telescoped and we are suddenly thrust into the present when, in the song "Next," we see the influence, particularly in things economic, that Japan today exerts over the rest of the world.

Sondheim ventures into the realm of Grand Guignol to present a considerably darker—even subversive—critique of socioeconomic culture in *Sweeney Todd, The Demon Barber of Fleet Street: A Musical Thriller* (1979), a near-operatic work with a libretto by Hugh Wheeler based upon Christopher Bond's updated version of one of the most popular British melodramas of the nineteenth century.[11] Complete with dumb show and masque, it has elements as well of the Elizabethan revenge play and of Jacobean tragicomedy. Here, Dickensian London becomes a lunatic asylum and a fiery inferno, peopled like Dante's hell by the rapacious, the venal, and the hypocritical. The capitalistic system in all its manifestations—political, legal, ecclesiastical, social, industrial—works on the principle of victimization of those down below by those up above; the great chain of being has been transformed, in Eugene Lee's drop curtain for the show's "Prologue," into an inhumane "British Bee Hive" or honeycomb.

Sweeney Todd, sent off to penal servitude fifteen years earlier for no other reason than the fact that his beautiful wife became the object of Judge Turpin's jealous lust, returns hungry for revenge to be accomplished by slitting throats. Mrs. Lovett, whose shop sits below Todd's tonsorial parlor, finds an ingenious use for his victims as free filling for her meat pies; in the face of a system that enslaves, her plucky entrepreneurial spirit, fed solely by profiteering on the misfortunes of others, seems deliberately intended to recall Brecht's Mother Courage. And the literalization of the cannibalism, the universal condition of man eating man, that lies at the heart of social (dis)order which measures everything by its commodity value, finds brilliant expression in the amoral glee of Todd and Lovett's exuberant duet "A Little Priest," replete with saucy double entendres ranking members of the upper social strata on the basis of their comparative delectability.

The binary patterning of the work's images and motifs—victim/victimizer, vengeance/forgiveness, lust/love, caged/free, sanity/lunacy, angel/devil, high/low—points, however, to the way in which boundaries are permeable as these opposites continually bleed one into the other. The ethical ambiguity that results can probably best be seen through the handling of Todd's daughter, Johanna, as a jewel to be treasured. After violating her mother, Turpin trapped Johanna in his home as his ward, and now has designs on forcing her to marry him. Mrs. Lovett proposes that she and Todd confine Johanna in their home in a condition hardly less imprisoning; and Todd's possessiveness of his daughter objectifies her as well; so the young sailor in love with her must talk of stealing her and even Johanna herself is left with no choice but to kill in order to save her rescuer from death. Ultimately, a disguised Johanna barely escapes murder at Todd's hands, as his wife and Mrs. Lovett cannot do when he apes the worst excesses of the system that once victimized him and his vengeance spirals out of control. In the play's Epilogue, even the audience is challenged to consider its own implication in the evil and destruction it has witnessed onstage. That some of the most rapturous and sensuous music Sondheim has ever written, especially the songs "Johanna" and "Pretty Women," is found within *Sweeney Todd* perhaps itself signals the continuation, however fragile, of beauty and innocence within an otherwise animalistic world. If these verities just barely survive, all other forms of hegemonic power are called into question if not completely undermined in this blackly humorous, well-nigh apocalyptic work.

In *Company* (1970, with book by George Furth), which in the 1970s was not just his most contemporary but also his most sophisticated score, Sondheim employs song in almost as radical a fashion as he later would in *Pacific Overtures*.[12] It has something of the unity and coherence, the repetition and reverberation of motifs, that we ordinarily expect only in a symphonic composition. Here, song is sometimes used for ironic comment, as in the brittle and cynically brilliant "The Ladies Who Lunch," that hymn to suburban matrons who fill up their empty days in empty ways, "Keeping house but clutching a copy of *Life* / Just to keep in touch" (106). Sometimes it is used to illustrate a scene, as in "The Little Things You Do Together." Other times it is used to be illustrated *by* (or parallel) a scene, as is the case with "Another Hundred People," a song that encapsulates the play's emphasis on the "lonely crowd syndrome," what Sondheim regards as "the increasing difficulty of making one-to-one relationships in an increasingly dehumanized society."[13]

At still other times, the song might exist outside of or divorced from the scene, perhaps for the purpose of character comment as in "You Could Drive a Person Crazy"—an affectionate parody of the Andrews Sisters. Or again, it might be, all by itself, a short, self-contained playlet, a structure which Hammerstein taught Sondheim to strive after as an ideal: "a song should be like a little one-act play, with an exposition, a development and a conclusion; at the end of the song the character should have moved to a different position from where he was emotionally at the beginning."[14] Probably the best example of this structure from *Company* is "Barcelona," in which Sondheim toys around with the tradition of the *aubade*: Robert, who does not even know the name of the stewardess with whom he has spent the night, and knowing that she must leave to catch her next flight, makes believe he would like her to stay. But she, unfortunately, succumbs to his insincere entreaties; as she "snuggles down" with him in bed, he can only bring this unlove duet to a close with a plaintive cry against even this little bit of permanence and commitment, "Oh, God!" (100).

From what has been said thus far, one should not conclude, however, that Sondheim only rarely uses song for its traditional function of revealing character, since he displays an especial affection for what he terms the "inner monologue song," as is particularly evident in both *Follies* (1971) and *A Little Night Music* (1973).[15] Though the latter, with a book by Hugh Wheeler, is adapted from Ingmar Bergman's film *Smiles of a Summer Night*, this stylish and delightful Chekhovian musical, with all its music in three-quarter time or some variation thereof, is vastly different in tone from its source, as Bergman himself observed: "I was surprised that it was possible to eliminate the shadows of desperation, eroticism, and caprice without the whole story collapsing. At the moment I forgot that this entertaining and witty musical had anything to do with my picture."[16]

Tonally and structurally, an even closer source would seem to be Shakespearean romantic comedy, especially *A Midsummer Night's Dream*. Both concern the lunacy of lovers—a topic pursued earlier in the number that was originally to have opened *Forum*, "Love Is in the Air," which cautioned, "Leave your house and lose your reason, / This is the contagious season."[17]

Both involve as well deserting the city with its artificial forms and strictures for the more natural couplings in the country. But if there are no magic love potions in *Night Music*, there is the "perpetual sunset" of Sweden that proves "rather an unsettling thing."[18]

The triptych of songs that begins the play, all essentially soliloquies complete with subtext or "subline," demonstrates the validity of Laurents' assertion that Sondheim "is the only lyricist who almost always writes songs that can only be sung by the particular character they are written for."[19] Each of these songs, like the play itself, concerns the nature of time. In "Now," we see the rational mind of the middle-aged lawyer Fredrik at work, weighing each side of every question in a lyric structured on the processes of logical reasoning and the literary allusions to be expected from an educated man. In "Later," the lyric is frenzied and the sound harsh, as befits his morose son Henrik, a life-denying, guilt-ridden ministerial student straining to break free of the self-control and repression that have brought him close to the edge of madness. And in "Soon," the sound is lilting and melodious and the sentiments dreamy and romantic, as is Fredrik's coquettish teenage bride Anne who sings it. Even the rhyming words are tailored to the individual, with Fredrik, for instance, characteristically rhyming "imbecilities" and "possibilities" with "facilities," and "arouse her" with "trouser," "penchant" with "trenchant," and "risqué" with "A."[20]

Sondheim believes that all the principles of writing apply to lyrics: "Grace, affinity for words, a feeling for the weight of words, resonances, and tone."[21] He carefully distinguishes, nevertheless, between lyric writing, which he considers "a craft," and the "art" of writing poetry for two reasons: first, because lyrics are written to be sung and heard, they "exist in time," meaning "you hear them only once," whereas poetry, which is written to be read, lies outside the bounds of time in the sense that it can be experienced, and if necessary reread, at one's own speed.[22] Second, and more importantly, while poetry stands alone, "lyrics go with music, and music," Sondheim feels, "is very rich, in my opinion the richest form of art."

> It's also abstract and does very strange things to your emotions . . . .
> There's a great deal to hear and get. Lyrics therefore have to be underwritten. They have to be very simple in essence. . . . essentially the thought is what counts and you have to stretch [it] out enough so that the listener has a fair chance to get it.[23]

Sondheim has a great affinity for and facility with words, as is indicated by the string of rhymes, the product of a controlling and shaping intelligence, that one finds in his lyrics. The number of rhymes within the lyrics to a single song often impresses just in itself. In *The Frogs*, for example, there is a twenty-two-line verse or stanza built around only eight end-line sounds, five of which rhyme *ababacccbbadadaeeebfgb.*[24] Or in *Anyone Can Whistle,* one finds a thirteen-line verse having a *aabbcdeeffgdg* rhyme scheme.[25] Finally, in one of the sung scenes in *Pacific Overtures,* one can count over a dozen words either at the ends of lines or internally that rhyme with one another: "day," "may," "bay," "convey," "away," "stay," "delay," "say," "array," "gray," "display," "sway," "pay," "stray," "pray," and "today."[26] Yet quality of rhyme takes precedence over mere quantity, for by Sondheim's own criterion, "You try to make your rhyming seem fresh but inevitable, and you try for surprise but not so wrenchingly that the listener loses the sense of the line."

> The true function of the rhyme is to point up the word that rhymes . . . .
> Also, rhyme helps shape the music, it helps the listener hear what the shape of the music is. Inner rhymes, which are fun to work out if you have a puzzle mind, have one function, which is to speed the line along.[27]

Here, for instance, are four extraordinarily apt and ingenious sequences of rhymes, again all from one song in *Pacific Overtures*: "Victoria," "Gloria," "euphoria," and "emporia"; "tentative," "representative," "argumentative," and "preventative"; "Czar," "caviar," and "ajar"; and "immorality," "neutrality," "extraterritoriality," and "nationality".[28]

Although in general Sondheim feels "suspicious" of alliteration and distrusts it for being too facile, he does recognize that if used "subtly, it can be terrific." "It's a great aid at times," he claims, "in speeding the line along."[29] The potential advantage can be amply proven by such a line as "It's a very short road / From the pinch and the punch / To the paunch and the pouch and the pension" from *Little Night Music.*[30] But it can also be equally effective in creating humor, as in "The bong of the bell of the buoy in the bay, / And the boat and the boy and the bride are away!" (51) from *A Funny Thing Happened on the Way to the Forum,* which belongs in the tongue-twister category with both "And any IOU I owe, you owe," and "Any sparerib that I can spare, I'd be glad to share!" from *Gypsy*—the last of which involves an allusive pun on Adam's rib as well.[31]

Like Cole Porter (the only other American composer–lyricist who can begin to touch Sondheim in artistry and ingenuity), Sondheim displays a fondness for allusions to real personages in his lyrics. He employs the device for comic effect in *Do I Hear a Waltz?* when a passenger on a jet plane at movie time bemoans that ". . . everywhere I look / Is a closeup of Doris Day! / Ninety minutes of Doris Day! / There was nothing to do but pray—" (20) and in *Follies* when a character prides herself on getting "through Herbert and J. Edgar Hoover, / Gee, that was fun and a half. / When you've been through Herbert and J. Edgar Hoover, / Anything else is a laugh" (59).[32] In the same show, he blends allusiveness with alliteration: "Some like to be profound / By reading Proust and Pound" (105).[33] Yet Sondheim normally succeeds even better than Porter ever did in suiting the lyric line to the character singing it, which may account in large measure for why relatively few of his songs have become popular hits when divorced from the musical drama for which they were written.

This appropriateness of Sondheim's lyric to his character is clearly evident in *Follies* (with a book by James Goldman), which centers on four major, well-developed characters and so, again, depends strongly on the interior monologue song. Its title carries both literal and metaphoric meanings, referring in the first place to a lavish stage spectacle à la Ziegfeld—a reference that ensures there is always an excuse for stopping the narrative line abruptly and breaking very naturally into a musical showcase number, as in the lavish Felliniesque "Loveland" sequence. Yet the title refers also to the folly or foolishness of love, as well as to the folly of thinking we can recapture the past and somehow live our youth over again, either as an individual person or as a nation, which Sondheim himself points to as the central theme: "the collapse of the [American] dream" and "all your hopes tarnish and . . . if you live on regret and despair you might as well pack up, for to live in the past is foolish."[34]

Follies, like *Night Music*, becomes a Proustian investigation about the nature of time: about the decay of material things like the theater building which is on the point of demolition, or of our aging physical bodies; about the changes in theatrical fashions; about the persistence of memory, and the way memory nostalgically embroiders fact, turning it into illusion and delusion. The past is palpably present on the stage, both to the ear and to the eye: to the ear in Sondheim's music, a pastiche of the show music of the past, with the composer–lyricist commenting on the various styles at the same time that he imitates them; to the eye in the presence of the ghostly showgirls, larger than life, as well as in the presence of the earlier, younger selves of the main (and even of some minor) characters, who are dimmer than life and who recall what the older people dreamed of becoming but did not. These earlier selves are utilized much more fully here than the similar chorus of Liedersingers in *Night Music*, where the equivalencies between characters and alter egos are not consistently or extensively worked out. The audience thus sees past and present, then and now, simultaneously before them.

The play's central thematic statement, expressed through Ben's song "The Road You Didn't Take," concerns the relationship between the passage of time and the possibility for human choice to alter the future. As one grows older, one's options grow progressively fewer, so life becomes a matter of ever diminishing possibilities. Every choice we make limits every future choice: to choose option A over option B means not only to reject B, but also to cut oneself off forever from all the possibilities that would have existed had one chosen B. So with each choice we make, we in effect cut in half our future options.

This notion of choice as determinism, what I like to call "the road not taken syndrome" after Robert Frost's famous poem—and which Sondheim evidently also had in mind—recurs frequently as a motif peculiar to American drama, recently, for example, in Jean Claude von Italie's *The Serpent* and Robert Anderson's *Double Solitaire*. But its most complete formulations are to be found in O'Neill's *Long Day's Journey Into Night* and Albee's *A Delicate Balance*. In the former play, Mary Tyrone speaks of "the things life has done to us":

> They're done before you realize it, and once they're done they make you do other things until at last everything comes between you and what you'd like to be, and you've lost your true self forever.[35]

And in the latter play, Agnes echoes Mary's words:

> Time happens, I suppose. To people. Everything becomes . . . too late, finally. You know it's going on . . . up on the hill; you can see the dust, and hear the cries, and the steel . . . but you wait; and time happens. When you do go, sword, shield . . . finally . . . there's nothing there . . . save rust; bones; and the wind."[36]

Ben Stone, who understands the anguishing dilemma that "one's life consists of either/or" (37), tries to fool himself that "the road not taken" would not have made any difference, would not have led anywhere anyway: "Chances that you miss, / Ignore. / Ignorance is bliss" (39). Finally, the only way to live with regret over missed opportunities is to anesthetize yourself to the pain, to rationalize away everything but what you have been—and become:

> You take your road,
> The decades fly,
> The yearnings fade, the longings die.
> You learn to bid them all goodbye.
> . . . .
> The worlds you never see
> Still will be around,
> Won't they?
> The Ben I'll never be,
> Who remembers him? (40)

That Sondheim can be seen in conjunction with such major American dramatists as O'Neill and Albee demonstrates, I think, the qualitative difference between him and nearly every other writer for the American musical stage.

Related to Sondheim's notion that it finally becomes "too late" for effective human choice must be its obverse: the implication that at some point(s) in his or her life the character can make the existential choice to appreciably alter the course of his or her destiny. And it is this pattern and conflict that recurs most frequently in Sondheim's musical dramas, and is usually expressed most pointedly in the penultimate song. Typically, the Sondheim musical focuses on unresponsive, vulnerable characters psychologically afraid of participating fully in life, of committing themselves to actively developing their full potential as *feeling* human beings.

One of the earliest extended developments of this theme occurs in *Do I Hear a Waltz?* (1965, with music by Richard Rodgers and book by Laurents). Leona Samish, "lost in her thirties" (3), uptight and lacking the courage to be, travels to "magical" (3) Venice where she falls in love with Renato Di Rossi, who is "in approval of living" (88) and counsels her, "Relax and the world is possible" (59). Like *Pacific Overtures*, *Waltz* concerns a clash between two cultures. In this instance, American materialism and puritanic scruples and guilt meet Mediterranean carefree-ness and lust for life. Di Rossi claims everyone is hungry for "something simpatico" (91) between two people, and when it comes we must grasp it, or perhaps lose it forever:

> Take the moment,
> Let it happen.
> . . . .
> Or the moment
> Will have passed.
> All the noises buzzing in your head,
> Warning you to wait—what for? (91-2)

Even though Leona and Renato break off their relationship, she has become a changed woman, vowing: "I still have time. And I'm going to see it all," the "it" referring not just to Venice but to her whole life (147-48).

Anyone Can Whistle (1964—also with book by Laurents) is subtitled "A Musical Fable" and is built around two premises that Shakespeare reworked again and again: first (as the lyrics to one of the songs say), that "No one's always what they seem to be" (53); and, second, that reason is not necessarily the highest good (that which appears to be sanity is often lunacy in disguise), and that the lunatics, the seeming fools, might turn out to be the saviors of the world. Nurse Fay Apple has charge over the Cookies, the residents of the Cookie Jar for the Socially Pressured, the local loony bin. These inmates (who bear the surnames of such famous artists and philosophers as Brecht, Chaplin, Engels, Freud, Gandhi, Ibsen, Kierkegaard and Mozart [171-72]) have been committed because "they . . . made other people nervous by leading individual lives" (34).

Eventually, they are proved to be as sane or saner than those running free on the streets—or those sitting in the audience when, in a Pirandelloesque sleight-of-hand accomplished through lighting effects at the end of act 1, the actors become the audience and the audience become the characters in the play. Sondheim, himself an inveterate game player, uses lyric word puzzles or nonsense syllogisms to illustrate the premise that the reasonable is often unreasonable: "The opposite of Left is right, / The opposite of right is wrong, / So anyone who's Left is wrong, right?" (71).

Fay, a firm believer in science, reason, control, cannot let go of her inhibitions and live, and so desperately needs a miracle to show her the way. She pleads with Dr. Hapgood (who is actually a loony in disguise and who knows that "Either you die slowly or you have the strength to go crazy" [158]):

> . . . show me
> How to let go,
> Lower my guard,
> Learn to be free.
> Maybe if you whistle,
> Whistle for me. (109)

Hapgood convinces her that just "Being alive" (107) is miracle enough in itself, but that if you want more, you must perform your own miracles; against all the nay-sayers and life-deniers, he says "Yes" to life, he urges "Do":

> Walk on the grass, it was meant to feel!
> . . . .
> Laugh at the kings, or they'll make you cry.
> . . . .
> Fall if you have to,
> But, lady, make a noise! (122-23)

Under his guidance, Fay learns that the nonconformists are the strength of the world, that we must change the world to accommodate people and not vice versa; and for herself she learns to dance, to commit herself to Hapgood, and finally even to whistle, as a real, miraculous rainbow of water gushes from the rock to underscore her change. Although *Whistle* was neither a popular nor total artistic success, it has developed a cult following over the years. If its concept is overly complex and in need of simplification, if its music is overly derivative of Bernstein, and if perhaps it is ultimately the victim (if such a thing is possible) of an excess of imagination, it was, nevertheless, undoubtedly a pivotal experiment in Sondheim's development as an artist.

In *Company*, every bit as much a landmark musical as *Oklahoma!*, the thirty-fiveish bachelor Robert is psychologically afraid of committing himself to marriage. Instead, he defensively chooses to be a visitor, an appendage in the lives of his married friends, used by them as confidant, visitor of the sick, eater of leftovers, babysitter for their kids, and amateur analyst and marriage counselor, and using them in turn as substitutes for a wife and children of his own. But he moves from being on the outside looking in to a decision to marry, and this despite what he sees as the faults of the institution: the male/female power struggles; the loss of identity; the lack of deep feeling; or, what is just as bad, too much cloying affection and possessiveness.

He opts for marriage in a brilliantly dramatic soliloquy song called "Being Alive," in which he works to a new position intellectually and emotionally, from shying away from "Someone you have to let in, / Someone whose feelings you spare" (114), to desperately pleading that "Somebody crowd me with love, / Somebody force me to care" (116), since "alone is alone, not alive" (116). He does not reach his affirmation easily or facilely because he possesses the maturity to see the darker side of committing oneself totally to another person: the risks of being "used" selfishly or of being "hurt," of being encroached upon, or of being emotionally naked. (The show's unromantic and unsentimental treatment of marriage would, by itself, make it stand out from most other musicals.)

Company, which might be seen as a modern psychomachia, ends as it began, with the other characters wishing Robert a "Happy Birthday" as the new light comes up at dawn. It is a *birth-day* for Robert; he has "put on the new man," become more fully human. As Joanne, the chief catalyst, says, "you'll [n]ever be a kid again, kiddo" (114). Perhaps, in light of *Company*, we can even see how *Pacific Overtures* relates to Sondheim's more personal musicals. To move from isolation always implies the risk of compromise, of some loss of integrity and individuality; yet it also includes possibilities for development that never existed before, and the opportunity for real growth outweighs the risks.

Finally, in *Night Music*, a minor character, Petra the maid, rather than a major figure, expresses the recurrent thematic motif through the song, "The Miller's Son." In the song, she reveals that she will eventually submit herself to the rhythms of life and, through the ritual of marriage, assume her proper place in the social and cosmic orders. But "in the meanwhile," she will "celebrate what passes by," so that when she dies she will at least have lived:

> There are mouths to be kissed
> Before mouths to be fed,
>
> . . . .
>
> There's a lot I'll have missed
> But I'll not have been dead when I die! (174)

This emphasis on celebrating everything in life, no matter how small or seemingly trivial (which Sondheim shares with the William Saroyan of the

Preface to *The Time of Your Life* and the Thornton Wilder of *Our Town*), should be seen as more than simply a hedonistic, *carpe diem* attitude. This attitude—and similar ideas expressed in *Waltz*—really stand closer to the Shakespearean notion of things brought to completion in the fullness of time. For the awareness of death as the fitting culmination of Nature's unending process of birth, life, and love hangs over the end of *Night Music*, since Madame Armfeldt dies in the third smile of the summer's night, accepting death as the final thread in life's fabric, secure in the knowledge that she has passed some of her store of wisdom on to her young granddaughter Fredrika. She also knows that the foolish lovers are now wiser, too, as they waltz across the stage "*at last with their proper partners*" (185), in a ritualized dance symbolic of regeneration. Nature's pattern, seen even in the temporarily unsettling condition of perpetual sunlight, becomes, therefore, the real hero of the play.

II

In their 1985 Pulitzer prize-winning musical, *Sunday in the Park with George*, lyricist–composer Sondheim and librettist–director Lapine express the notion of the artist as seer. As the basis for their reflection upon how personal and aesthetic problems merge for the creative genius, Sondheim and Lapine turn to an imaginative recreation of the creative processes of a real artist, George Seurat, painting his masterwork, *A Sunday Afternoon on the Island of La Grande Jatte*. Even more obviously than O'Neill's *Long Day's Journey into Night* (with which it might be compared), theirs is a work about the nature of the creative process itself, and as such reflects something of a turning point for Sondheim. As Frank Rich (who calls Sondheim "as adventurous and as accomplished an author, playwrights included, as Broadway has produced over the last two decades") rightly claims, " 'Sunday' is itself a modernist creation, perhaps the first truly modernist work of musical theater that Broadway has produced."[37]

The image of what Peter Brook calls "the empty space" is an extremely potent one in the modern theater.[38] It is the stage space that must be peopled through the artist's imaginative faculty as he or she makes what wells up from his or her mind and heart visible to an audience. *Sunday in the Park* begins—and ends—with "a white stage," here the painter's "blank page or canvas" waiting to be filled.[39] "The challenge," says George, is to "bring order to the whole. / Through design. / Composition. / Balance. / Light. / And harmony" (17-8).[40] In the brilliant *coup de théâtre* that concludes act 1, the audience literally sees, through a magical combination of real characters and painted cutouts, Seurat's most famous painting created and frozen on the canvas that is the stage.

But if art is permanent, it is not life, which is never so ordered, composed, and harmonious. The characters in the painting understand that the gain in conquering time involves a diminution in lived life—that to remain forever "frozen" is the price they pay for their artistic apotheosis. Even Dot, George's mistress and the mother of his child (at whom he will not even glance, so absorbed is he in his work), feels used by the artist who is "so cold," so "controlled," sufficient unto himself, and so she moves on to someone else (29). Her very name, of course, indicates that she will be "studied," objectified and distilled into the dots of "color and light" that Seurat put on his canvases—so that the viewers' eyes would fuse and harmonize them—in a technique that came to be known as Pointillism (135-36).⁴¹

In a similar manner, the musical notes and lyrics, often of one syllable, are the "dots" through which Sondheim composes *Sunday*: "blue / Purple yellow red water"; "green / Orange violet mass / Of the grass" (88). Just as the museum-goers find Seurat and his paintings without "passion" and conclude that he lacks "life in his art" or even "life in his *life*" (30), so critics of the American musical theater oftentimes judge Sondheim as too emotionally detached, as a songwriter who, like the Seurat he creates, is "All mind, no heart" (30), so his and Lapine's fictionalized artist may be partly self-portrait and self-explanation. Paradoxically, then, one of Sondheim's most deliberate and reserved scores might also be one of his most personal, an analogue for the way that the artist sometimes must bring his feelings under strict control so that others might feel. Sondheim will continue to develop this theme in his most recent works.

Understanding character like understanding painting (or any work of art) is all a matter of the perspective from which one looks. When Dot accuses George of "hid[ing] behind painting because [he] care[s] about nothing," he responds, "I am not hiding behind my canvas—I am living in it" (73-4)—apparently finding it necessary to deny himself a full emotional life outside of it. Seurat, and by implication any artist, must simultaneously be both connected and detached; there must always be a part of him standing aside and looking, for his "mission [is] to see" (76)—and to see well always to some degree requires treating objects as people and people as objects, animating the first and deanimating the second. *Seeing* forms the necessary prelude to creation, to making, if not from nothing as the archetypal creator–artist did, then from "flecks of light": "Look, I made a hat . . . / Where there never was a hat . . . " (67), Seurat sings with wonder and fulfillment.

The second (and less innovative) act of *Sunday* jumps forward a century, from 1884 to 1984, when another young artist named George—presumably the great-grandson of Seurat and Dot—demonstrates his Chromolume, a huge domed machine from which emanates a spectacular sound and laser light display (Seurat himself always preferred to be called a chromoluminarist). Here the chic world of art and high culture is deservedly satirized. The artist is now lionized and fawned over, himself turned into an object who is as much on exhibition as are his creations; it is a world of celebrities and promoters and hype, and to sell himself, to survive, the artist must often compromise his integrity.

Feeling that his gift has faded, George returns to Paris, where high-rise buildings obscure the park of his ancestor. In his artistic dark-night-of-the-soul, he feels "alone" "afraid," "adrift," "aground," doubting whether he will leave behind any work of value since he has stopped "stretching his vision in every direction" (167). He reads "Lesson #8" of Dot's grammar book, left him by his grandmother Marie, where he finds still visible on the endpapers the loving notes Dot wrote about Seurat. Because Seurat once taught Dot how to concentrate on reality and "see," she will now, in turn, act as George's muse. All that is necessary is that he, as artist, keep seeing so that he can help others to see. She encourages him, "Stop worrying where you're going—/ Move on. / If you can know where you're going, / You've gone. / Just keep moving on" (169).

Even if the choice of what to create next proves wrong, the act of choosing is itself a good, for life itself means moving on, and so the artist as seer must "look forever" (173). The newness of what he has to say is neither important nor unimportant; the obsession with newness as an end-in-itself in art is, indeed, just a fad. All that matters is that he create "harmony" (172) out of chaos, that he impose a meaning upon existence by taking the infinite number of "possibilities" (174), the dots, and arranging them in an ordered pattern of "color and light" (34) on the once blank white canvas—just as Sondheim and Lapine create a play text by composing dots of sound and sense to fill the empty space of the stage; just as the audience members existentially write the text of their own lives by choosing and moving on.

Eugene O'Neill's *Long Day's Journey into Night* also defines the artist's vocation in terms of "seeing," although Sondheim and Lapine's vision of the artist is, finally, very different. O'Neill's artist figure penetrates through the surface to reveal the reality, or better, suprareality, already there beneath it and to help the audience share in the illumination by seeing it, too. Sondheim and Lapine's artist figure, on the other hand, uses experiences impressionistically received in order to construct a new reality not there before; in this way, he is much more actively the creator guiding the audience to perceive phenomena from a new angle of vision, but one which potentially changes with each viewer. It is the difference, in short, between the Romantic conception of art and the Modernist.

O'Neill's Romantic image of the poet's vision as parting the veil of fog to reveal what lies beneath—analogous to the Biblical concept of seeing things face to face rather than as reflections in a mirror—has several antecedents in traditional Western thought, among them the writings of Plato, Nietzsche, Emerson, and Shelley. Sondheim encapsulates his quite different image of the artist in the first act song, "Beautiful," sung by Seurat and his mother. His mother seems bewildered by change, by time passing, and by "towers" (specifically, the Eiffel Tower) "Where there were trees" (77). Whereas she can discover beauty only in the natural, Seurat can see it in the manmade as well: "What the eye arranges / Is what is beautiful" (78). The artist not only "holds the mirror up to nature" (Plato's words) by reproducing reality, but "revise[s] the world," constructing a new reality of his own (78). Along with stopping time by bringing permanence where once there was change, the Modernist artist, rather than just shadow forth pre-existing forms, revealing their beauty, actually devises new forms that are beautiful in themselves. The Modernist artist, as maker of a new reality that did not exist before, sees that it is good, precisely because, though it harmonizes, it refuses to deny "tension" and remains open-ended: "White. A blank page or canvas . . . . So many possibilities . . ." (174).[42]

III

If *Sunday in the Park* concludes on a note of "possibilities," increasingly in the eighties and nineties Sondheim's lyrics describe "a darkening earth," as for example, in *Into the Woods*.[43] With a book by James Lapine that draws upon several classic fairy tales, *Into the Woods* (1986) may well be Sondheim's most thematically integrated musical play. And its central theme—the necessity to embrace the unknown and welcome opportunities for change if there is to be any possibility for growth and realization of potential—is much the same as that incessantly espoused by Edward Albee in plays from *Who's Afraid of Virginia Woolf?* (1962) through *Seascape* (1975) to *Three Tall Women* (1991). The journey the mythical characters take "into the woods," fearful of what dangers may await them there, is one that they—and the audience—have no choice *but* to take, since no one can "stay a child" (60) forever. For this is nothing less than the archetypal journey into selfhood and psychological and moral maturity; the safe and secure shelter must be left behind to risk (ad)venturing "out there in the world" (60). The woods are the site of temptation and testing, of selfishness and sexual madness, and of chaotic misrule where the natural order is broken and a giant threatens.

Yet they are a place not only where one is forced to develop moral discrimination, but also where certain qualities that are sometimes repressed or forgotten in the getting and keeping of day-to-day existence, such as "sharing" and "open-heart[edness]" and "consider[ation]" and "trust" (54-6), can be released and blossom. Since "wishes are children" (136) in that they grow and burgeon in totally unexpected and even frightening ways, presenting unforeseen conundrums that demand answers, the words "I wish" that frame the play signal the characters' desire to break free of the tethers of a life ruled by "shoulds" and "shouldn'ts" (112). They want to be able to experience not just "either" one thing "or" the other, but a plentitude of "both/and" (112). So the woods, then, are where people "learn" the complexity of moral choice, as well as gain a renewed appreciation of the possibilities in life, for now "the 'or' "—which previously had seemed too limited—comes to "mean more" (113).

In many ways, Sondheim's and Lapine's woods seem akin to the green world of Shakespearean romantic comedy; and the characters' journeying into them becomes an analogue for the audience's going to the theater. In both instances, too, there must be the parallel "return" out of the woods and out of the theater back into the world one left, but now knowing "many valuable things . . . that [you] hadn't known before" (35) and made substantively "different" (35) by being better equipped emotionally and ethically (35). That the characters, after the "happy ever after" that concludes act 1, must begin over again and take a second, even more perilous journey "into the woods" in act 2 indicates that life must be a continual process of growth rather than stasis, of learning by accretion. To enter the woods is, finally—for both the characters and the audience—to come under the "spell" of the storyteller's tale, his "Once upon a time" (3) linked irrevocably with the listener's "I wish" (3, 138) that begins and ends the play. The Narrator of the metatheatrical *Into the Woods* describes himself as possessing a near-godlike vision, as the "objective observer" (102) who (like the modernist artist in *Sunday in the Park*) can harmonize and "order" the world of "chaos" (103) since he alone possesses the key to "how [the] story ends" (102). And he attributes to the tale or work of art an almost talismanic power over its hearers as they are instructed in the need for commitment and engagement, for mutuality and togetherness; as one of the songs insists, "It takes two"—at least. The created story is, ultimately, a shared experience, the accumulated wisdom of the community that helps bond each human being to every other, demonstrating, in the words of the penultimate song, that "No one is alone" (128-32).

The journey undertaken in *Merrily We Roll Along* (1981, revised 1994), rather than the archetypal–mythic one of *Into the Woods*, is the more literal upward climb through the landscape of American society from the Eisenhower to the Reagan eras, when being "rich and famous" equates with being "happy."[44] Like the source on which George Furth's book is based, Kaufman and Hart's original 1934 comedy—and indeed like Harold Pinter's *Betrayal* (1978) which, as Michael Billington has noted, also concerns the gradual waning of commitment into compromise—*Merrily* moves backward in time over twenty-five years. Framed by two high school commencement ceremonies, it probes the question, "How did we get here from there?"[45] Exploring how seemingly limitless opportunity ("opening doors" [29], "following every star" [29]) must inevitably undergo a reality check ("flowers wilt" [19], "apples rot" [19], "thieves get rich and saints get shot" [19]), it asks whether any middle ground can exist between the extremes of youthful idealism and adult pragmatism: can the sense of diminishment that comes with time, the realization that life usually turns out to be *less* (as one song laments, "Nothing's the way that it was" [14]), be somehow accommodated without our falling into cynicism and negativity? Since two of the central characters start out as composer and lyricist of rather avant-garde and minimally-melodic

musicals that their producer faults for being short on "hummable" (30), toe-
tappable tunes, Sondheim can even indulge himself in some metacritical
commentary along the way about demands on the creative artist to sell out by
sacrificing personal vision—the unique ability to "Tell 'em things they don't
know!" (33)—to popular success.

Merrily's central metaphor of the journey along the road allows Sondheim to linger again over some very Albee-esque questions, as he earlier had
in *Follies*. The jaded, early middle-aged Franklin Shepard's insistence on giving in to practicality, on being satisfied with "doing the best you can" (8)
rather than unequivocally "doing the best" (8), may well recall the motto Tobias adopts in *A Delicate Balance* that accepts loss of purpose and enshrines
complacency: "We do what we can" (19).[46] Yet even more pertinent here may
be Albee's interrogation of Agnes' position in the same play that ultimately a
time may come when it is "too late," when options for choice are so severely
reduced that change becomes virtually impossible.[47] Just as the Kennedy era
seemed to announce a new beginning for the country, at that time in their lives
the characters in *Merrily* blithely thought that if one path was closed off to
them, they always had another, that "An exit from one place" inevitably
opened up "an entrance to another" (19). Temporary setbacks, both professional and personal, could always be managed without much introspection.
Later in life, however, they begin to ask each other the existential question of
"How did you get to be you?" (12). If there was, indeed, a decisive, determining moment in the making of who they now are and what they have become,
how did they miss it? *Merrily's* answer is not to deny the impossible dream,
but to caution us instead not to "confuse" it with illusions that may all too easily become delusions. Instead, be ready to make a mid-course adjustment and
"bend the dream with the road" as it moves through time and space.

Sondheim's most daring and audacious work, *Assassins* (1990)—with a
book by John Weidman—forms a kind of diptych with *Merrily* in that it, too,
plumbs, albeit more disturbingly, the dark underside of the American Dream,
even employing Arthur Miller's *Death of a Salesman* (1949) with its "independent, proud . . . decent man who tries and tries but never gets a break" as
an explicit intertext.[48] Using the stories of nine historical figures, most no-
tably John Wilkes Booth and Lee Harvey Oswald, who between 1865 and
1981 either attempted or succeeded in taking the life of a president, this brilliantly astringent and ironic work delves into what happens when people feel
that the egalitarian ideal of anyone "Rich man, poor man, / Black or white"
(13) becoming anything "from a mailman to a President" (82) is simply not
operative for them, and the promised "liberty and justice for all" gives way to
"Another National Anthem" that "says 'Never!'" (84). If it supposedly remains true, as the jaunty opening number in the carnival shooting gallery
affirms, that "Everybody's / Got the right / To their dreams . . ." (7), what
happens to these outsiders—the disaffected malcontents; the have-nots who

could not "work [their] way / To the head of the line" (50, 53); the over-looked, "misguided nobody" (93); or those who feel "unworthy" (59) and in need of "earn[ing] your love" (59) like John Hinckley and Squeaky Fromme, who sing so vulnerably and tenderly to Jodie Foster and Charlie Manson? Perhaps reminiscent of *A Chorus Line* (1976) in its denial of unlimited possibility and a "prize" day for all (there can, after all, only be a single star, "One, singular sensation . . . and you can forget the rest" who are simply supporting dancers), *Assassins* already accepts some limitations to achieving life's goals.[49] But if one is "Not the sun, [then] maybe one / Of its beams" (13) is the least to which one should legitimately aspire.

In order to achieve that, those who feel somehow powerless, perhaps even previously anonymous, will use a gun, the ultimate weapon of those to whom "no one listens" (81), to enter into history. Although the history of the country is too strong a story to be "stop[ped]" (15), they can at least halt it for a day and effect the narrative, and in so doing ensure that their personal history is not robbed of meaning; no longer "ignored" (67) they will now be "remembered" (68) and "immortal" (100). If, as Booth argues when he appears to Oswald, every assassin brings back from the past and "empower[s]" (101) all the others, then the musical itself might be seen as examining the whole question of what options the disenfranchised powerless have for gaining power. It cogently recalls, as well, the concern of writers as far back as Alexis de Tocqueville and as recent as Tony Kushner over whether democracy's championing of untrammeled individualism does not, at the same time, nourish the seeds of a narcissistic egoism that threatens any notion of responsibility to the larger community and so, instead of connecting, only divides.

Sondheim's most recent musical, *Passion* (1994)—with a spare libretto by James Lapine based on Ettore Scola's film that was itself adapted from Iginio Tarchetti's novel of a century earlier—is the most nearly operatic of all his works, charting in a ritualized, epistolary form the education of the dashing soldier Giorgio in matters of the heart.[50] The play opens with the post-coital Giorgio and the married Clara naked in bed, celebrating the state of "so much happiness" (3) that comes with sexual abandon. A love based on surface beauty is, however, subject partly to the enemy Time, and so later when Clara sits staring into a mirror and sees a gray hair, she laments it as "a milestone of [her] age" (88). Giorgio by then has been transferred from Milan to a provincial town, where he has met Fosca. In this gothic tale, if Clara is light and gay, Fosca—who first announces her presence by a distant scream—is dark and gloomy, the madwoman in the attic once tricked into marriage for her money and then quickly deserted. If "a woman's like a flower . . . . [whose] only purpose is to please" (84) and if when "you're a woman, / You're only what [the world] sees" (86), then Fosca, unlike Clara, has never been the object of the male gaze.

The reclusive Fosca's friendship with Giorgio begins in the sharing of his favorite novel, for she "read[s] to dream. / . . . to live" (22) through "other people's lives" (22); yet she recognizes the dangers of such escapes from reality into the world of fiction, for dreams may foster "expectations" (23) that only lead to "disappointment[s]" (24). Love alone could make "possible" (32) the ordinarily impossible bridging of life with dream. The tortured, physically austere yet intensely passionate love through which the hysteric captures and gradually wins over the soldier to her side is an obsessive one; Giorgio, nevertheless, comes to honor and value it as "without reason, . . . or shame" (122), as not subject to "wisdom . . . [or] blame" (122), as having no concern "with being returned" (122), while Fosca discovers through it that she is "someone to be loved" (130). "Reason" (122) and practicality, the minutiae that ordinarily rule and restrict, and therefore diminish, everyday life, are not for Giorgio; as Fosca says, "They hear drums, / You hear music" (35). The bed on which their passion is finally consummated becomes within a few days Fosca's deathbed, as she tutors Giorgio in an all-consuming "love as pure as breath, / As permanent as death, / Implacable as stone" (61). The imagery recalls nothing so much as the stone effigy on a tomb, a marble monument transporting us into another realm of permanence and Art, where Giorgio's "love will live" (131) forever in Fosca. The haunting subtext of *Passion* may well be a memorial to love-in-the-face-of-death in the age of AIDS—a time when the "being alive" of *Company* gives way to the even more vital imperative of "feeling loved" (128) that alone can assuage aloneness and conquer the ravages of time.

IV

Stephen Sondheim continues to write for the American musical stage. Although his work is better known now than it was in the 1970s, it still has generally eluded the kinds of critical comparisons to other dramatists—to O'Neill, Albee, Williams, Miller, and Pinter, for example—who are his real peers in the theater, and it continues to challenge serious consideration for its literary as much as its artistic value. With his taste for words, wit, passion, and especially that very rare ingredient in a musical, the "glow of thought," Sondheim offers us gifts in abundance throughout the musical dramas to which he contributes.[51] It is probably no exaggeration to claim that the American musical theater has him to thank today for "being alive," and what is more, for being *adult*, which is to say, for being mature in a way not often visible in American popular culture.

NOTES

[1] Earlier sections of this chapter first appeared in Adler 1978, 513-25, and Adler 1987, 149-152. Permission to reprint material from these sources is hereby gratefully

acknowledged. For *The Frogs*, see Shevelove and Sondheim 1975. For *Forum*, see Shevelove, Gelbart, and Sondheim 1991.

[2] Shevelove and Sondheim 1975, 76.

[3] Zadan 1994, 42.

[4] Zadan 1994, 59.

[5] Zadan 1994, 52.

[6] Gottfried 1973, 90.

[7] Zadan 1994, 117.

[8] Azenberg 1973, 99.

[9] Aronson and Rich 1987, 46.

[10] Sondheim and Weidman 1991a, 22.

[11] Sondheim and Wheeler 1991a.

[12] Furth and Sondheim 1970.

[13] Zadan 1994, 117.

[14] Kanfer 1971, 72, 74.

[15] *Time*, March 1973, 58-9.

[16] Prince 1974, 178.

[17] Shevelove, Gelbart, and Sondheim 1991, 143.

[18] Sondheim and Wheeler 1991, 134.

[19] Michener 1973, 55.

[20] Sondheim and Wheeler 1991, 32, 34.

[21] Zadan 1994, 231.

[22] Zadan 1994, 231.

[23] Zadan 1994, 231.

[24] Shevelove, Gelbart, and Sondheim 1991, 79-80.

[25] Laurents and Sondheim 1965, 142.

[26] Sondheim and Weidman 1991a, 31-2, 34-6.

[27] Zadan 1994, 232.

[28] Sondheim and Weidman 1991a, 74-6, 79, 81.

[29] Zadan 1994, 232.

[30] Sondheim and Wheeler 1991, 173.

[31] Richards 1973, 367; 347.

[32] For *Waltz*, see Laurents, Rodgers, and Sondheim 1966. For *Follies*, see Goldman and Sondheim 1971.

[33] Goldman and Sondheim 1971, 105.

[34] Zadan 1994, 136.

[35] O'Neill 1956, 61.

[36] Albee 1967, 169.

[37] Rich 1984, 53.

[38] Brook 1980.

[39] Lapine and Sondheim 1991, 17.

[40] Cf. Lapine and Sondheim 1991, 172, where we read: GEORGE: "Design." / "Tension." / "Composition." / "Balance." / "Light." Dot, I cannot read this word. /

DOT: "Harmony." In other words, when young George reads from the French grammar book of his grandmother, the word "tension" has been added. There is an interesting enactment of this addition in the CD liner notes where we read, in the lyrics to the earlier passage: "The challenge: bring order to the whole. / Through design. / Composition. / Tension. / Balance. / Light. / And harmony." See Lapine and Sondheim 1984, 5. The liner notes insert the word into the earlier list itself. [SG]

[41] Pointillism was a "technique of employing a point, or small dot, of colour to create the maximum colour intensity in a Neo-Impressionist canvas." See Block 1996, 78. George offers a discussion of pointillism on 135-36. [SG]

[42] See note 40 above.

[43] For "darkening earth," see Shevelove and Sondheim 1975, 124. For *Woods*, see Lapine and Sondheim, 1992.

[44] Furth and Sondheim 1982, liner notes, 12.

[45] Cf. "How did you get there from here, Mr. Shepard? / How did you get to be you?" Furth and Sondheim 1982, liner notes, 12, and "How did you get here from there, Mr. Shepherd?" Furth and Sondheim 1982, liner notes, 14.

[46] Albee 1967, 122-23.

[47] Albee 1967, 19.

[48] Sondheim and Weidman 1991, 93

[49] Bennett et al. 1995, 116.

[50] Lapine and Sondheim 1994.

[51] Shevelove and Sondheim 1975, 124.

CHAPTER 2

Maternity, Madness, and Art in the Theater of Stephen Sondheim

Allen W. Menton

This essay began as an inquiry into two themes that seem nearly ubiquitous in Sondheim's work: 1. a domineering or repressive mother figure locked in a cycle of dependence and rivalry with her (often grown) children (such as Desirée and her mother, Madame Armfeldt, in *A Little Night Music*); and 2. the arrival of a madness at climactic moments that is often rooted in that troubled mother-child relationship.[1] This madness often leads to its own resolution to it, and with that resolution an end to the vicious cycle of dependency. As I further explored the relationship between maternity and madness, however, I discovered the role of art as an intermediate step between the two. In Sondheim's work art serves in this context as a temporary refuge in which to bury the various tensions of the troubled relationship until madness brings it to a point of crisis.

In the essay that follows, I will begin by looking closely at Sondheim's characterization of maternal figures, and then turn to the role of art. Finally, I will take up the role of madness in bringing about an end to the cycle of dependency.

I

Maternal figures in Sondheim's work tend to be matriarchal and domineering. In some plays, maternity even borders on evil: the Shogun's mother in *Pacific Overtures*, for example, who poisons her own son, and Mrs. Lovett in *Sweeney Todd*, who assumes a maternal role for the street urchin Toby, yet will not hesitate to sacrifice his physical well-being (or even his life) for her own material gain.[2] In *Anyone Can Whistle*, the degree of power assumed by the matriarchal "mayoress" approaches that of a domineering parent insofar as she regards the townspeople as children, subject entirely to her ubiquitous intrusion and control.[3] Like absolute monarchs of the past, she recognizes no boundary between her own person and her constituency, as she sings "Love me, / Love my / Town!" (7). More often, the exercise of matriarchy is subtler. One way for the mother to maintain her power and authority is to deny that her child has in fact grown up. By promulgating the fiction that her offspring is a helpless child who cannot survive without a mother to protect it, the mother makes herself indispensable, and thus all-powerful. In many Sondheim musicals, we further note that the dominance of the matriarch coincides with a weak or absent father whose active role would presumably be to help the child towards independence.

The first act of *Sunday in the Park with George* was originally performed as a lengthy one-act musical tracing the relationship of painter George with his mother and with his mistress, and our current discussion will be confined largely to the present act 1.[4] From the beginning, George's mother haunts the margins of the stage. Her initial complaints about the missing tree and the swimming boys seem like bits of local color until much later in the play, when we realize who she is and appreciate the greater significance of her comments.

Observing the scene with his sketch pad on his knee, George mutters, "I hate this tree" (19), and behold, the tree vanishes into the flies—our first clue that what the audience sees on stage is not, in fact, the park on La Grande Jatte, but rather the island as seen and reconstructed by George's painterly eye. Now his mother enters, immediately casts a suspicious look at George, and complains, "Where is our tree? . . . Someone has moved it" (19-20). By the end of the act, after a revealing duet between George and his mother, we understand that a central characteristic of her psyche is the inability to cope with change, especially change as it is embodied by George and the island. For most of the act she has addressed her son as "Monsieur" (32), barely acknowledging this grown man as her son. She adds her voice to the others who dismiss George as "crazy" (43) and compliments George's mistress Dot for having the good sense to leave the "deluded" (43) artist for a baker.

In her final scene with George, we see her clinging to a vision of her son as a small child running out for a swim. Addressing him as "Georgie" (77) she speaks of his childhood as though it were an immediate presence, which for her it is. In the duet "Beautiful," we learn more about her objection to change: for her, the artist's role is one of preservation. She laments the changes that time has brought—"how I long for the old view" (79)—and wants George to capture this past and preserve it: "Changing, / As we sit here—/ Quick, draw it all, / Georgie!" (78). For George, however, the essence of the artist is change, the possibility for the artist to impose his vision on the world, to change red and blue into violet in the viewer's eye, to make a hat "Where there never was a hat . . . " (67). As he sings "What the eye arranges / Is what is beautiful" (78), his mother stares at him in incomprehension, no less so than George's friend and fellow painter Jules, who cannot understand his work any more than the others and exclaims in frustration, "Always changing! Why keep changing?" (56). As his mother once again turns her gaze to the world of her own memory, George looks at her fondly, but sadly, longing for her comprehension, or even just a momentary retreat from her self-absorption to look at him and see him for the accomplished and innovative artist he has become. At the same time, he is aware that her refusal to see him grow up is a part of a madness that he cannot penetrate.

The closing line of the duet is a single word from George, "connect" (82). Although George and his mother are clearly unable to connect, "connection" is a running motif throughout the play, beginning with the very nature of La Grande Jatte, an island of flirtation and assignation, a modern day Cythera, the mythical island of love depicted by so many French painters before Seurat.

The theme of connection brings us to the second of the mother's early complaints, about the boys bathing so early on a Sunday morning. Her remarks remain enigmatic until near the end of the act, when she wistfully recalls how George, as a small boy, used to rise early on a Sunday morning, and, accompanied by his father, go out swimming on the island. Her eyes fixed firmly on this untroubled vision of the past, she refuses to listen as George gently reminds her that his father was not faithful to them, and his anxious insistence leads us to suspect that his accompanying George to the island was only a cover for the adulterous liaisons he would pursue there. In this light, the mother's yearning for the past and obsessive return to the same spot on the island acquire an added dimension. Her resistance to change is a resistance to knowledge, a denial of the reality that her marriage had succumbed to the same hypocrisy that characterized so much of nineteenth-century bourgeois morality. In the play, George's first major work, "Boys Bathing at Anières," complements his second major work, "La Grande Jatte," in that they present two sides to the family drama: the innocent story of the boys bathing and the illicit assignations on the island.

George's response to his mother, "connect" (82), is immediately followed on stage by the dalliance between Jules and his servant's wife Frieda, even as Frieda is supposed to be supervising his daughter Louise. The placing of this scene and the disturbing chromatic music which underscores it lend it an eerie quality, suggesting at once memory (since the manner of Jules's adultery so closely resembles that of George's father), and a cycle of eternally frustrated connection. Jules moves from one woman to another in search of connection, yet each conquest leads only to boredom and the desire for a fresh conquest. If Jules is presented as George's alter-ego (the successful painter) throughout act 1, the statement in act 2 that George was very much like his father leads us to wonder whether, for George, the possibility of "connection" also represents the danger of falling into the same frustrating pattern of behavior as his father and Jules.

II

If George's avoidance of connection is an internal obstacle rooted in his parents' troubled relationship, other mothers are more overt in their blocking of children's relationships, as an indirect means of maintaining a cycle of dependency that keeps them in a position of power. A common feature of maternal figures in Sondheim is their desire to prevent the child's independent development, to control and shape every aspect of their child's life, especially when it involves the possibility of developing outside relationships. The child grows dependent on the mother as the sole source of interpersonal contact and cannot develop mature social skills, thus having great difficulty with interpersonal relationships as an adult.

Madame Armfeldt, in *A Little Night Music*, for example, strongly disapproves of her daughter's financial and amorous independence. Like the aging geisha of "Welcome to Kanagawa" in *Pacific Overtures*, or the aging prostitute of "I Never Do Anything Twice" in *The 7% Solution*, Madame Armfeldt understands only one kind of relationship, one in which the exchange of money and sex are scrupulously negotiated—"a pleasurable means / To a measurable end" (68) as she puts it.[5] Forever rooted in the bygone world of the nineteenth-century courtesan, she laments the passing of "liaisons," and heaps scorn upon the long-standing object of her daughter's affections, the lawyer Egerman, because he offers her nothing more than love and happiness on a middle-class budget. Having given up trying to control Desirée, she turns to her granddaughter Fredrika, but without success; her ideas of how to raise a young girl are no less relics of the past than she herself, and the young girl can only dream of the day when her independent mother will come to her rescue.

In *Company*, the various women in Robert's circle of married friends take on a collective role as surrogate mother to describe Robert as their "Poor Baby."[6] Juxtaposed with their lyrics "Robert ought to have a woman" (88), are their catty barbs directed against every potential partner he brings home, effectively undermining his attempts to build relationships outside his close circle of married friends. Like so many other domineering mothers in Sondheim's work, their primary desire for the child (Robert) is for him to continue keeping them company in order to maintain the delicate symbiotic balance that keeps their own precarious marriages alive. All the couples finally join in singing to Robert, "What would we do without you?" (83).

In *Sweeney Todd*, although it is Judge Turpin who keeps Johanna locked in her room, it is Johanna's mother (as the old beggar woman) who stands guard below, warning the young sailor away. If Johanna and Anthony are as foolish and naive as Sweeney and his wife once were, then the unintentionally complete collaboration of the elder generation (Sweeney, Mrs. Lovett, Turpin, the old beggar woman) in obstructing their relationship sends a clear signal: do not venture into romance and suffer the elder generation's terrible fate.

The Witch of *Into the Woods* takes similar precautions with her daughter Rapunzel, the fruit of an illicit union with a roving neighbor who abandoned her.[7] Determined to protect Rapunzel from the same fate, she locks her away in a tower. When, despite these precautions, she finds Rapunzel entertaining an amorous Prince, the Witch musters a variety of arguments (in the song "Stay With Me") to convince Rapunzel to remain with her and keep her company rather than venturing into the world with strangers: that only her mother can properly shield Rapunzel from the dangers of the world, that the world is full of people who will do her harm, that no one will love her as much as her mother does, and finally, that she should hang on to childhood as long as she can—"Stay a child while you can be a child" (60).

Her overprotectiveness bears its bitter fruit in a cycle of dependency. Even after Rapunzel has left with her Prince and become a mother in her own right, she regards her mother as the primary determining force in her life: "Because of the way *you* treated me, I'll never, *never* be happy!" (95). To be sure, the Witch is only too happy to assume the role of perpetual mother, and when Rapunzel is crushed by the Giant, the Witch laments:

> Children can only grow
> From something you love
> To something you lose . . . (106)

The notion that this cycle of dependency lasts unto death is reinforced by two other stories from *Into the Woods*, that of Little Red Ridinghood and that of Jack and the Beanstalk. Sondheim and Lapine have acknowledged their debt to Bruno Bettelheim's interpretation of traditional fairy tales in *The Uses of Enchantment* (1977), and accordingly, Little Red Ridinghood and Jack and the Beanstalk form a matched pair, as allegories of the onset of sexual maturity in girls and boys.[8] In Sondheim's version, both stories moreover cast the death of the overprotective mother as a necessary (if symbolic) result of this maturity.

If Little Red's adventure represents the discovery of adult sexuality, then the mother, who functions as an unseen character, forms the principal obstacle; it is she whom Little Red must disobey in order to grow up. The mother's admonition not to stray into the woods, talk to strangers, or even look away from the path carries a metaphorical message: the woods symbolize the unknown, the world outside the family circle. If one never ventures into this world to talk to strangers, one will never develop an independent personality, and the child will remain bound in a cycle of mutual dependency with the mother.

The Grandmother in contrast facilitates the girl's initiation into maturity. Because the Grandmother lives in the woods, Little Red must go there in order to bring her sustenance, and this same journey brings her in contact with the Wolf, a two-dimensional caricature of male lust. When she emerges

from the consummation of their relationship (literal as well as figurative: she
has been consumed), she sings of her initiation:

> And he showed me things,
> Many beautiful things,
> That I hadn't thought to explore.
> They were off my path,
> So I never had dared.
> I had been so careful
> I never had cared.
> And he made me feel excited—
> Well, excited and scared (35).

In short, Little Red Ridinghood has been initiated into a new kind of
knowledge: things that previously lay outside of her purview—"they were off
my path" (35)—and which are at once beautiful and exciting, but also a little
scary, precisely because they are new and unknown. At the same time, this encounter returns her to the familiar:

> And when everything familiar
> Seemed to disappear forever,
> At the end of the path
> Was Granny once again. (35)

In the middle of what has become a coded narration of sexual initiation,
the Grandmother reappears as a symbol of female sexual maturity. Little Red
has learned how her grandmother became a grandmother (sexual knowledge)
and, more importantly, that she can rediscover herself as a sexually mature
woman, for whom the grandmother is the archetype. The mother is unsuited
for this role because she functions as the obstacle to her daughter's maturity—warning her not to talk to strangers. Little Red's new self-image is con-
firmed when she returns to her childhood home only to find it in ruins and her
mother gone.

In Sondheim's version of Jack and the Beanstalk, his mother asserts her
control by treating Jack as a little boy and dismissing the father's absence
with a vague lyric, "Your father's not back" (15). Observing a similar *wan-
derlust* in Jack, his mother forbids him to leave the house. Under such restric-
tions, the only relationship he can develop is with the cow, Milky-White.
Even as Jack insistently refers to the cow in masculine terms, the relationship
displays a peculiar intimacy. Jack urges his friend, "Please, pal—Squeeze,
pal" (4-5), while his mother dismisses the relationship as a childhood phase:
"Children can be very queer about their animals" (50).

No sooner has Jack ventured into the forest with Milky-White than he
encounters the Mysterious Man, who chides him for being such a mama's

boy and suggests exchanging the cow for a sack of beans. As the character of the Mysterious Man develops throughout the play, we come to know him as a symbolic father figure, periodically accessible to those in need of a father, such as Jack and the Baker. Having once bequeathed the "magic beans" to his son the Baker, he now looks on as the Baker gives them to Jack in exchange for the cow. If the cow represents a phase of adolescent sexuality, the beans represent the possibility of sexual initiation and maturity—the magic bean which a boy (or man) carries in his pocket and which can suddenly become a large thick stalk. As the Baker drops the beans into Jack's hands, the importance of this exchange is emphasized by the musical underscoring, which quietly articulates the musical theme later associated with another mother's lament over her lost child: "Don't you know what's out there in the world?" (60). Indeed the woods (and the beans) represent the dangerous world of adulthood, the world which all children must eventually enter. With the exchange of the beans, Jack has taken the first step towards independence ("The difference between a cow and a bean / Is a bean can begin an adventure" [40]) even as his mother dismisses his new-found independence with a cynical putdown: "Slotted spoons don't hold much soup" (42).

Indeed, the beginning of more mature relationships is possible for Jack only when he disobeys his mother and pursues the new independence afforded by the beanstalk:

> You're free to do
> Whatever pleases you,
> Exploring things you'd never dare
> 'Cause you don't care (43).

As Jack continues to sing, he describes his sexual initiation with the lady Giant in terms reminiscent of Swift's description of Gulliver among the Brobdingnagian women. After Jack has killed her husband and deserted her, the lady Giant comes looking for him, as a threatening symbol for the sexual adulthood that Jack has unleashed. Even as his mother defends him, her angry confrontation with the lady Giant assumes the added dimension of a mother jealous of her son's girlfriends. Only with the mother's death is Jack finally forced to be independent and confront the consequences of his actions as an independent adult.

III

Death is a radical solution, to be sure. In much of Sondheim's work we find the child of a domineering mother using art—and often theater—to avoid the mother's oppression and escape from the related difficulties in interpersonal relationships.

In *Anyone Can Whistle*, Nurse Apple can escape the mayoress and explore a relationship with Dr. Hapgood only by donning an outlandish costume and temporarily assuming a new identity. As the romance unfolds in act 2, Hapgood questions her reliance on this mask, while she pleads her inability to function on an interpersonal level without such artifice: "What's natural comes hard" (109). She has internalized Mayor Hooper's repressive regime to the point that she cannot accept Hapgood's *carpe diem* argument that merely "being alive" is enough of a miracle to warrant liberation (107).

In *Gypsy*, Rose's children (including those she abducts) all grow up to be artists of one sort or another.[9] Under the repressive regime of Mama Rose, even the untalented Louise channels her emotion into art. Unable to openly express her sadness at being forgotten on her birthday, she projects her emotions onto the pets and toy animals that surround her, transforming them into a mask through which she can express her true feelings: "Little cat, little cat, / Ah, why do you look so blue? / Did somebody paint you like that, / Or is it your birthday, too?" (348-49).

Rapunzel, locked away in her tower in *Into the Woods*, turns to music, singing her wordless refrain *ad nauseam*. In *A Little Night Music*, Henrik also turns to music, as a refuge from the confusion of young adulthood. Tormented by alternately passionate and platonic affection for his stepmother (not to mention the coquettish teasing of the maid Petra), he embraces instead his cello, whose body lies between his legs as he strokes it vigorously with a long, stiff bow.

Desirée Armfeldt uses theater, the "glamorous life" of her stage career, both to avoid dealing with her frustrated affection for Fredrik and as a mask through which to conduct the various sexual liaisons which she pursues in its place. Sex becomes a staged performance, as she describes in "Bang," a duet she sings with her latest paramour (dropped from the final version of the show).[10] In this respect, she follows the example set by her own mother, who regards life as a succession of scenes to be staged—Mme Armfeldt even designates the props for her own funeral. Theater is also the primary mask of relationships in *Follies*, in which the characters' efforts to conduct relationships are supposedly mediated but are in fact hindered by the stylized representations of love in the various numbers from their former "Follies" stage roles that keep interrupting the narrative flow.[11]

If Sweeney Todd is described as an "artist with a knife" (37), we should not be surprised to find that his razors are his chief companions as well. As he sings "These are my friends" (41), he ignores Mrs. Lovett's pleading counterpoint, "I'm your friend too, Mr, Todd" (42). The play, however, which most thoroughly explores the use of art as a way to avoid the difficulty of relationships is *Sunday in the Park with George*. The unusual title of the musical succinctly outlines the central conflict of the drama. George, as already noted, has a fear of connection which is rooted in his father's adultery and his mother's reaction to it. At the same time, La Grande Jatte (the park of the title) seems primarily a setting for illicit liaisons.

Moreover, the temporal setting of act 1 is defined as a series of Sundays, "the day off" (49), when people of various social classes are released from their civilized obligations and mingle freely on the island, in a kind of discreet bourgeois Bacchanal. At one point, George thumbs through his series of sketches and reviews the musical phrases associated with each assignation: "Ah, she looks for me . . . " (Franz flirting with the Nurse [54]), "Second bottle" (Frieda waiting for Franz to get drunk so she can meet with Jules [54]), "Mademoiselles!" (the two soldiers hooking up with the two shopgirls [63]), and "Yapping . . . Ruff! . . . " (the two dogs exchanging canine small talk [65]).

After reviewing these relationships, George sings (in "Finishing the Hat") about his position in relation to them: he is the outsider, "watch[ing] the rest of the world / From a window" (65). George essentially restages his own position as the outside observer of his father's adultery. Unlike the flirtatious habitués of La Grande Jatte, George can only connect to people, indeed, to the world, through the medium of the aesthetic: "Reaching through the world of the hat / Like a window" (66). In other words, his artistic creation (the hat in his painting) is the window through which he relates to the world. Even the staging of the musical reinforces this point: the characters are often seen through a large frame covering part of the stage, with George positioning them and sometimes singing along with them. Thus, the characters are not fully independent, but rather derived from the thoughts and motivations which George, the creative artist, gives them.

Many characters in the play interpret George's aesthetic detachment as a form of madness: "Artists are so crazy" (43) and (in Dot's opening song) "Artists are bizarre. Fixed. Cold" (22). At the same time, this aesthetic distance enables George to hold at bay another kind of madness, one which we perceive through his eyes and ears: the madness of connection, the sometimes deafening cacophony of all the flirtations, pursuits, and assignations taking place on the island. Only at the end of act 1, following George's command, "Order" (87), do they cease. In fact, the characters cease "connecting" and become figures of light and shadow—a *tableau vivant* created on a stage which, we are reminded, represents not a park after all, but rather George's artistic vision of the park. As serenely pulsing music softly begins, George moves among the characters, who are now oblivious to him, and arranges them in such a way that they can no longer connect in any meaningful way to each other, but rather form a harmonious and balanced composition. The song's lyrics contain no reference to connection; they mention only abstract artistic values: colors, shapes, shadows, and light. As the song concludes, a large frame drops down from the flies to enclose all the characters, now frozen in position. Only George stands outside the frame. Just as the play's opening monologue defined the artist's task as bringing order to the whole, so has George been able to remain outside the madness of connection and reduce the amorous characters to "arrangements of shadows" (88).

George even relegates himself to the status of an outside observer in his own relationship with Dot. Like his father, George rises early to go to the park and meets his mistress there. However, George's liaison is entirely aesthetic. In her opening song, Dot advises the members of the audience not to get involved with an artist if they want "connection" (23). Indeed, although George stares at her no less than any of the other would-be couples stare at each other on the island, Dot chides him, "There is someone in this dress!" (21), for George's gaze emanates from the eye of a painter fascinated only with color, light, and shadow.

At the same time, George remains always intensely aware of Dot. Even as he works on a canvas, his thoughts continually turn towards her, but he forces them out of his mind with self-reproach: he must finish his painting. Although Dot accuses him of using his work as a way of avoiding her, she comes to recognize that George has channeled his passion for her into his art. George tells her that he cannot give her the words she wants, only his painting, which he hopes she can be a part of, since for George art is the only realm in which he can make connection. And though it pains Dot that he cannot look away from his sketch pad to say good-bye to his own child, George is in fact preparing to put the baby, complete with its surrogate father Louis and his waffle-stove, into the finished painting as a permanent tribute.

In "Finishing the Hat," George expresses his ambivalence about using art as a vehicle for connection, since it often comes to serve as an obstacle to the very relationships it is intended to facilitate. He sings that any woman who would have a relationship with an artist like himself must understand that "There's a part of you always standing by, / Mapping out the sky" (66). Dot does indeed appreciate this aspect of George; even though she will bear his child, she still wants a painting he did of her as an expression of his passion.

Still, Dot has a sensuous side that George cannot satisfy. An unabashed hedonist, she purrs, "The less I wear, the more comfortable I feel" (35), and her fantasies of attracting George's attention all revolve around her physical appearance. Finally tiring of George's involvement with his work, she takes up with Louis the baker, who presents her with more physically gratifying words of art: "Louis' art is not hard to swallow" (60). Whereas George's painting was cold and cerebral, her new lover "bakes from the heart" (59). His cream puffs are as sensuous as they are edible, and Dot proclaims that, unlike George, Louis makes a connection that she can *feel*. Louis has several flaws, however—"Louis drinks a bit, / Louis blinks a bit" (60)—and even as Dot announces "Louis it is!" (60) with her mouth stuffed full of cream puff, she drops the rest on the ground in disgust.

Although she must acknowledge her need for the physical connection afforded by Louis ("Louis is what I think I need" [69]), she recognizes that it is George's intense, aestheticized passion that continues to exercise its spell over her. His refusal to settle down with Dot—to grant her the connection that she longs for—keeps them both in a state of eternal desire. Unlike George's successful friend Jules, who has long since settled into a routine and lost any interest in sketching (or remaining faithful to) his wife, George remains as fascinated with Dot as she is with him. In act 1 they sing passionately, "I could look at her/him / Forever" (40), and in act 2, we learn that George has tirelessly placed Dot in at least four different places in the finished canvas. The aesthetic distance which prevents their connection allows them to remain an eternal mystery to each other, and thus eternally faithful. In this way, their love can be permanent, unlike the other relationships George has observed—witness his adulterous father and his adulterous friend (and alter-ego) Jules. Indeed, George's intuition is correct: Dot never ceases loving George, and she even returns from the grave in act 2 to sing, "We should have belonged together" (75).

IV

In most of Sondheim's works, however, this refuge in art is temporary at best. What works for the rare artistic genius like George cannot work for others, and art cannot ultimately contain the tensions underlying characters' attempts at interpersonal relationships. The moment in which these tensions burst forth is typically staged as a moment of madness, and Sondheim constructs climactic moments in his work around them.

For example, the Loveland sequence in *Follies* culminates in the mental breakdown of Ben Stone, as the old Follies tunes—the mask through which Ben and the other characters have tried to understand each other and on whose platitudes they have tried to build their relationships—appear as jumbled and incoherent fragments, just as so many of the relationships of the past now lie in ruins.

Madness plays an important role throughout *Anyone Can Whistle*, since the matriarchal mayor asserts her power and authority by dismissing anything which threatens her power as madness and those who try to live freely in her town as "cookies" (madmen). Her efforts culminate in the "Cookie Chase" of act 3, in which she wheels on a large animal cage (foreshadowing Mrs. Lovett's oven in *Sweeney Todd*) and begins randomly throwing people in:

> Are they breathing? Then they're Cookies.
> Are they moving? Then they're Cookies.
> Are they living? Then they're Cookies.
> So get on with it! Quick, get on with it!
> Are they human? Then they're Cookies. (165)

Nurse Apple's efforts to help them escape create a parallel between her role and that of the old beggar woman leading the lunatics' escape in *Sweeney Todd*. Both Nurse Apple's lyrics and music remind us of that similarity:

Fire!
Hurricane!
Everyone off of ze streets!
Run for your lives! Run for your lives!
Ze dam has burst!
Run for your lives, run for your lives!
Ze lion's loose! (167)

When Mayoress Hooper finally rounds up the last of them and orders their names read aloud, the list of these so-called madmen (and women) includes a variety of social and creative visionaries: Ibsen, Kierkegaard, Engels, Mozart, Brecht, Chaplin, Freud, and Susan B. Anthony. Despite the heavy-handed symbolism, Sondheim and Laurents have made their case for the necessity of madness as the only way to overcome the paralysis of a repressive regime. Not only does Nurse Apple address them as "the hope of the world . . . all the crazy people like you" (173), but Dr. Hapgood drives the point further home in the show's final song with the lyrics "Crazy business this, this life we live in" (176). A little madness is necessary to liberate oneself from the paralysis of matriarchy (or any other totalitarian regime) and become truly alive.

In *Sweeney Todd,* the release of the lunatics from Fogg's Asylum brings the representation of madness to apocalyptic levels:

City on fire!
Rats in the streets
And the lunatics yelling at the moon!
It's the end of the world! Yes! (187)

Indeed, the connection between madness and the apocalyptic runs throughout *Sweeney Todd.* Sweeney makes his entrance, by rising out of a grave, his face chalk-white, to sing "Attend the tale of Sweeney Todd. / He served a dark and a vengeful god" (25). Other lyrics of "The Ballad of Sweeney Todd" suggest an ongoing connection with a demonic underworld: "Sweeney heard music that nobody heard" (25). In fact, Sondheim does let us hear Sweeney's demonic music: several melodic themes associated with Sweeney are derived from the traditional Gregorian chant *Dies Irae,* which recounts the biblical apocalypse. A distinctive and oft-quoted musical theme (for example, in the "Witches' Sabbath" section of Berlioz's *Symphonie Fantastique*), Sondheim uses it to construct the melodies for "Swing your razor wide, Sweeney!" (24), and again for "These are my friends" (41). Even the opening theme, "Attend the tale of Sweeney Todd" (23), is a musical inversion of the same melody.

The release of the lunatics from Fogg's Asylum likewise recalls the release of the dead from the underworld. The disturbing noise they make is in fact a musical compilation of many different fragments of musical material from the score, all sung to one word: "Sweeney," so distorted as to become unintelligible. At the end of the evening, when we feel relieved to know that he has been put out of his misery, the chorus arrives to announce that Sweeney is always with us, always beside us—"Isn't that Sweeney there beside you?" (203)—and brings this effect to a hair-raising climax by pointing into the audience and shouting, "There! There! There! There! / There! There! There!" (204). As though their belief in the myth of Sweeney were powerful enough to bring him to life again, Sweeney once again rises from the grave, an eternal symbol of revenge. His pronouncement, "To seek revenge may lead to Hell" (204), drives home the demonic nature of the cycle of revenge: to engage in revenge is to live in hell.

The motive for this revenge is the wife whom he presumes to be dead. However, Sondheim gives his audience a series of clues that she is in fact alive, as the "half-crazed beggar woman" (31) On first seeing Todd, she peers at him intently and anxiously asks, "Hey, don't I know you, mister?" (30), at which Todd cuts her off.[12] Sondheim also gives us a musical clue as to her identity: the vulgar song which the old beggar woman sings employs the same melody as the minuet played during the rape of Lucy (in "There was a Barber and his Wife"). And as soon as the beggar woman finds herself in Todd's tonsorial parlor, we hear this theme again as fragments of her distorted memory return and she pantomimes opening a window and cradling her baby, while humming a lullaby set to the same melody.

So intent is Todd on his revenge against Judge Turpin that he overlooks her constant presence and ultimately kills her when she gets in the way of this revenge. Indeed, Lucy has been pushed aside and marginalized throughout the play, even as she continues to haunt the scenes of her trauma—Judge Turpin's residence and Todd's barbershop, where Mrs. Lovett periodically complains "What about that looney?" (148). Even as she represents madness, the beggar woman also represents the truth, the secret that will be revealed at the end of the play when Sweeney at last looks in her face and recognizes her. In short, madness has become the carrier of truth, of a truth that needs to come out, a true apocalypse (from the Greek *apokalupsis*, meaning 'revelation').

Revelations occur as the culminating moment of other plays as well, often in the form of testimony, confession, or confrontation. At the end of *Gypsy*, the mental breakdown of Mama Rose is staged in the number "Rose's Turn." Mama Rose first confesses that her dominating treatment of her daughters is rooted in her own frustrated ambitions, and as she mimics their complaints against her, she suddenly recalls her own mother's mistreatment of her and the suffering that was part of her own childhood.[13] Only after this confrontation can she recognize her own matriarchal habits as a futile attempt at revenge against the memory of her own mother, and let go of them. Mama

Rose is now capable of reconciliation with her own daughter, treating her as another adult without lapsing into domination or matriarchy.

In "Send in the Clowns" in *A Little Night Music*, Desirée Armfeldt confronts the folly (another word for madness) of her attempt to avoid intimacy by escaping into theater. Owning up to the mistakes of her past, she calls for an end to the "merry-go-round" (183) of flirtation and illicit assignation. Fredrik likewise confesses to a kind of madness—"Me as King Lear" (183)— and proposes that they begin a new, more "coherent" existence (183). Even Madame Armfeldt numbers herself among the foolish as she reveals that she rejected her one true love because he gave her a wooden ring.

V

The long final sequence of *Into the Woods* takes up all the major preoccupations of Sondheim's work and weaves them into an elaborate musical tapestry: oppressive mothers, children locked in rivalry with their mothers, difficulty in interpersonal relationships, confrontations with the past, madness, apocalypse, and finally, reconciliation.

The sequence begins with "Your Fault" (114), in which characters look for a single scapegoat on whom to blame their collective fate. This behavior stems from a common pattern of parent-child relationships in Sondheim: one's dependence upon the other for the fulfillment of one's wishes. When those wishes turn out badly, the other becomes the target of blame. Rapunzel, the child, blames all her problems on her mother, while the parents in the play—the Baker and his Wife, the Witch, Jack's mother—expect their children to solve all of theirs.

The song's rising intensity is suddenly interrupted by "The Last Midnight," a song which bears the same weight of revelation as "Rose's Turn" or "Send in the Clowns." Mocking the other characters' obsession with finding blame, the Witch exposes the supposedly magic beans as nothing more than a symbol for wishes, as she pulls handfuls of them from her pockets and scatters them wildly—to suggest that the unchecked proliferation of wishes is the ultimate cause of unhappiness. In ironic reference to the traditional superstition of blaming witches for everything that goes wrong in human affairs, she volunteers herself as the center of blame, and reminds us of the link between wishing and blaming. If people blame her when things go wrong, they also seek her help in making wishes come true. The revelation that wishing and blaming belong to the same cycle of dependency marks an end to the era of wishing, the end of an enchanted view of the world, in which parents hold magic power over their children and in which children have the magic power to fulfill their parents' dreams. At the end of the song, the Witch finally disenchants herself by revealing the source of her magic as a punishment visited upon her by her own mother, thereby exposing this magic as nothing more than the largely symbolic vestige of a stubborn rivalry between mother and child.

In this newly disenchanted world, characters begin to regret their wishes. The Baker tries to renounce wishing and make a clean break with enchantment in "No More." Suddenly, his own father, the indestructible and ubiquitous Mysterious Man, reappears to remind him that such radical change is not possible. Indeed, the last lyric of the play, a repetition of the opening lyric "I Wish," confirms that human desire, the tendency to wish, cannot be overcome by a simple act of will.

The next song proposes a communal response to the problem of wishing, "No One Is Alone." The lyric begins with a commentary about children growing up and learning to be independent—"Mother cannot guide you. / Now you're on your own" (128). This advice then overlaps with the Baker's advice to Jack that one must first recognize oneself as a wishing subject in order to recognize others as wishing subjects, to see the "other" side of the menacing Giant (or rival), for whom the parent is always the prototype: the story of Jack and the Beanstalk is meant to remind us that all grown-ups are giants in the eyes of children. By further casting the Giant as an external force threatening the community, Sondheim reminds us that all adults carry traces of their own childhood around with them, and this inner child often determines how we react to the world, or, indeed, how we parent our own children.

The all-too-human tendency to overlook the subjectivity of the other and turn others into "A blank page or canvas" (17) (from the opening lines of *Sunday in the Park with George*), an empty vessel into which we pour our own wishes, is driven home by the final song, "Children Will Listen." As always, the parent–child relationship is the paradigm for all others: the lyric "Wishes are children" (136) reminds us of the tendency of parents to place unrealistic expectations on their children. Such expectations teach children to disregard their own subjectivity, and thus to disregard the subjectivity of others, a lesson which brings innumerable difficulties in adult relationships. In Sondheim's work, only when parents and children learn to accept and live with each other as adults can the isolated child move beyond rivalry with a smothering parent and an obsession with solipsistic art and move on into mature relationships with others.

NOTES

[1] Sondheim and Wheeler 1991.
[2] Sondheim and Weidman 1991a. Sondheim and Wheeler 1991a.
[3] Laurents and Sondheim 1965.
[4] Lapine and Sondheim 1991.
[5] Sondheim 1976.
[6] Furth and Sondheim 1970.

[7] Lapine and Sondheim 1992.

[8] Zadan 1989, 338. Bettelheim 1977, 182-84. *Editor's note:* Sondheim comments as follows [in taped remarks to Sandor Goodhart]. "No, I don't think we did. . . . James has talked about Bettelheim. But, in fact, mostly . . . we relied on . . . Jungian interpretations. I read some of Bettelheim's book, and I guess James read all of it. But that was not . . . our springboard."

[9] Richards 1973, 331-90.

[10] Sondheim and Wheeler 1991, 202-05.

[11] Goldman and Sondheim 1971.

[12] In the original Broadway production, however, the actor playing the old beggar woman often continued under his line, so that audiences could hear that she did indeed recognize him as "Mr. Barker." Cf. Sondheim and Wheeler 1991a, 30-1, 192.

[13] *Editor's note:* Sondheim disputes this claim as well, of course [in the same taped remarks to Sandor Goodhart]. [Mr. Menton], he says, "is drawing conclusions from a mistake of Ethel Merman's. Not his fault, . . . but there it is. She is not recalling her own mother's mistreatment of her and the suffering that was part of her own childhood. I don't think she had much, frankly—suffering and mistreatment, I mean." See also Sondheim's comments upon the same issue in the Introduction, note 32.

CHAPTER 3

"Every Day a Little Death"
Sondheim's Un-musicaling of Marriage
Kay Young

> *It started off so swell*
> *This, "let's pretend."*
> *It all began so well*
> *But, what an end.*
> *The climax of the plot*
> *Should be the marriage knot.*
> *But there's no knot for me.*
> — GEORGE AND IRA GERSHWIN[1]

To begin at the beginning when thinking about the work of Stephen Sondheim means for me to think about the "end." More than any other writer of musical comedy, Sondheim problematizes what we take an ending to be. To enter into the world of a Sondheim musical means to experience the concept of "the end" as a live question. When does it occur? What is its nature? How are we to sort out the presence of multiple endings? Most of all, what are we to do with an ending which is not happy?

So critical, in fact, Zvi Jagendorf asserts, is the "happy end" to comedy, that "anything can happen."

> It is rather the absence of . . . necessity that characterizes the comic mode. Fundamentally, the end of comedy is determined by no objective structuring principle, only a conventional one. You must have a happy ending.[2]

In essence, then, what Sondheim compels us to consider is the following question: what is a musical comedy which resists the requisite happy end? How can it know itself?

I

Side by side, women and men on the stages of vaudeville from the 1890s to 1932, sang and danced routines, acted out sketches, and did "talking acts" as male-female comedy teams performing marriage. These teams chart a course. The immigrant humor of ethnic marriage routines of John and Maggie Fielding doing sketch acts like "The Tipperary Couple," the enactment in song and dance of courtship in elegant evening clothes of Hallan and Hart (who were precursors of the couples to be featured by Ziegfeld and personified by Astaire and Rogers), the carping shrewish wife and defenseless husband in the "talking acts" of Melville and Higgins, the featured "comic" marriage born from the woman's stupidity and the man's attempts to sort out "the mess in her head" in the routines of Ryan and Lee (who only slightly antedate Burns and Allen)—all these couples and their routines reveal vaudeville's interest in *marriage* as the central site for the display of male-female comedy.[3]

It is an interest generated by the desire to attract women into the audience and by an understanding of comic theater dating from the revolutionary plays of Menander of fourth century BC Athens. If Aristophanes' "old comedy" offers anarchic, often obscene political satire which ends with the lone social outcast as victor over the society against which he pits himself, Menander's "new comedy" offers a more staid, domestic plot of the obstructed lovers who must overcome the comic antagonists who block their desired end: marriage. From Plautus to Shakespeare, Mozart to Noel Coward, the comedy of marriage—how to get it, how to do it, how to get it again—has come to be the model of choice in comic theater.[4] Like the classical transition from old to new comedy, the Menander-inspired marriage acts of the male-female vaudeville team found their way into comic theater and film *after* that of the Aristophanic solo male clown of the vaudeville tradition: the marriage routines of a "they" eventually supplant the clowning routines of a "he."

If the acts of vaudeville performed marriage in pieces (as individual sketches, song and dance routines, and talking acts), near to vaudeville's Palace Theater on Broadway or far away in Hollywood, these pieces were woven together by the Gershwins, Cole Porter, Noel Coward, Rodgers and Hart, Jerome Kern, and Irving Berlin who made witty and romantic the "bumpy road to love" in their musical comedies of courtship. Musical comedy of the 1920s and 1930s in America made it its business this business of getting married. The comic twists which keep the lovers apart—in *Oh, Kay!*, *Anything Goes*, *Private Lives*, *The Girl Friend*, *Sally*, and *Top Hat*—are for the most part unmemorable, and deliberately so. What lingers about these works is their reliance on a farce which glitters with the rapid-paced dialogue reminiscent of the comedic exchanges of Shakespeare's lovers and upon melodic songs of women committed to finding someone who will "watch over them" and men who advance toward, maintain their freedom from, collapse under the disappointment of losing, or celebrate the attaining of a woman's love.

With the 1943 opening of *Oklahoma!*, however, Rodgers and Hammerstein shake loose from the musical the edgy wit of their predecessors and replace it with an ethical, even transcendent, vision of the relations between men and women. Marriage is no longer cause for farce. In the work of Rodgers without Hart, Rodgers and Hammerstein writing for an America at war, sanctify and sentimentalize marriage with ballads that make "forever" declarations of love, whether or not the object of that forever affection is worth it. *Carousel, The King and I, The Sound of Music,* and *South Pacific* come to define the "quality" of the musical of the 1940s, the 1950s, and the 1960s.

II

These creations of twentieth century America—the male-female comedy team of vaudeville and the musical comedy of Broadway and Hollywood— invented as the end toward which their action was directed new ways of performing the by now old end of comedy: the promise of a happy marriage. When, however, in Stephen Sondheim's *Company* all five of Bobby's married friends ask him "Whaddaya wanna get married for?" (53) and the closest he can come to a response is "Someone is waiting" (without in the end a "someone" materializing to fill that role), a profound shift asserts itself in what the musical has to say about marriage and itself (52-3).[5]

The 1970 *Company* is musical comedy as "other." Looking at marriage happening rather than looking at what comes before it, Sondheim casts the courtship plot against five flawed, quirky, evolving marriages. If Bobby courts not one, but three women, his inability to choose "the one" stems from a willingness to question both how one is to choose and why one would choose at all. The marriages to which Bobby acts as witness function as the foreground of the text. Bobby's hesitant amorous pursuits work as responses to what he sees played out before him. If the pre-Sondheim musical designed itself around the frame of the call and response between lovers—as his feedline set up her punchline, her lyric inspired his song, his dance step challenged her tapped response—*Company* recasts the musical's fundamental frame. The female lover is replaced by five marriages and the male lover is replaced by Bobby who acts as passive questioning audience to them. His attempts to reproduce what he witnesses, to find the girl and do the marriage, lead him to find the girl*s* and do *nothing*.

The illusions of the musical's plot created by the singularity ^f ^:-sion—that for everyone there is a someone, that such a som〈 found, and that the world around the lovers functions always as 〈 or destructive background to them—disappears in *Company*. Tho are held to be just that. In their place emerge questions: what if there isn't a someone who's waiting? Or as Bobby sings it, "Would I know her even if I met her? / Have I missed her? Did I let her go?" (53). Or other questions: what if these marriages are whole, functioning worlds apart from the lover so that the lover's relation to them is that of an outsider? "What would we do without you?" (83) Bobby and his couples parry. "Just what you usually do!" / "Right!" (84).

Three plots present themselves as coexistent: the marriages apart from Bobby, Bobby in pursuit of marriage, and Bobby in relation to his married friends. The marriage plot with its unity of vision and direction splinters in this proliferation of a triple plot when the topic is not the happy end of marriage but its questioning. Sondheim further destabilizes the musical in his shaking up of comedy's drive toward pairing. Shakespeare's double couple and Rodgers and Hammerstein's solitary couple become in *Company* the ongoing repetition of threes, Bobby and five couples set "side by side by side": "One's impossible, two is dreary, / Three is company, safe and cheery" (82). But how safe is it? Without a fourth side, the musical teeters—will it fall or just remain inertly destabilized?

In his exploration of the looks and sounds of marriage happening, Sondheim removes the fairy tale "happily ever after" lens from its construction. As Elaine Stritch croons: "It's not talk of God and the decade ahead that / Allow you to get through the worst."

> It's "I do" and "You don't" and "Nobody said that"
> And "Who brought the subject up first?"
> It's the little things . . . (32)

That there is a "worst," that it is about "the little things," that marriage is fundamentally ordinary, "unmusicalizes" its ontology. Love and marriage, as the ends in an aesthetic which normally carry with them the discovery of meaning and truth from out of the chaos which is life, become themselves the chaos, or just small moments which interact with other small moments that when taken collectively compose a life.

Bobby refers to the couples who share these lives as "Those / Good and crazy people, my friends, / Those / Good and crazy people, my married friends!" (13-4). He gazes at them with fascination and horror. If Aristotle asks, "what is the end toward which we direct our lives?" and answers "happiness," when Bobby asks his male friends about the end toward which they have directed their lives, their answer is different.[6] Happiness for them is the subject of wonder and doubt. "You ever sorry you got married?" he asks and they respond:

> You're always sorry,
> You're always grateful,

You're always wondering what might have been.
Then she walks in.
And still you're sorry,
And still you're grateful,
And still you wonder and still you doubt,
And she goes out. (35)

If *Company* suggests that to "be alive" is to be in the company of others, it never wholly decides what form that company should take. Is being married the company one wants to keep? Bobby's darkest question at the apparent end of *Company*—"What do you get?"—leads him to weigh the idea of a "Someone to hurt you too deep" (114) against that of a "Somebody" to "let me come through" (116). "I'll always be there, as frightened as you, / To help us survive / Being alive" (116), he sings, and then returns to his married friends. Where is the ending to *Company*? If the end is just survival, what has happened to the musical?

III

Ending act 1 of Sondheim's full treatment of the relation of the musical to fairy tale in a seeming state of closure in *Into the Woods*, Cinderella and Rapunzel have found their Princes.[7] The curtain goes down in the middle of the production with the Narrator asserting, "And it came to pass, all that seemed wrong was now right . . . and [all] those who deserved to were certain to live a long and happy life. Ever after . . ." (74). Strangely, the "musical of expectation" finishes in its middle and it becomes replaced by the Sondheim "musical in revision." Act 2 undoes the work of happily ever after. No one, it seems, is deserving of forever happiness or no certainty is possible of living a long and happy life. The Princes prove less than perfect: they can be unfaithful, unsatisfying, dead.

Gazing at the other side of the promise of "ever after," the daylight fairy tale marriages are replaced in act 2 by the darkness of disappointment and loss banished from act 1. Cinderella wishes for more than what she has found in the Prince. Rapunzel, let out of her tower, driven mad by her adulterous Prince, roams the earth screaming. What follows the hopes of "ever after" are the nightmares of children where the fear of abandonment and the deeper fear of not surviving that abandonment pervades the consciousness of the musical. Separated from their spouses by new liaisons and violence, Rapunzel, Cinderella, and the Baker must face their lives "de-married" as well as the demons which accompany the necessity of acknowledging the loss of one's partner to another or to death—the terrors of being alone. A new ending emerges out of the refuse heap of the disconnected. Sondheim acts as *bricoleur*.[8] The severed partners discover one another and in the reality of their pain discover a new vision of what it means to face tomorrow without the illusion of "ever after." Again what Sondheim asserts to be an end is not the happiness of marriage but that of survival. Those in *Into the Woods* who do survive and survive their fears find connection in loss and in the random acts of violence which join strangers.

IV

If act 1 of *Into the Woods* ends with the promise of happy marriage, and act 2 explores the failure of that promise, *Sunday in the Park with George* never even attempts a marriage.[9] It closes its first act with the composing into harmonious balance of a painting—the making into an "ever after" of a frozen image. The thorny ground of the relational is replaced here by the work of a solitary "I." Georges Seurat sings to his lover Dot:

> I am what I do—
> Which you knew,
> Which you always knew,
> Which I thought you were a part of! (75)

The pregnant Dot responds:

> No,
> You are complete, George,
> You are your own.
> We do not belong together.
> You are complete, George,
> You are alone.
> I am unfinished,
> I am diminished
> With or without you.
> . . . .
> You have a mission,
> A mission to see.
> Now I have one too, George.
> And we should have belonged together.
> I have to move on. (75-6)

Each must leave the other to be a complete self. That completion, Sondheim makes clear in *Sunday in the Park with George*, is dependent upon the rejection of marriage. While George and Dot each gain a kind of "inspiration" from the other (she is his model—literally, she is his Seurat "dot"—while he is the father of her child), for him there is no "being together" apart from his with his work, and for her there is only being diminished in being together. If departure signals the end or the necessary conflict for a later resolution, here the resolution of act 2 assumes the form of a repetition. The grandchild of the artist is an artist gazing at the painting of the grandfather. Sondheim poses an alternative end for musical comedy. There is the possibility of an "ever after," it would seem, not in marriage, but in children and art. For Sondheim, if we find a way to "survive" through marriage, we achieve a generativity, a promise of something that lives beyond the self, in the creations of a self alone.

V

Sondheim's revision of how musical comedy plots closure and what constitutes the end toward which it is directed has, he asserts, grown out of his close collaborations with the book writers of his musicals—George Furth, John Weidman, and James Lapine. However, if those collaborations worked to generate new ideas about how to plot the old ends of comedy, Sondheim's musical and lyrical creations transform these ideas into new ways of hearing, new ways of experiencing plot. His "avoidance of musical inevitability" enables the plot to surprise, disrupt, and make uncomfortable our notions of how comedy is supposed to move.[10] Sondheim music privileges accompaniment over melody, or what he calls "what's going on inside the music," meaning according to Stephen Schiff (whose language on Sondheim's music I'm borrowing here), "the specific pattern of chords and bass line that will ride underneath the melody" (86).[11] Whereas most songwriters begin with the melody, Sondheim begins with the accompaniment, that which "gives a song dramatic form," and the dramatic form his songs take are difficult, open-ended, nonrepeating.[12] As a result, Sondheim's melodies move amidst an unpredictable context without themselves settling or repeating. If the melody of a song works as a kind of plot in miniature, Sondheim's melodies avoid the clarity of progression: they swerve, advance, float, circle back like the very plots which they sing. He adds to these arrangements musical surprises or "variations for the sake of variation," which further undermine the sense of a predictable end toward which they move.[13] Precisely where a Sondheim song ends is not determined along the way—as it often is in other composers. Without repeating refrains throughout an act, without building inevitability into a song through the way it advances with rising emphasis or a quickened pace, for example, a Sondheim song can just end. Or it can close the first act with an intensity expected for the show's close. Or it can close the show itself with a haunting, complex quiet. Plot acts most often in a musical as accompaniment to music and in a Sondheim musical the dissonant, unexpected, atmospheric, complex sound of his score insists that the plot mirror the musical resistance. The promise of the happy end that is marriage is never promised musically.

Further, the way in which Sondheim makes a dialogue in song between
lovers distinguishes his work and redefines the musical, much as the topics
about which they sing. Banishing the songs of "forever" infatuation, devotion, and commitment, Sondheim writes of love tinged with regret, disappointment, incompletion, loss. The complexity of Sondheim's love lies in its
earth-boundedness, temporality, mutability. This love must be worked at if it
is to survive the fact of its being made between two changing, separate
people. Yet, informing one another of their love, working at it collectively,
creating a language between them to make a flexible space for the marriage or
love is not for the most part possible in the way Sondheim composes his
music. Whereas the high water mark of the musical before Sondheim is the
ballad sung between the lovers who discover that they know the same words,
notes, and arrangements—a knowledge which distinguishes them in sameness—Sondheim refuses to shed the boundaries of his lovers' individualism
in unison singing. It is as if he is asking as metaphysician, "can the other mind
be known?" and responding as skeptic, "no."

When singing alone, Sondheim's characters express doubt, confusion,
and hesitation about what they know and feel, as often as they express insight.[14] The soliloquizing voice uses the solo as an opportunity to work
through a kind of Henry Jamesian preoccupation with where the soliloquizer
is "at." George's singing of "Finishing the Hat," for example, enables him to
come to terms both with the making of his art and the loss of the woman he
loves. He sings as if in conversation with himself as if he doesn't know what
the next thought and so lyric will be:

> Yes, she looks for me—good.
> Let her look for me to tell me why she left me—
> As I always knew she would.
> I had thought she understood.
> They have never understood.
> And no reason that they should.
> But if anybody could . . .
> Finishing the hat,
> How you have to finish the hat.
> How you watch the rest of the world
> From a window
> While you finish the hat. (65)

VI

When singing together, Sondheim's partners continue to sing as if they sing
alone, still in solitary conversation with themselves, as they give voice to different words, rhythms, and sentiments. In *A Little Night Music*, Sondheim's
adaptation of Bergman's fairy tale-like *Smiles of a Summer Night*, all the

characters begin by being attached to the wrong partner.[15] The work of the narrative is to move them ahead or back to the appropriate "other." Fredrik, Anne, and Henrik sing together and in isolation from one another, separated from their early inability to know just with whom they should sing:

(Simultaneously)

ANNE:	HENRIK:	FREDRIK:
Soon.		
I want to.	"Later". . .	Now,
	When is "later"?	As the sweet imbecilities
	All you ever	Trip on my trouser leg,
Soon,		
	Hear is	
Whatever you		
Say.	"Later, Henrik . . ." (39)	

Destabilized into a singing "partnership" of three, they become engaged in individuating themselves from one another, declaring their difference, and ultimately declaring their resistance/attraction to each other, gestures that are set to the distinguishing lyrics of time and musical rhythms that define when sexual fulfillment is desired or likely for each (moments which, importantly, do not yet overlap).

When the men sing with the men and the women with the women about their partners in *A Little Night Music* (or any of Sondheim's works), they discuss their sense of the couple's losing ground, not of the bliss of their partnerships. What these men and these women know, therefore, is the experience of loss in relation to marriage; for that they have a shared language and music, although not for fulfillment. Significantly, the women who sing "Every Day a Little Death" can hear each other's words, add their own verses to fill out the song begun by the other, and come ultimately to sing the words together:

CHARLOTTE:
　　Ah, well . . .
　　Every day a little death,
ANNE:
　　Every day a little death,
CHARLOTTE:
　　In the parlor, in the bed,
ANNE:
　　On the lips and in the eyes,
CHARLOTTE:
　　In the curtains,
　　In the silver,　　　　　　　　　　ANNE:
　　In the buttons,　　　　　　　　　　In the murmurs,

In the bread.   In the pauses,
                                       In the gestures,
                                       In the sighs.
Every day a little sting   Every day a little dies,
In the heart
And in the head.
                                       In the looks and in
                                       The lies.
Every move and
Every breath,
And you hardly feel a   And you hardly feel a
Thing,   Thing,
Brings a perfect little   Brings a perfect little
Death.   Death. (83-4)

If Charlotte begins by seeming to instruct Anne in the meaning of marriage, Anne's quick ability to respond reveals that this song works not so
much as a speech act of instruction as an awakening within Anne of what she
already knows, without ever having articulated it. Thus music coaxes the revelation out of her; the women alternate who initiates and who responds; and
they come finally to sing as if one mind, one voice.

That the women share this knowledge (as do the men in "It Would Have
Been Wonderful") underscores just how "other" the other is in a marriage.
Sondheim's marital partners are deaf to one another. Singing in unison
(though different songs), Sondheim's couples do so in a bounded space where
neither can hear the other's voice or chooses not to. It is revealing that "Send
in the Clowns" is Sondheim's only popular hit. It is one of the few instances
where partners sing a love ballad to one another. Even in this ballad, however, the lovers only alternate phrases, until they finally sing together the concluding line—which is about their achieving at last a mutual presence to one
another:

FREDRIK:
    Make way for the clowns.
DESIRÉE:
    Applause for the clowns.
BOTH:
    They're finally here. (184)

It is significant that Fredrik and Desirée have not yet married.

VII

Left with a world of broken second acts, the musicals of Stephen Sondheim ask whether there is such a thing as the second act or an act to follow. Marriage is a structure of second acts. With its promise of more to come in repetition, return, and renewal, marriage has constituted the structure of musical comedy. If comedy's dependence on a happy ending insists on the coupling of marriage and happiness, to do a critique of marriage is to do a critique not just of musical comedy but of the very possibility of comedy—that which depends on marriage for its archetype of renewal. With the guarantee of an unseen happiness swept aside—that which is the promise of marriage and so too the promise of comedy—what emerges instead is a series of questions. What is marriage? Is it desirable? What is comedy? Is it possible?

Destabilized, fundamentally "unmusicalized," marriage and comedy in the works of Sondheim wear faces of confusion and self-doubt. To know themselves again, they must meet as if for the first time. ". . . the suddenly wind-shaken wood springs awake for the second dark time this one Spring day."[16] The "end" of musical comedy, like the promise of "Spring," we must at last acknowledge, carries with it the problems of the dark.

NOTES

[1] An alternative version of the song appears in Gershwin and Gershwin 1991: "It all began so well, / But what an end! / This is the time a feller needs a friend, / When ev'ry happy plot / Ends with the marriage knot, / And there's no knot for me."

[2] Jagendorf 1984, 13.

[3] See Staples 1984 for an overview of the evolution and decline of the male-female comedy team in vaudeville.

[4] Aristophanes' delight in the anarchic, political, obscene, and the fortuitous rise of the witty, often corrupt, loner finds itself replicated more often in narrative than in theater—his comic ethos is echoed in the narratives of Rabelais, Cervantes, and Fielding, not in the theater of Shakespeare. Why it should be in narrative and later in the early solo male clown films of Chaplin, for instance, or the male team films of the Marx Brothers that the Aristophanic form finds its heirs raises interesting questions about genre difference. The picaresque novel, like clown comedy in film, lends itself to the nonlinear merging of comic bits which constitute the anarchic tradition. This was a specifically male comic form set on the road or framed as a contest between the conventional dwellers within a society and its critic poised outside of its boundaries. The early comedic novel, like that of early film, found a solution to its production in the stringing together of jokes: these novels developed from a "storytelling aesthetic," while early silent and sound comedy emerged from the "vaudeville aesthetic" which Henry Jenkins defines in fine detail in *What Made Pistachio Nuts.*

[5] Furth and Sondheim 1970.

[6] Of course, Aristotle's notion of this "end" which he calls happiness has nothing to do with how the musical defines it. Where the musical turns to marriage, Aristotle discusses the "good life," a life lived between states of extreme as that which enables happiness. The most content life of all, he concludes, is that of the solitary philosopher who pursues contemplation. The notion of happiness, therefore, could not be more radically different.

[7] Lapine and Sondheim 1992.

[8] A *bricoleur* is a handyman or tinkerer, someone who can find a way to make do. The term was made popular in the 1960s by French ethnologist Claude Lévi-Strauss who used it to describe the way in which cultures organize their material surroundings. See Lévi-Strauss 1966. [SG]

[9] Lapine and Sondheim 1991.

[10] Schiff 1993, 86.

[11] Schiff 1993, 86.

[12] Schiff 1993, 86.

[13] Schiff 1993, 86.

[14] Schiff 1993 accounts in part for the "unhummability" of Sondheim's music from the musical expression of the character's sense of doubt—as the characters "hem and haw," the music does so too (87). (I, however, contest this claim of "unhummability." I can think of few other composers' works I get more satisfaction out of humming than Sondheim's, and I don't take this capacity to be just the result of repeated listenings.)

[15] Sondheim and Wheeler 1991. Bergman 1960.

[16] Thomas 1954, 95.

CHAPTER 4

The Funeral of *Follies*
Stephen Sondheim and the Razing
of American Musical Theater
Ann Marie McEntee

Frank Rich titled his commendatory review of the 1971 production of *Follies* "The Last Musical."[1] Both Clive Barnes and Walter Kerr failed to see, perhaps, the irony in Rich's title, for in their own reviews they panned the production as a plotless trendy "concept" musical.[2] Such an indictment—in which "concept" dismisses "book"—was perhaps more a reflection of the theater-going public's reluctance to accept a new perception of culture and theatrical techniques than a valid criticism of the work of Stephen Sondheim and Harold Prince. "Hal told us . . . to maintain a tension," Sondheim noted (93). "*Follies* does have a story, many stories, but it has no plot: it's Chekhovian, everything happens underneath the surface."[3]

Simply put, the production team of Prince, Sondheim, Goldman, Aronson, and Bennett replaced the formulaic musical comedy which came to fruition under Rodgers and Hammerstein with a postmodernist treatment of the same subject matter. *Follies* presented a seemingly cinematic collage of two middle-aged couples whose thirty-year reunion with one another and their younger selves proved to be their undoing. Unlike more traditional memory pieces, during which performers recounted in a chronological sequence their respective histories (only to grow all the wiser at the conclusion of the evening), this "concept" musical was conceived and staged as a fragmented destabilized collection of memories and events of the present evening which followed more a Brechtian than an Aristotelian time construction. And in place of offering clear and stable visual boundaries, Aronson's dilapidated set offered spatial ambiguities, contradictions, and resonances. As a result, no singular, integrated, positive image or character was able to emerge from the "Loveland" sequence, the extravagant finale during which the four leading characters played out their own "follies" to a cacophanous conclusion.

Thematically and theatrically, in other words, *Follies* ushered in a new paradigm in the American musical theater, a treatment of the disillusioned

American culture which jeered at the happy ending of the Rodgers and Hammerstein musical rather than supported it. The critics panned the play, perhaps not because they were unable to follow the fragmented story, but rather because, like many members of its audiences, they were unwilling to experience the stripping away of the illusions and fantasies about love that for most of the current century the American musical theater has sustained.

I

Originally a murder mystery entitled "The Girls Upstairs," *Follies* evolved into a surrealistic tribute to and obituary for the musical-theater style of the Ziegfeld era. Its staging at the Winter Garden Theater, a Shubert temple of musical comedy and revue from 1912 to 1924, furthered the production's dualistic goal of reverence for and dismissal of an exhausted art form. This aging theater thus served as a "concrete exemplification, an objective correlative, of [that] period of American musical] history, with all its associated hopes, despairs, and aspirations."[4]

Two images galvanized this dual-edged concept for the production team. The first presented the glamorously dressed, but obviously aging Gloria Swanson, posed amid the rubble in the skeletal remains of the recently demolished Roxy Theater, the New York movie palace which premiered during its glory days (1927-40) many of Ms. Swanson's films. Her posturing and facial expressions, suggesting both triumph and defiance, expressed for Prince the poetic essence, the indomitable human spirit that he wanted the production to project. (One is also reminded of Swanson's remark to William Holden in the film *Sunset Boulevard*, "I am big. It's the pictures that got small!") A still from Fellini's film *Juliet of the Spirits* presented the mixed mood of glamour and gloom, past and present; the posturing of the would-be suitor and the actress warmly accepting the kiss on the hand corresponded to the aging Dmitri Weismann greeting his aging chorines in front of the staircase. The staircase, in turn, supported the *tableau vivant* created by the "girls" during the "Beautiful Girls" number. The outsized statues of Greek goddesses appeared as six-foot tall chorus-girl "ghosts," who drifted languidly through the set during the performance, suggesting both the characters' romanticization of their past and the glory days of the musical-revue theater. A goddess-like showgirl's statue—a cracked Miss Liberty actually—served as the logo for the *Follies* poster. And, although such an image betrayed national and political dimensions of the disillusioned early 1970s which the production did not necessarily portray, it encapsulated the thematic concept for which Prince was striving.

> Metaphoric rubble became visual rubble. A theatre is being torn down. On
> its stage a party in celebration of that. The celebrants for whom the theatre

represents youth, dreams lost, a golden time, are to be orphaned. Is the theatre torn down? Will it be torn down tomorrow? Or was it torn down yesterday? Keep it ambiguous, a setting for the sort of introspection that reunions precipitate, a mood in which to lose sight of the present, to look back on the past.[5]

The stage itself thus became a spatial representation of the Plummers and Stones, four individuals who have begun to experience the ravages of time. Fighting the battle of middle age, they foolishly cling to the past which clutters up their present like the rubble and crumbling edifices scattered around the stage. They dismiss the rubble—the real, the follies of their youth—because their selective memories of nostalgia recall only the golden illusions they entertained as chorines and stage-door Johnnies. As Prince explains, "*Follies* suggests *Ziegfeld Follies*, but also, in the British sense, foolishness, and in the French 'folie,' which is madness."[6]

This threefold connotation of follies was realized through Aronson's set.[7] Asymmetrical in design, the stage picture depicted a semidemolished theater. A collection of architectural bits and pieces, including a gaping hole located up center stage, which looked out on the New York theater district, evoked the thematic disconnectedness. Youth and middle age remained separate entities, never permitted to merge. Aronson created his set as representative of a culture intolerant of age: "In this country things become old-fashioned within half an hour . . . . Cities have no time to develop a patina. As soon as a building goes up, they make plans to tear it down."[8] Architecturally, youth supplants age, and thematically, the characters cling to their youth instead of accepting the patina of middle age. A former apprentice to Alexandra Exter, Aronson turned to his Russian formalist roots to realize such disjointedness.

Memories arrive in bits and pieces—they're evocative . . . . I used these leftovers, these remnants very purposefully. If you see a statue and a hand is missing, or the nose is broken, it leaves so much more to the imagination than if it is complete. This very [fragmentation] creates a positive-negative relationship between the missing pieces and the elements that remain.[9]

Fragmentation of memory thus leads the characters into their follies, and this stage picture, a milieu characterized by disjointedness—the structures no longer "fit" together—facilitates the very collision that the characters experience during their confrontations with their respective pasts.

What Aronson's stage designs realized, Sondheim accomplished with the score and lyrics. He established two distinct styles of music, the so-called "book" numbers which the characters sang as middle-aged persona, and the pastiche numbers which were entirely separate in style. These latter songs evoked musical theater revues and show tunes. Sondheim captured the essence of Kern, Porter, Gershwin, Da Sylva-Brown-Henderson, and Herbert-Friml. It was with these pastiche numbers that the characters enacted their youthful fantasies which precipitated their mid-life crises. As Sondheim explained, "there were two kinds of music going on in *Follies*. I was splitting the attention, but that was the idea. It's a schizophrenic piece and it's supposed to be."[10] Such a split aurally established the mosaic of character dissolutions and disintegrations which Aronson's set rendered visually.

II

"Who's That Woman?" and the "Loveland" sequence demonstrate how this thematic schizophrenia developed theatrically. "Who's That Woman?", better known as the "Mirror Number," conveyed the primary thesis of the production—namely, that superficial affairs cannot hold back the ravagement of time. Sally, Phyllis, and several of the other women performed this tap dance number in their younger, "Weismann girl" days. Led by an overweight Stella Deems, the decrepit middle-aged women recreated their old dance number downstage. Meanwhile, their younger selves, "ghosts" actually, dressed in black and white mirror-laden costumes which "flashed and sparkled as they moved," replicated the dance upstage.[11] Their monochromatic appearance contrasted sharply with their present day, "Technicolor" selves. Male chorus members, tapping underneath the stage, created an echo effect, which was miked over the stage to further the ghostlike quality established visually by the younger chorus girls upstage. Past and present, youth and age, collided during the number's climax as the ghosts moved downstage to dance with their older "selves."

Illusion and reality thus interacted during this production number. The aging female performers—Alexis Smith, Dorothy Collins, Yvonne DeCarlo, Fifi d'Orsay, and Mary McCarty—themselves relics of an earlier age of entertainment, embodied the *Follies* theme. Ethel Shutta was actually a member of the 1925 *Ziegfeld Follies*. These actresses recalled, for the audience, its own past. As Martin Gottfried commented, "these [actresses] are aging and we see them aged, and 'Follies' is aging and age. In a sense these [women] were used as people rather than as performers."[12] Like the historically significant theater—the revue house—in which they performed, these women enacted the youthful follies of their earlier promising stage careers.

To heighten the poignancy of the presence of these performers, Prince and Bennett cast six-foot tall Vegas showgirls as the "ghosts." As Bennett explained, "I wanted those girls to be bigger than the Ziegfeld girls could ever have been. It was like looking into a mirror and seeing the past—not the *reality* of the past, but the glorification of it."[13] The juxtaposition was nothing less than devastating. James Goldman remarked, "to see the decay of the flesh—all those bright, young beautiful girls and their lovely bodies with all the sense of youth and the promise of what's to come contrasted against what *actually* became of it."[14]

One of three "memory" numbers staged approximately halfway through the production, "Who's That Woman?" disclosed further the ironic nature of Sondheim's score. Performed between the thematically related "Broadway Baby" and "I'm Still Here," this number presented the false set of values which arose from the chorine's pursuit of tinsel, glamour, and gaiety. And although "Who's That Woman?" led to Stella's resolution with her past, "I'm Still Here," performed by the vamp Carlotta Campion (Yvonne DeCarlo), returned the audience to that world of the hoofer who wades through life, knowing the "big break" is just around the corner. The big break—a part in a Broadway show that sustains a long run, fame, glamour, and fans—was show business's version of the American Dream. *Follies* was, in essence, Sondheim's version of *Death of a Salesman*.

The production raced toward a mini-Ziegfeld follies during which the show's musical idioms collided as Buddy, Sally, Phyllis, and Ben performed pastiche numbers which expressed their mid-life crises. "Where musical performance in the Ziegfeld era was its own justification, in this latter day Follies it is double-edged, intensely self-regarding in its use of music as metaphor . . . both tribute to and an obituary for a musical-theatre style [Prince and Sondheim] helped to make obsolete (98)."[15]

"Loveland" opened with a burst of light and color upstage of the four principals, lost in arguments with the ghosts of their younger selves. Aronson's darkened, asymmetrical shell of a theater space transformed itself into a two-dimensional, symmetrical set which typified the musical revues of the Ziegfeld era. A fan-shaped structure suggesting a Fragonard valentine, "Loveland" represented the rosy, sugar-coated fantasy rising out of the rubble and ruin: color, panache, and light supplanted the gloom and doom of the principals' reality. Aronson conceived of the set as a collection of boxes which denoted the shifts in time from present to past, reality to fantasy.

> The boxes represented the mind . . . . What happened outside them was real: it happened at the party. What occurred *inside* the boxes were the memories, fantasies, and thoughts of our characters . . . . The boxes were a kind of house of the past, and at the end our four leads had to move out of that house.[16]

As the "Loveland" box descended from the flies, chorines dressed as Dresden dolls and cavaliers sauntered downstage to welcome the principals to "Loveland," "where everybody lives to love (83)."[17] Thus "The Folly of Love" unfolded, revealing bewigged chorus girls dressed in extraordinary thematic costumes. Froufrou abounded. "Music," the "First Love," wore a hoop skirt "encrusted with lutes and harps, entwined with strands of pearls and swags of silk and God-knows-what."[18] Additional "Loves" such as "Romantic," "Young," "Pure," and "Eternal" wore costumes decorated in a similar manner, ornamented with three-dimensional Cupids, huge bows, and jewels, recalling for the audience the opulent production numbers of musical-revue theater. As these "loves" moved languidly under the weight of their headdresses, the male cavaliers recited lines reminiscent of a Hallmark valentine:

> To lovers' lips, a lover's lips are petals,
> A velvet promise budding like a rose.
> . . . .
> Two lovers are like lovebirds in devotion,
> If separated, they must swoon and die. (84)

As the chorus struck decorative poses upstage, the "Folly of Love" brought on the young, pink-cheeked, dewy-eyed Ben and Phyllis and Buddy and Sally. The lovers sang innocently of romance, their lyrics simultaneously recreating the histories of the older couples and belying their present lives: "You're gonna love tomorrow, / As long as your tomorrow is spent with me" (89), and "Love will see us through / Till something better comes along" (91). The couples' "Folly" presented a world of idealized love, "a world that the American musical theater encouraged its audience could be found, yet one that the disillusionment of maturity had proved to be a pipe dream."[19]

Their sentiments and hopes, derided by what has become of these young lovers, then shifted to the present-day lovers who, in turn, performed their own "follies." Each of the principals performed a revue number reminiscent of the 1920s and 1930s musical idioms. Buddy's "God-Why-Don't-You-Love-Me-Blues," a fantastical echo of his earlier book number, "The Right Girl," recalled the comic's patter song, traditionally performed in front of the main drape. The comic, who was costumed in baggy blue suit and oversized derby hat, kept the crowd occupied as set and costume changes occurred behind the curtain. A cut-out miniature car hung from Buddy's waist, and his routine involved inept maneuvering of this prop. He continually bumped into a parody of his mistress, Margie, as he pursued his wife Sally. Prince and Bennett staged this number under a strobe light to suggest the madcap adventures characteristic of Mack Sennett films.

As Buddy scooted off the stage, the curtains parted, revealing Sally. Dressed in "a clinging, beaded silver gown" (100), she played out her Helen Morgan fantasy. Her boudoir number, "Losing My Mind," reminiscent of a Gershwin torch song, recalled her earlier book number "In Buddy's Eyes."

The follies of Phyllis and Ben, unlike those of Buddy and Sally, revealed alter egos which did not appear until they entered Loveland. Their respective numbers, in fact, contrasted sharply with their earlier book numbers. Phyllis' folly, staged on an art deco set, recalled the glitzy burlesque houses of the

1920s and 1930s. She sauntered out on the stage wearing a sexy, red fringed flapper dress and as she gyrated in hootchy-cootchy fashion, belted out "The Story of Lucy and Jessie," a tribute to Cole Porter. Revealing the struggle within herself, this song juxtaposed juicy Lucy (her naive, younger self) to dressy Jessie (her present unfeeling self).

Ben's "Live, Laugh, and Love," evoked the Fred Astaire dance numbers of the 1930s. Dressed in white tails and top hat, and sporting a clear plastic cane, John McMartin appeared to be the dashing man about town who could indeed dance on the ceiling. Surrounded by a kick line, Ben tried to reject his material success for the values of "life, laughter, and love," values he so clearly lacks. As the number picked up its tempo, he stumbled, calling to the conductor for his lyrics. Racing from chorine to chorine, as the chorus line continued to dance, he shouted justifications for his callous treatment of Sally thirty years before. Suddenly, the "Loveland" set flew out, revealing the shell of the Weismann theater. Platforms shifted back and forth, carrying ghosts, party guests, and house musicians, all moving and dancing to the rhythms of their own respective songs. The kick line continued its routine downstage. This animated finale—the madness located inside Ben's mind—peaked as he screamed for Phyllis. The cacophony receded as the lights dimmed, suggesting his inability to find his own way out of this chaos.

A vilification of their lives, the "Loveland" follies insured a release of the nostalgia with which Buddy, Sally, Phyllis, and Ben had distorted their memories and their lives. Conversely, a "vaudevillification" of American musical theater, the follies within *Follies* dismissed the formulaic, happy ending musical which had supported the theater's star system for over fifty years.

III

The critics objected to these thematic disparagements. Walter Kerr claimed, "the legitimacy in love-stories that ought to give the evening its solid foothold is skimpy and sadly routine."[20] Clive Barnes also focused upon the story line, asserting that "by the faded beard of Pirandello [James Goldman] has gone too far."[21] Martin Gottfried appeared undecided in his assessment, stating that " 'Follies' was not quite ready to rely completely on concept as the organizational replacement for a book."[22] After learning that his colleagues Kerr and Barnes panned the show for that very reason, the critic retracted his original criticism.

Its importance as a *kind* of theater transcends its interest as an example of a musical . . . 'Follies' is a *concept musical*, a show whose music, lyrics, dance, stage movement and dialogue are woven through each other in the creation of a tapestry-like theme (rather than in support of a plot).[23]

These three critics seemed overly concerned with the relationship between the book and how effectively the production executed it; other critics, however, conveyed the intentions of Prince and his production team. Stanley Kaufmann remarked that "the big-time theater seems to be running out of the ability to nourish itself on society, so it's feeding on itself, chewing its left leg or right arm."[24] *Time*'s review cogently expressed the significance of the production:

> The best of *Follies* indicates that the art of theater, like all art, must renew itself by destroying tradition or by using it in fresh ways. *Follies* amply demonstrates that the musical—America's single greatest contribution to the history of drama—need not become the exclusive province of the antique dealer or the rock group. In style and substance it can be flexible as a film, as immediate as a street scene.[25]

Read alongside that of Kauffmann, *Time*'s critique offered a new definition of the musical as a viable art form which had to change in order to survive. This reading of *Follies* revealed the cinematic essence which Prince wanted to stage. Concomitantly, it referred to Brecht's famous essay entitled "Street Scene," a seminal treatise which presented directorial techniques that Prince himself has incorporated into his own directing oeuvre.[26] Kerr, Barnes, and Gottfried, I would submit, misunderstood the purpose of *Follies*, while the latter critics realized the tribute to and funeral for the musical revue theater which Prince, Bennett, Sondheim, and Aronson saw as paramount to their development as theater artists.

Follies represented, in fact, a "swan song" for these artists whose work was strongly attributed to theatrical art forms—musical comedy, the revue, and the chorus line—from which *Follies* was conceived and realized. Harold Prince, whose apprenticeship was served under the renowned producer George Abbott, came to directing after a brief stint of producing. His radical career, which included such memorable hits as *The Pajama Game*, *Fiddler on the Roof*, and *Cabaret*, enabled Prince to strike out in a direction that ran counter to the traditional Rodgers and Hammerstein bill of fare. As Prince explained,

> There is a kind of deliciously unmotivated musical, a cherished memory of yesteryear, which some of our critics lament the loss of. Not I. I think that shows in which songs are utterly unmotivated, in which characters react inconsistently for laughs, mindless and pleasantly entertaining though they may be, through overpraise dangerously inhibit the future of the musical theater.[27]

Follies furthered the notion of the concept musical which *Cabaret* had introduced several years earlier: as Prince explained during an interview with then *Los Angeles Times* theater critic Joyce Haber, "'Follies' isn't about will the guy get the girl? or will the boat arrive in the harbor on time? It's about this country, marriage, affluence, the loss of spiritual standards."[28] Prince staged *Follies* at the midpoint of his career, a time when he chose to reflect on the direction his work had taken him, and so jokingly likened the production to *8-1/2*, Fellini's quasi-autobiographical film.

The codirector and choreographer Michael Bennett emerged through the ranks as a "hoofer." Although a difficult show for him because of his artistic differences with Prince, *Follies* nonetheless represented his tribute to such theatrical icons as the Radio City Rockettes. And, like Prince, who saw *Follies* as a turning point in his career, Bennett developed styles of choreography that would be more fully realized in *Chorus Line*, and *Dream Girls*.

For Boris Aronson, whose work in the theater began under the tutelage of Alexandra Exter at the Kamerny Theater, Moscow, *Follies* entailed resurrecting the doctrine of Cubism: " 'The fascination of the empty stage.' It is a question—not of how you fill that emptiness—but rather, what you can extract from the existing space."[29] Aronson thus designed the set as a celebration of disjunction which coalesced in its ambiguous collage.[30] Like Prince, Aronson read the production as a metaphor for a disillusioned postmodern society which resonated with moral and spiritual conflicts and contradictions. And, for Aronson who knew firsthand the work of Meyerhold, theater was the one venue by which to examine such a metaphor. He also knew, however, that theater, and in particular Broadway, had devolved into a row of museums which simply remounted traditional family dramas and musicals. "In *Follies*," Aronson explained. "I wanted to pay tribute to the institution of theatre, as the process of its dismantling is becoming more than fantasy."[31]

Stephen Sondheim, who deems Oscar Hammerstein his greatest teacher and influence, treated *Follies* as a tribute to his musical theater roots. The pastiche numbers, such as "Loveland," "One More Kiss," and "Losing My Mind," revealed the composer's acute understanding and love of the music and lyrics of early twentieth-century composers. By refracting his score through an analogous theatrical form like the Ziegfeld revue, Sondheim created a conflict. Whereas the older forms reminded the audience of what theater could do, what the culture of an earlier time valued, the ironic and sometimes satiric lyrics impinged upon those forms, coaxing the audience to accept the disillusionment of the leading characters and, conversely, the culture of the early 1970s.[32] Such a dislocation of style and content, like the set's dissonances and ambiguities, established an ambivalence, a sense of feeling two things at once. Sondheim defined *Follies* as an opportunity to "[get] away from the linear and the naturalistic."[33] Like the other members of the production team, this composer-lyricist, who has often been accused of writing unhummable songs, refocused the lens with which the theater-going public perceived musical revue theater. For Sondheim, the selective memory of nostalgia, which recalls only the good, but never the real, became *Follies'* central theme.[34]

IV

To no one's surprise, *Follies* lost money. And yet it remains the one Prince-Sondheim musical which has undergone two revivals, a concert version in New York, and a London production, neither of which Prince directed.[35] Ironically, both revivals, venues for aging entertainers whose careers needed a financial boost, recirculated the original production's underlying message of the foolishness of clinging to the past. As a piece of theater, *Follies* offered lavish show-stopping numbers, but as a cultural critique, it remains a sardonic exposé of American culture of the early 1970s. The "selective memory of nostalgia" thus lost itself in theatrical forms, while dismissing the ideological indictment. The original Prince-Sondheim production argued that nostalgia focuses upon only what is pleasing, even distorting cultural myths. Evidently the revivals found a new way to pay old debts amid the rubble of the musical revue known as *Follies*.

NOTES

[1] An abbreviated version of this paper was presented at a Special Session on Sondheim at the annual meeting of the Modern Language Association of America in Toronto, December, 1993. For Rich's remarks, see Prince 1974, 170.

[2] Barnes 1971, 44, and Kerr 1971, 1

[3] Hirsch 1989, 93.

[4] Gordon 1990, 80.

[5] Prince 1974, 159-60.

[6] Prince 1974, 100.

[7] For photographs of Sondheim's productions, see Gottfried 1993.

[8] *Boris Aronson* 1981, 15.

[9] Aronson and Rich 1987, 234.

[10] Sondheim 1978, 13.

[11] Goldman and Sondheim 1971, 51.

[12] Gottfried 1971, 311.

[13] Zadan 1986, 139.

[14] Zadan 1986, 141.

[15] Hirsch 1989, 98.

[16] Aronson and Rich 1987, 232.

[17] Goldman and Sondheim 1971, 83.

[18] Goldman and Sondheim 1971, 83.

[19] Gordon 1990, 110.

[20] Kerr 1971, 2:1.

[21] Barnes 1971, 44.

[22] Gottfried 1971, 311.

[23] Gottfried 1971, 1:1.

[24] Kaufmann 1971, 24.

[25] Kanfer 1971, 74.

[26] Brecht 1964, 121-29.

[27] Prince 1974, 23.

[28] Haber l971, 11.

[29] *Boris Aronson* 1981, 2.

[30] Aronson and Rich 1987, 30.

[31] Aronson and Rich 1987, 250.

[32] Gordon 1990, 10.

[33] Hirsch 1989, 85.

[34] Gordon 1990, 77.

[35] Since this writing, there has been a third revival—at the Papermill Playhouse in Millburn, New Jersey, in 1998.

CHAPTER 5

Difference and Sameness

Tarchetti's *Fosca*, Scola's *Passione d'Amore*,
and Sondheim's *Passion*

Shoshana Milgram Knapp

"We're the same," sings Fosca to Giorgio, trying to persuade him to be her
friend and ultimately her lover. "We are different."[1] Putting aside the context
in which these words are uttered, the student of Sondheim could readily employ these statements to describe a remarkable body of work in which each
musical is different both from musicals by other artists and from other Sondheim musicals, while at the same time displaying the intellectual grasp, emotional strength, and artistic craft we have come to expect.

Sondheim's most recent musical, *Passion* (1994), is a tragedy built on
the comic material of *Forum* where love is disease and beauty is destiny. It
has its origins in Ettore Scola's film *Passione d'Amore* (1981), which in turn
was based on Iginio Ugo Tarchetti's novel *Fosca* (1869).[2] Yet *Passion* explicitly and persistently addresses exclusivity, singularity, the new, the unknown,
the never-before. Regardless of its roots, it is unique, and it celebrates uniqueness. Comparing and contrasting in broad outlines the novel, the film, and the
play, I propose to show in this paper how a key theme—that of sameness ver-
sus difference—at once permeates all three works and yet remains crucial to
the analysis of the passionate relationships in *Passion*.

I

In all three stories, the beautiful Clara (whose name means "light") and the
ugly Fosca (whose name means "dark") are contrasted. Married and a
mother, Clara encounters the handsome Captain Giorgio Bachetti, and the
two decide to meet regularly in a flower-filled room in Milan for love in the
afternoon. The captain is reassigned to an obscure army outpost where his romantic life is complicated by Fosca, his colonel's cousin, who reads to live,
borrows his books, and seeks first his friendship, then his love. Repulsed by
her relentless and increasingly manipulative pursuit, he nonetheless feigns

love on the advice of the military doctor who believes that Fosca's passion for him has brought her so close to death that only Giorgio can save her. Instead of making Fosca well, however, Giorgio makes himself sick. His relationship with Clara becomes attenuated and problematic. Hoping to save Giorgio from the ravages of illness, the doctor arranges his transfer. Upon hearing the news, Fosca reveals her passion publicly, and her cousin challenges Giorgio to a duel. Hours before the duel, Giorgio goes to Fosca's room, proclaims his love (which he discovers with amazement to be genuine), and joins her in bed—an act the doctor has said could kill her. The next morning, Giorgio wounds (but does not kill) the colonel, collapses with a cry similar to Fosca's repeated howls of agony, and regains consciousness in a hospital, months later, to learn of Fosca's death.

Iginio Tarchetti's novel (which was serialized in a Milanese periodical) is apparently autobiographical. Its details are presumably borrowed from the author's happy romance with a married woman and his unhappy romance with a sickly relative of his military commander. *Fosca* consists of a first-person narrative composed five years after the fictional events it describes and incorporates journal entries and letters. It is presented for anonymous publication not by Giorgio himself, who seems to have outlived his suffering and experienced public success, but by a friend. (The novel itself, coincidentally, was completed after Tarchetti's death by Salvatore Farina, a novelist and a friend.) In other words, doubly removed from the events it recounts—by the five years between the history and the story, and by the difference between the narrator–writer and the alleged presenter of the material—*Fosca* remains nonetheless "quivering" and "hypersensitive." It is as if Giorgio has indeed been infected by Fosca's disease, as if Fosca's agonized howl has become itself the tonality of the novel in which it is described. The incoherence and fervid emotionalism of this fiction may be as much the result of Tarchetti's enmeshment with his subject matter as it is of his attempt to create a diseased narrator, or of his own raging illness, one which killed him at the age of twenty-nine before he completed the book. His Fosca, we are told, survived him by many years.

Tarchetti's Giorgio is absorbed by his own uniqueness. "I often gaze about me as if I were the only person left in the world," he writes (6-7). "What fills me with horror is the solitude of emotion" (7).

> I was born with exceptional passions. I could never hate or love in moderation; I could never lower my affections to the level of other men's. Nature rendered me a rebel against common standards and common law. It was therefore just that my passion should have exceptional causes, means, developments, ends (7).

Giorgio recognizes that his love for Clara is ordinary in its blissfulness: "Relating it would be the same as repeating the story of every affection" (8).

He includes the ordinary story of Clara to contrast it with the extraordinary story of Fosca, which he regards as "the diagnosis of an illness." "I do not know," he writes, "whether any earthly creature ever submitted to such a test, or whether in the circumstances wherein I endured it; I do not know whether they survived" (8).

Giorgio's relationship with Fosca in Tarchetti's novel begins with the books he lends her—not only the epistolary novel of romantic love, Rousseau's *La Nouvelle Héloïse*, but as well the appropriately entitled *L'Homme Singulier* by La Fontaine (which Fosca reads and annotates) and the ominous *Les Confessions à la Tombe* (which she returns to him immediately). His feelings for Fosca are complicated by his awareness that in some respects—and not solely those of culture and sensitivity—she is like him. In Tarchetti's novel, Giorgio is already ill when he meets Clara, and her love for him temporarily restores his health. "What was I, a year ago?" he asks. "The conclusion I drew is distressing, but just: I was loved out of compassion; am I not obliged to love Fosca for the same reason?" (89). He imagines himself, therefore, we may say, in Clara's role.

Giorgio's descriptions of the two women highlight their differences even when he is using the same words. Clara is physically "robust" (20), whereas Fosca has "an intelligence that is robust" (41). Giorgio explicitly notes the parallels. Both women fill their rooms with flowers; both are tall, with dark hair; both are associated with birds; both indulge as adults in childlike pleasures. At the same time, he also notes that walking with Fosca makes him remember and yearn for Clara, as the scent of one woman reminds him of all women (48-9), and that the sensation of feeling Fosca's skeletal thinness reminds him of holding Clara's voluptuous roundness. "She was so thin, so wasted that I could feel her skeleton beneath the folds of her silk dress, and I shuddered. How different from those days when I playfully carried Clara about our little room, and felt her full, dense, yielding forms press against my body!" (135). Clara reminds him of his mother: "My mother possessed her same beauty, and at just the age when I was born" (20). Fosca reminds him of Mary, mother of God, a wax Madonna: "Her white waxen face, mane of black horsehair, and eyes of polished glass. . . made her resemble Fosca" (82).

Who, then, is like whom? Fosca dictates to Giorgio a love letter addressed to herself. She is, in effect, making Giorgio resemble her (in that he is speaking her words) and making herself resemble Clara (in that she is to be the object of the endearments she has scripted for him). Clara lies awake at night, wishing she could watch Giorgio sleeping (115-16). Lying by Giorgio's side, Fosca has a waking dream of Giorgio as her guardian angel, awake by her bedside when she was a child (84). Fosca herself as a schoolgirl, we are told, lay awake to watch the sleep of a fellow schoolgirl to whom she was passionately attracted (95). Fosca used to steal the schoolgirl's ribbons and handkerchiefs in the same way that she now cherishes Giorgio's scarf (92), and that Giorgio viewed his mother's handkerchief as a "relic of her holy scent" (49) and yearns for one of Clara's ribbons or a dress (18).

To be sure, undeniable contrasts emerge. "I was born sick," moans Fosca (93), and Clara admits "I was born happy" (116). In their letters, Fosca and Clara speak for themselves, and no one would mistake Fosca's history or story for Clara's. For Giorgio, however, the parallels he sees everywhere serve to exacerbate disparity, and vice versa. He spends a day in the country with Clara at places they have visited before, and he thinks back on a day he recently spent with Fosca. "I think—scornfully, almost angrily—of the strange conformity that Fortune has established between several scenes of my two very different loves. What points of comparison! What analogies in this antithesis!" (160). Yet Giorgio ultimately does not achieve insight. He relates the diagnosis of an illness without learning from it. To paraphrase T. S. Eliot, he has had the experience but missed the meaning.

This failure is dramatically plain in his reaction to Clara's final letter. In Tarchetti's novel, Giorgio reads Clara's letter after Fosca's frenzied reaction to the news of his transfer has led to the inevitability of a duel between Giorgio and the colonel. Clara writes that her family has become impoverished, and that she must devote herself to her husband and son. She would not want her son to learn of her adultery, to feel himself dishonored, and to form a negative opinion of her and of all women. And, having placed her son ahead of her lover, she reminds her lover that he thought she resembled *his* mother: "love me in her and like her" (175). Giorgio responds by noting (with respect to Clara) "I had loved a monster" (177) as he has earlier seen Fosca to be, and that he himself is entirely changed: "There was a moment when the mirror seemed to reflect the face of another person, who was standing behind me, bending over my shoulder to gaze at his image" (176-77).

After receiving Clara's letter, Giorgio asks the doctor to arrange for him to meet privately with Fosca: "That woman loved me, she alone truly loved me. I shall not abandon her without throwing myself at her feet, without thanking her with my tears" (181). Although the resolve is clearly his own, he remains uncertain of the degree of his responsibility. "Am I responsible for the deeds I committed that night? Was I aware of my actions? I do not know" (181). When he sees Fosca later that night, she becomes both Clara and his mother. When she asks him who is the woman he loved above all others, he answers "My mother" (186). When she asks a second time, he refuses to answer. Giorgio and Fosca both think of Clara—until she asks once again, and he answers "You" (187). At this point she asks him to do "what you would do with a woman you love, what you did with women you loved, what you did with Clara" (187)—and she runs "her thin hands through my hair, twisted it around her fingers as one does with children," to which gestures he "surrendered like a child" (188).

They make love, he shoots the colonel in a duel, he falls ill with a Fosca-like disease, Fosca dies, and his mother arrives. Tarchetti's novel offers a profusion and confusion of blurred and exchanged identities filtered through a character–narrator who no longer exists as a consciousness at the time the fictional narrative is published by a "friend." The Giorgio who wrote the words did not attempt to grasp their meaning; the Giorgio who, five years later, has recovered and continued with his life does not appear to care about their significance. The final words of the novel are those of the doctor who hopes that Giorgio will not reproach him for his contribution to the "misfortunes" and who, almost in return, assures Giorgio that "blind fate" alone was responsible. No one is to blame.

Tarchetti's version of the Fosca story conspicuously lacks a clear focus, yet we can see in it several features central to Sondheim's *Passion*: the romantic triangle, the transmission of disease, and the suggestion that the important characters are not purely and simply the same as they initially appear. Although Sondheim first encountered the Fosca narrative in Scola's film, he subsequently became familiar with the novel as well, even arranging for a translation while composing *Passion*. And it is from *Fosca* rather than *Passione d'Amore* that he and James Lapine draw the most, not only for the details of Fosca's prehistory, but for the timing of the end of Giorgio's relationship with Clara.

II

Scola's *Passione d'Amore*, like Tarchetti's *Fosca*, is a framed narrative, although the nature of the frame is not clear until the very last scene. Scola expands the implicit political context, compresses the philosophical discussions in which Fosca and Giorgio engage, reduces Clara primarily to an image, and heightens Fosca's frightening intensity through grotesque closeups of a face painful to contemplate.

The most salient cinematic technique is juxtaposition, both through voice-overs which contrast with the scene in view, and through sudden cuts between simultaneous or sequential scenes. As we hear the words of Giorgio's first letter to Clara, for example, we see him crying on the train and arriving at the outpost, and we see her retreating from her husband and dinner guests, to sit alone in her room. As the camera shows us military exercises, we hear Giorgio telling Clara: "During the absurd exertions of military discipline, an art that deadens the mind through physical strain, and saps the soul by means of violence, I take refuge in my memories of you, your name, your letters." During the same exercises, we hear her report of having a portrait made of herself, which she sends to him, and we see him reading the letter and kissing the portrait.

The camera does not show the spectator the portrait, however, until, during Giorgio's first five-day leave, he writes to Fosca, as promised. We see him kissing and embracing Clara in Milan, with the voice-over rendering his letter to Fosca, who is at the outpost. Then, just after he says to Clara, in the frame in real time, "How beautiful you are," we see Fosca at the piano, hitting discordant notes, running from the room. Back to Giorgio's voice-over: "Suppose the woman I loved was you, Fosca? How would you feel if I betrayed you?" We see him in bed with Clara. The camera cuts to the outpost. Fosca enters his room, runs her hands over his uniform (as Giorgio is running his hands over Clara's body), rummages through his desk, finds Clara's picture, stares at it, and weeps. Only then does the camera show us the picture: Fosca, Giorgio, and the spectator are simultaneously contemplating Clara's beauty. Scola cuts to the train whistle, and to Clara, in real time, walking beside the train.

The screenplay supplies additional density of information: the facts about Giorgio's rescue of a fellow soldier in the Crimea, the substance of the officers' conversations regarding horses and women, the apt passage marked by Fosca in Rousseau's *La Nouvelle Héloïse*: "Heavenly powers, since I have a soul for pain, give me one for joy. Tortured love provides a disturbing pleasure that replaces happiness."

Scola also performs narrative subtractions, modifying, for example, the facts of Fosca's marriage. Whereas the marriage of Tarchetti's Fosca endures for eleven months (111) and leads to the birth of a child (although Fosca was not able to be a mother, for reasons that are not explicit), Scola's Fosca is deserted by her husband on her wedding day, once he has collected her dowry. In the novel (and in Sondheim's version), Fosca's husband declares that he has fulfilled the terms of a bargain into which she knowingly entered (111). Fosca's past in Scola's film is more clearly that of a naive victim.

She is, however, also presented in Scola as powerful, overwhelming, even brave in her pursuit of passion. When Giorgio, on doctor's orders, departs for Milan on another leave, he looks out of the window, as if he fears Fosca will follow him. It is raining. No Fosca. We hear the train whistle. When Fosca's reflection suddenly appears in the window, we see and share Giorgio's shock. We then hear her furious declaration, nearly verbatim from the novel: "When I've smothered you under the weight of my feelings, when I've followed you, step by step, wherever you go, like your shadow, when I've died for you, you'll be compelled to love me!"

It is at this point that Giorgio confronts the contrast between Fosca's uncompromising, enraged, enraptured passion and the simple (even simpleminded) feeling that constitutes Clara's love. For no special reason—no financial disaster, no concern for her son—Clara gives Giorgio up. "I need you to be happy," she says to him. "She, to survive. I'm beautiful. You've told me a thousand times. That should be enough. Christmas is in a week. That's the gift I'll give my husband." So much for Clara. No letter delivered at a strategic moment, no anguished decision on Giorgio's part, no need for

Giorgio to render judgment on Clara. She vanishes in the smoke at the train station.

Immediately after Clara ends the relationship in Scola's film, we find ourselves at the regiment's Christmas party, where Fosca publicly reveals her love for Giorgio, breaking down when she learns he has been transferred. Although the doctor attempts to explain the truth (or as much of it as he knows), Giorgio resists his interventions, and explicitly claims responsibility. The doctor begs him: "Speak up! Go ahead, say it. How you were forced . . ." and Giorgio responds: "Not at all. Nothing was forced on me." As in the novel, there now follow in quick succession the colonel's challenge to a duel, Giorgio's realization that he loves Fosca and his formulation of a plan to spend the night with her, the night itself, the duel, Giorgio's subsequent illness, Fosca's death, and the passage of some years.

But *Passione d'Amore* concludes with a peculiar scene that finally explains to whom the voice-over reminiscences have been spoken, and that conveys an ugly counterpoint to the meditative melancholy of Fosca's romantic fulfillment and Giorgio's romantic discovery. "For five years," says Giorgio, "it has gnawed at my soul and body." We see him smoking in a sordid tavern. "I relish the havoc that time, little by little, is playing with my memory." We see that he is drunk. His drinking companion, the audience for his story, pushes him another drink; the camera pulls back to show that his companion is a lame hunchback dwarf, who laughs at him:

A jolly story! What did you hope to do? Change the eternal laws of nature? What an absurd tale! It would make sense if Fosca had been a great beauty, and Giorgio . . . like me. Everyone would have understood that "passionate affair" [*passione d'amore*]. But this way . . . Giorgio and Fosca. What an absurd tale!

Still laughing, and assisted by a cane, he walks slowly and awkwardly out through the archway. In the film's final image, we see the dwarf's bent shadow on the stone pavement suggesting the doubt cast on Giorgio's emotional perspective and ultimate judgment.

III

Sondheim's musical removes the narrative frame and presents Giorgio's romantic choices (and the women themselves) more directly. There is no cautionary narrative apparatus at the beginning, as in the novel; no cynical dwarf at the end, as in the film. Although much of the dialogue is taken from the novel, the film, or both, it appears here stripped down, elliptical. Absent Giorgio's effusions, the words of conversations, whether spoken or sung, slash through the silence. Words and melodies echo each other as we hear them sung, spoken, thought by different characters, and with different meaning. *Passion* takes us from Clara's opening words, in bed ("I'm so happy, / I'm afraid I'll die / Here in your arms" [1]) to Fosca's closing words (not counting the letter Giorgio receives after her death), as she leads Giorgio to her bed, knowing that the act of love will kill her: "To die loved," Fosca says, "is to have lived" (123).

Sondheim has said that at one point he planned to end the play with the same song with which it began—with Fosca and Giorgio in bed singing Clara and Giorgio's song. Ultimately, however, he decided that "bookending the story was too on the nose," and "James [Lapine] wanted me to explore the change in Fosca, not just in Giorgio."[3] What survives from the original plan of the repeated song is a musical motif that pervades the play, "in a thousand different guises, in inversion and in retrograde in both major and minor keys" (7), as well as words and melodies quoted and modified. To hear the same thing in a different setting stresses the changed circumstance.

Passion concludes with Giorgio's reading of Fosca's farewell letter: "Now at last" (128) (an account of Fosca's feelings after the night of love-making, unique to the musical) and a partial reprise of the dictated letter, ending with "Your love will live in me" (131). When Fosca dictated the letter, in approximately the middle of the play, the sentence that meant the most to Giorgio, the line he repeated, appeared to be "That doesn't mean I love you" (60), the denial of love. Now what Fosca sings (and what he hears) is the affirmation of eternal love in spite of death.

> And should you die tomorrow,
> Another thing I see:
> Your love will live in me. (130)

For Fosca to sing these words in her own voice, and for her own sake, in the earlier dramatic context, makes no sense. Why would she imagine that Giorgio is in danger of dying? The only "you" who might die "tomorrow" is Fosca herself. When Giorgio later sings in his own voice, and for his own sake, the words she earlier scripted for him, he embraces not only Fosca herself, but her view of what is essentially important in love. This embrace is the climax and conclusion of a long journey.

Giorgio's romantic odyssey in the Sondheim musical, has a beginning, middle, and end, and at each point, questions about sameness and difference, typicality and singularity, are asked and answered. The play starts with Clara and Giorgio: is their romance the same as an ordinary love story? The middle of the play shows Fosca pursuing Giorgio and replacing Clara: is she the same as either of these characters, or different? The play concludes with Giorgio's resolve to end his romance with Clara and to declare his love for Fosca, and with the consequences of this decision: how can we explain Giorgio's choice, and how does it change Giorgio and Fosca?

Is the initial Clara-Giorgio romance the same as an ordinary love story? We notice that their duet is led by Clara, who sings first. They overlap, sing in unison, and, on several occasions, disagree. Clara attributes their union to a "miracle" (2); Giorgio prefers "inevitable" (2) (and Clara acquiesces, but without conviction: "Then inevitable, yes" [2]). "So much happiness," she sings, "Happening by chance" (4); again, he disagrees: "Not by chance, / By necessity" (4) and adds that this necessity is "the sadness that we saw in each other" (4), which recalls his earlier line, "We were both unhappy" (2). This time Clara does not disagree, but we notice that Giorgio is attempting to assert a similarity where there is not in fact a perfect match. Clara was attracted by Giorgio's sadness, but was he attracted by the sadness in her? "You pitied me" (2), he sings—but did he pity her? When they sing "How quickly pity leads to love" (2), are they describing mutuality or asymmetry? Or are they in too much of a hurry to get to the soaring melody to bother with technicalities?

Are they in fact the same at all? They sing separately of what they had differently imagined love to be—"yearning," "kindness," and "shame"—and, although they believe they have reached a shared understanding about the identity of love, their definition of love is the relatively inarticulate "It's what I feel with you, / The happiness I feel with you" (4). They are united, too, in asserting that their love is unique. They sing together, in defiance of the imagined perspective "they" would assert:

> Just another love story,
> That's what they would claim.
> Another simple love story—
> Aren't all of them the same?
> CLARA:
> No, but this is more,
> We feel more!
> BOTH:
> This is so much more—! (4-5)

And then they undercut themselves, smiling: "Like every other love story" (5). They go on to contrast the permanence of their love with transience.

> Some say happiness
> Comes and goes.
> Then this happiness
> Is a kind of happiness
> No one really knows. (5)

Their own words betray them. No one—not no one *else*, they say—really knows this happiness. Within a few seconds, we see evidence of trouble in the relationship. Giorgio has known the whole time that he has been transferred, and has said nothing. Only when Clara guesses that something is wrong does he tell her. When Clara learns that Giorgio has been transferred, she sings of the happiness (moments before, "*Endless* happiness" [6]) as "*Ended* by a word in the dark" (8; emphasis added). When Giorgio sings "I will always be here" (9), Clara sings, to their familiar melody, "So much happiness / Wasn't meant to last" (8). A scene that begins with drums, the act of love, and Clara's evoking her own death—"I'm so happy, / I'm afraid I'll die / Here in your arms" (1)—ends in the same way, as Clara sings "I don't know how I'll live" (9) and, in the stage directions: "As they begin to make love again, military drums join the orchestra" (9).

Giorgio tells her that they will "always have each other" because, in their letters, they will make love with their words. Yet his words, immediately following, are not distinctively eloquent: "God, / You are so beautiful. / I love to see you in the light, / Clear and beautiful" (7). He gives her the same compliment ("beautiful") twice, and, in a sense, "light" and "clear" and "you" are also synonymous because the name "Clara" means "light" and "clear."

The opening scene, in other words, shows us the lovers' rapture, and also foreshadows its limitations. They are not as much like each other, or as unlike other lovers, as they wish to think. The hints of difference prepare us to reserve judgment on the lovers' claims of a "superior kind of love" (32) (during a letter they sing together, as Giorgio later tours a castle with Fosca):

> CLARA [*singing the letter*] and GIORGIO [*singing to* FOSCA]:
>   Love that fuses two into one,
>   Where we think the same thoughts,
> GIORGIO:
>   Want the same things,
> BOTH:
>   Live as one,
> GIORGIO:
>   Feel as one,
> BOTH:
>   Breathe as one. (32-3)

They will learn. At their eventual parting months later, the language, melody, and confusions will recall the warnings implicit in this scene that the two of them struggle to evade and escape (114-18). Giorgio ultimately concludes that theirs is "A temporary love story" (115), hence in fact "Just another love story" (115).

Giorgio and Clara begin the play romantically united, yet on the verge of geographical separation. By contrast, Giorgio and Fosca begin their relationship in geographical proximity, yet apparently divided romantically, not only by Giorgio's affair with Clara, but also by Fosca's refusal to expect, hope, and love.

When Fosca first meets Giorgio, she tells him her appearance precludes all romantic expectations.

> How can I have expectations?
> Look at me. (23)

She insists that he face, as she has, her unlovely face.

> No, Captain, look at me—
> Look at me!
> I do not hope for what I cannot have!
> I do not cling to things I cannot keep!
> The more you cling to things,
> The more you love them,
> The more the pain you suffer
> When they're taken from you . . . (23)

The last four lines could almost be warnings to Giorgio and Clara, who have been singing in their letters about their longing, their tears, and their pain at their distance from each other. The previous two lines are sung in an "exalted" manner, as if Fosca is expressing her deepest conviction. The lines are, perhaps, true for now: she does not hope, does not cling. Subsequently, however, the lines appear to be false. As Fosca pursues a relationship with the reluctant Giorgio, hoping for what she cannot have and clinging to what she cannot keep, she abandons discretion, violates propriety, and ignores his blatant rejection of her passion. But in the end, when the unlikely has taken place and the impossible is fact, when Giorgio recognizes that her love will forever "live" in him (131), it seems that Fosca was indeed able to have what she hoped for and to keep what she clung to.

Giorgio's relationship with Fosca, however, is more distinct from his relationship with Clara than it is similar—because Fosca, not Clara, is the one who in significant ways is like Giorgio. The play's long and painful midsection belongs to Fosca.[4] Over and against the union of Giorgio and Clara, Fosca asserts a different oneness: she claims to be like Giorgio (in their difference from the soldiers and their *uni*forms) and therefore wants to replace Clara.

How is Fosca like Giorgio? To begin with, she is introduced as resembling him in her love of reading—as described in the play's first use of the word "passion." (The word appears only once more [54]). "My cousin," the Colonel tells Giorgio, "loves to read—it's her only passion, really" (13). "I also love to read," responds Giorgio—but does he share the passion? It is somewhat ominous that Fosca's passion for reading is insatiable ("I can't find enough books for her," says the Colonel) yet also unselective ("She's been given to reading military handbooks. I've no doubt she will welcome anything in print").

Yet even in the area where Fosca is the same as Giorgio, she is defiantly different. He suggests that books require and reward meditation; she disagrees. When they meet, they quickly move from a discussion of Rousseau's *La Nouvelle Héloïse* to Fosca's explanation of why she reads: not to think, not to learn, not to search for truth, but to live *and* to get away from life (21-2). Note the paradox. The music stresses "I read to live," which we hear in two sentences, by pausing after "I read to live" *before* completing the thought: "In other people's lives."[5] They love reading, but they love it differently. Not a strong similarity.

Fosca is also like Giorgio in evoking pity. In the novel, Giorgio dwells upon the parallel. He was sickly, enervated, unhappy, and the robust Clara took pity on him and cured him. Should not he, in a sense, return the favor by curing another sick, pitiable, person? (In the novel, moreover, Clara herself becomes ill through curing Giorgio.) The play raises the connection of pity only to downplay it. The comparison highlights the contrast. Yes, he pities Fosca—as Clara understands ("You showed pity" [37]). In this context, however, the lines from Clara and Giorgio's opening scene—"Unhappiness can be seductive" and "How quickly pity leads to love" (2)—do not apply. Instead, Fosca's "wretchedness," "suffering," and "desperation" move him to "embarrassment" (27); with "all that self-pity" (27), in his view, she does not need his pity. As Fosca points out when she says that working in poorhouses did not alleviate her melancholy ("I felt no different"), pity "is nothing but passive love. . . . Dead love" (30). She does not seek or achieve a bond on the basis of pity. Another weak connection.

Fosca's view of her *strongest* link with Giorgio appears in her song at the ruined castle.

> They hear drums,
> You hear music,
> As do I.
> Don't you see?
> We're the same,
> We are different,
> You and I are different.
> They hear only drums. (35)

They are the same, she claims, in being different from the soldiers, who are "all alike," as every dinner-table conversation is alike, with the talk of horses and women, food and routine, maneuvers and gossip.

The melody here, however, with its stressed rhythms, is military in contrast to the flowing "Chopinesque" music associated with Fosca (13). Her song is powerful, intense, and not entirely accurate. For Giorgio is a soldier, too, albeit a "soldier who cries" (13), and he hears drums as well as music (perhaps implied in Fosca's corrective "They hear only drums" in the same-but-different repetition of "They hear drums"). To hear music instead of "only drums," metaphorically, is to be refined:

> You with all your books,
> Your taste,
> Your sensitivity,
> I thought you'd understand. (35)

And, as well, benevolent:

> I saw that you were different then.
> I saw that you were kind and good.
> I thought you understood. (35)

But does she really think he is kind and sensitive, or does she merely wish to think so? Notice that she brings up his "taste" and "sensitivity" at the very moment she is accusing him of cruelty and naïveté (in speaking to her of love). Notice, too, that she apparently hoped he would "understand," yet she simultaneously expected her appearance to repel him:

> Thinking we'd meet,
> Thinking you'd look at me,
> Thinking you'd be repelled by what you saw. (35)

How kind, good, sensitive, tasteful, and understanding would such a person be? The paradox, to be sure, is not beyond resolution. Fosca sees Giorgio as essentially different from the other soldiers, essentially like herself, and she demands that he depart from accident or habit or whatever has caused him to betray his truest self, and to sing with her instead of with Clara. She gets her wish, musically, only when he reads her letter to him after her death.

Fosca's wish to replace Clara in Giorgio's affections, to be treated by him in the same manner as Clara is treated, is actually based on difference. Giorgio, singing-writing to Clara as he walks with Fosca at the castle, wonders: "How could anyone . . . So unbeautiful . . . Stir my memory of you?" and imagines his associations triggered by the warmed fragrance of silk (30-1). The link is weak, the contrast salient.

Throughout the play (and, for the most part, the novel, and the film), the apparent points of contact between the women only highlight the contrasts. Both have been married. Fosca's husband abandoned her with debts, Clara refuses to leave her husband (and, in the novel, her rejection of Giorgio is connected with her husband's financial ruin). Clara sends Giorgio a single grey hair; Tarchetti's Fosca bequeaths to Giorgio all her hair.[6] Both are associated with flowers. They fill Clara's little room. Fosca brings them to Giorgio and to the dining table. Ludovic courts Fosca with them. Fosca poignantly says that "a woman is a flower" to exclude herself (in a way that the beautiful Clara is not excluded). Fosca asks Giorgio to dream together with her, and Clara writes a letter upon arising from a dream of him. Clara writes "How I wish I could just lie by your side and watch you sleep" (58); Fosca awakens and stares at the sleeping Giorgio (58-9). Yet Giorgio is in Fosca's bedroom only because the doctor has asked him to save Fosca's life by feigning love as convincingly as he can. We have to assume, moreover, that this is the only reason he complies with Fosca's request to kiss her goodbye "like you kiss her" (62). To *pretend* to be Clara is not to *be* Clara. In fact, it makes being Clara impossible. Pretense precludes identity.

Ultimately Fosca's claim on Giorgio is based not on being like Clara, but on being different from her. After the train station song ("Loving you"), she asks: ""Would Clara give her life for yours? Would she, Giorgio?" (101). In the stage directions we read "A beat; he doesn't answer, realizing the truth of his situation" (101). And that truth is not the truth of which he spoke *before the song* when he said: "Fosca, you have to face the truth. Please. You have to give me up." (100). Her song and her question make him face a very different truth.

Fosca's song at the train station is the sparest, barest number in the play, and one of the few sung by only one character. In its simplicity, it expresses Fosca's single-minded, undivided passion, and its integrity is unique to her. No one else could sing "Loving you / Is . . . who I am" (100). "This is why I live . . . why I do / The things I do" (100-01). (Clara's trite version—"I don't know how I'll live when you're gone!"—is hardly the same.) Yet Fosca's integrity embodies a disturbing combination of activity and passivity. Loving Giorgio gives her a goal and a purpose, yet she says, twice, that it "is not a choice."

For Giorgio it must be a matter of choice, and the play's denouement depends on his embracing choice—a sharp contrast with Tarchetti's attribution of causality to "blind fate." When Giorgio asks Clara to run away with him, taking her child, she says: "We have no choice." "We have a choice," he counters. "Yes, I suppose that's true, Giorgio," she answers. "Just as you have chosen to forgo your sick leave." (109)

When, in the following scene, she asks him to wait for her until her son goes off to school, he angrily rejects the suggested "logical and sensible / Practical arrangement." Any "foregone conclusion," one which is "convenient," "scheduled in advance," "guaranteed," cannot in his view be love (116). In an angry echo of the complacent attitude he assumed initially ("We feel more" [4-5]), he now sings "Love is more, I want more" (117). When

Clara tells him "You decide" (117), he does. The difference between them is insuperable, and all the more obvious because the music and words in this sequence echo the opening scene. We note, too, that although he is singing alternately with Clara, in response to her letter, they are not together. Does he even answer the letter, which he he crumples?

In his decision, Giorgio rejects the notion of love as a "negotiation." Love as negotiation appeared, in its ugliest form, in the farewell of Count Ludovic, Fosca's fraudulent husband:

> We made a bargain, did we not?
> And we got
> What we bargained for.
> . . . .
> You gave me your money, I gave you my looks
> And my charm.
> And my arm.
> I would say that more than balances the books.
> Where's the harm?
> Now it's through. (83)

In refusing to bargain, Giorgio is declaring his difference from Ludovic. He will not, moreover, repeat Ludovic's poisoned statement ("But you as well must face the truth" [83]), a statement that has inspired Fosca's retreat from truth. "I know the truth," she sings. "The truth is hardly what I need." (22)

And what is the truth? After placing his love with Clara in the emphatic past ("I did love Clara"), he sings "No one has truly loved me / As you have, Fosca." (122)

This is the first time he sings her name. True, deep love is "unconcerned / With being returned" (122). He is denying what he told her earlier on the mountainside: "Love is what you earn, / And return . . . " (91). True love is now described primarily in terms of negatives—"without reason," "without mercy," "without pride or shame," "No wisdom, no judgment, / No caution, no blame," "not pretty or safe or easy" (122). Giorgio considers Fosca's love to be based on a genuine knowledge of him: "No one has ever known me / As clearly as you" (122). "Clearly" becomes Fosca's word now, no longer Clara's. He loves Fosca in part because her love has led him to conclude that Clara's love is inadequate.

Giorgio is not choosing a future with Fosca. She is going to die. He is going to fight a duel. He has, however, learned the meaning of the letter Fosca dictated: he has learned not only to see her "in a different light," but also to see love "Like none I've ever known."

> A love as pure as breath,
> As permanent as death,

> Implacable as stone.
> A love that, like a knife,
> Has cut into a life
> I wanted left alone. (61)

Although he does not *sing* the letter at this point, the letter remains an important part of the present context. The colonel has challenged Giorgio to a duel because of this letter, and Giorgio refuses to save himself by denying it: "Nothing was forced on me" (120). In claiming responsibility, he also honors Fosca, and asserts another connection with her. Contrary to the colonel's belief that no man could desire Fosca, Giorgio *does* desire her. Contrary to the colonel's belief that Fosca is nothing but a passive victim, Giorgio accords her full autonomy. "You don't know your cousin. She is not a child! She is not just a sick person. Signora Fosca is as responsible for her actions as am I for mine" (119). To the extent that he accepts this letter as the expression of his own emotion, he admits that, in his relationship with Clara, he was still alone. "Love within reason—that isn't love. / And I've learned that from you . . ." (122).

He has apparently learned how to understand Fosca, as she had hoped he would. On their first night together, her letter (dictated by her to him, but worded as if addressed by him to her) had sent him running from the room. When he hears it again, in the closing scene, he sings the words himself. "Your love will live in me" (131), words which formerly appeared as a threat, now return as a promise.

The same is true for his complaint when she follows him to the mountainside:

> Everywhere I turn,
> There you are.
> This is not love,
> But some kind of obsession.
>
> . . . .
> Yet everywhere I go,
> You appear,
> Or I know
> You are near.
> This is not love,
> Just a need for possession.
> Call it what you will,
> This is not love,
> This is the reverse,
> Like a curse,
> Something out of control.
> I've begun to fear for my soul . . . (91-2)

He comes to see Fosca's constant presence not as a burden but as his permanent and enduring desire. As he reads her final letter, they sing together: "Everywhere I turn / You are there" (129).

Death ends Fosca's life, but it does not end Giorgio's relationship with her. Clara lives on, but not for Giorgio. She foresaw the end of their relationship before he told her.

> At times, these past few days together,
> I would wonder whether
> You were here,
> Really here with me.
> I thought, was I naive
> To believe
> We'd continue year by year?
> Is it over forever?
> It seems to me the answer rests with you. (114)

His answer of course is "No"—and that he learned from Fosca. What has Fosca learned from him? She has learned, she sings, to "see things clearly" (Clara's word again), to love the world, to let go of the "vain / And bitter self-concern" of "tears" and "pride," to receive love, to see herself as "someone to be loved" (128-130). "Everywhere I look, / Things are different" (130).

What does it mean for things to be "different"? Fosca and Giorgio continue together "Everything seems right, / Everything seems possible" (130). Their sentiments echo Giorgio's early letter to Clara:

> Love that thinks
> Everything is pure,
> Everything is beautiful,
> Everything is possible. (32)

But everything was *not* possible for Giorgio and Clara. "Let's have a life together," he suggested. "Giorgio, you know that's not possible," she replies ("slowly") and he remarks "Everything is possible." (108)

Where Clara surrenders to inevitabilities, Giorgio believes in possibilities. So does Fosca. She began without this belief: "How can I have expectations?" (23). But now she has profoundly altered her view:

> But though I want to live,
> I now can leave
> With what I never knew:
> I'm someone to be loved.
> And that I learned from you. (130)

She believes herself loved, whereas she used to think her appearance made that response impossible. But is not loving Fosca hazardous to Giorgio's health? As Fosca's cousin falls wounded in the duel, Giorgio "releases a high-pitched howl—a cry that is clearly reminiscent of Fosca's" (125). Will her pain and disease live in him as well as her love? He once dreamed "She was dragging me down into the grave with her. She was hugging me. Kissing me with her cold lips. Those thin arms pulling me, drawing me, like icy tentacles" (97). Has his dream come horribly true? As he prepares to enter Fosca's bedroom, he refers to his "disease" (120), and he ends the play in a hospital. What is ahead for him? Giorgio is ill and alone, spiritually and physically, and the warm, beautiful Clara is gone. Is this in any sense a happy ending?

The happiness of the play's ending appears questionable not only from the standpoint of its outcome, but from the perspective of method (how Giorgio reached it). In choosing "love without reason" over "love within reason," Giorgio has removed himself from rational deliberation. And if Giorgio continues to view "love within reason" as no love at all, will he consistently denigrate the standard of reason in defining and seeking his values?

Whatever it means for Fosca's love to live in Giorgio, he now grasps that, with Clara, everything was not possible, and he wants everything. He wants more, even if that more is dangerous, deadly, destructive, diseased. "When choosing between two evils," Mae West said, "I always pick the one I haven't tried before."

Never do anything twice. Fosca's love, Sondheim tells us, is "something that destroys you in order to rebuild you. Giorgio gets destroyed by Fosca, and in so doing breaks through into something huge."[7] Now, truly, everything looks different, everything seems possible. He sees love, Fosca, himself, and perhaps life itself, in a different light. "A blank page or canvas. His favorite. So many possibilities. . . ."[8]

NOTES

[1] An earlier version of this article was delivered at a session on Stephen Sondheim in conjunction with the annual meeting of the Ars Lyrica Society in Chicago at the Modern Language Association Convention on December 30, 1995. For the quotation from *Passion*, see Lapine and Sondheim 1994, 35.

[2] The film was released in Italian 1981. My source is the 1982 subtitled videotape, also known as *Passion of Love*. Tarchetti's novel is entitled *Fosca*. The English translation by Lawrence Venuti is entitled *Passion: A Novel*. Venuti, who also contributed a useful introduction, began work on the translation independently of Sondheim's and Lapine's work on the play. All quotations are drawn from this edition, which is also my source for information about Tarchetti's life.

[3] See *Dramatist Guild Quarterly* 1994, 7.

[4] See *Passion* 1994. Musical references are drawn from this recording.

⁵ The play version connects Fosca with the audience, giving us her point of view, in one prominent departure from the earlier version. In the novel and the film, the reader–spectator knows early that Clara is married and a mother; in the play, however, we do not learn this fact until Fosca does, after Giorgio returns from a visit to Milan.

⁶ Sondheim intended to include this detail, and dropped it only because of audience incomprehension. See Besner 1994, 5, and Sondheim's letter in Sondheim 1994, 2.

⁷ *Dramatist Guild Quarterly* 1994, 9.

⁸ Lapine and Sondheim 1991, 174.

CHAPTER 6

"It Takes Two"
A Duet on Duets in *Follies* and *Sweeney Todd*
Paul M. Puccio and Scott F. Stoddart

Puccio:

The *duet*, most elementally defined, is a composition for two performers, vocal or instrumental.[1] In the plays of Stephen Sondheim, as in other musical theatre, the duet is typically a song during which two characters sing simultaneously or in dialogue.

Stoddart:

"Now, there are two possibilities." A, the two voices may share the dramatic moment, recognizing one another's presence within the narrative, and singing to, or with, each other.

Puccio:

For example, Fredrik and Desirée's conversational duet, "You Must Meet My Wife," in *A Little Night Music*—a musical discussion about the woeful inadequacies of Anne, which occurs within the play's world.[2]

Stoddart:

Or B, the two voices may share only the theatrical moment; that is, they enter the musical score without narrative awareness of one another's presence.

Puccio:

For example, "One More Kiss," Heidi's duet with her younger self in *Follies*, in which, the stage directions tell us, "an old voice and a young one twined about each other"; this dreamlike song comments on the events of the narrative, and may or may not be a part of the diegetic songs of the Follies reunion itself, though it is surely a part of *our* experience of the play.[3]

Stoddart:

As these two dramatic and/or theatrical illustrations demonstrate, the duet allows for the fusion, the interlocution, or the collision of two voices, two characters, or two levels of consciousness within the same character. Such musical *doubling* reflects Sondheim's fascination with duplicity in narrative: unconscious or conflicting motivations within a single character, oppositional or ironic layers of plot.

Puccio:

So, the formal and conceptual dialogics of the duet are not only suited to Sondheim's characteristic subtexts and ironies, they embody those qualities. We can uncover these (musical and narrative) dialogics throughout his scores, for in so many songs, there are two expressive levels of consciousness or feeling: the lyric, a relatively explicit articulation of a character's thoughts and emotions; and the music, which employs a rhetoric of its own to communicate perceptions, desires, responses that are often unavailable to the character's consciousness.

Stoddart:

This kind of duality is especially conspicuous in solos where the music virtually undermines the lyrics: for example, "Me and My Town" from *Anyone Can Whistle*, in which Cora proclaims her concern for "the populace," while the bluesy rhythms suggest that this song is actually all about Cora's ego; or "Everybody Loves Louie" from *Sunday in the Park with George*, where the agitated musical line reveals that Dot, in her extravagant praise of Louie, protests too much.[4] In other words, these solos are all "duets," insofar as they have two distinct voices—one a lyric-voice, one a music-voice.

Puccio:

You might say . . .

Stoddart:

. . . we do . . .

Puccio:

. . . that the binary form of the duet provides Sondheim with an objective correlative to what he does in so much of his writing: namely, to construct a musical space where two narrative or expressive voices meet. In poststructuralist terms then, the "duet" is a single text within which multiple, sometimes competing, discourses are constructed. These discourses are articulated by and in the binarism of music and lyrics, the dialogue between distinct characters, and the counterpoint between distinct song lines.

Stoddart:

Before we focus on *Sweeney Todd* and *Follies*, we'd like to examine "Barcelona" from *Company*, which shows in sharp relief how Sondheim's work, both formally and thematically, can depict the "duplicity" of human emotion, motivation, and situation.[5] In this duet, Bobby and April volley niceties after their night together, but the music, with its unresolved chords, suggests that this conversation is going noplace, that their situation is itself unresolvable, as they desire conflicting outcomes from this date, and that this conversation could, indeed, proceed in the same fashion for hours with no happier or more decisive conclusion.

Puccio:

Their duet functions on two levels: there are the two voices (Bobby's and April's) that are themselves not only disparate but potentially disputatious, and there is the "duet" between the lyrics and the music—one articulating the attempts to turn a one-night stand into a relationship, the other expressing the futility of this attempt.

Stoddart:

In *Sweeney Todd*, where so much of the drama is musically scored, and where the musical motifs provide clues to the unraveling of some of the narrative mysteries, we see this binary approach most clearly in two duets: "Pretty Women" and "A Little Priest."[6] In "Pretty Women," the lyric itself operates at two levels: rhapsodically praising the beauty of women in general, and evoking erotic thoughts about Lucy and Johanna in particular. It functions as a sort of homosocial lovesong—in which two men draw treacherously close to one another through their mutual sexual regard for women who figure as the apex of their erotic triangle. Yet, while it appears to be a lyric pause in the progress of the thriller narrative, agonizingly postponing Sweeney's actions, the music for this duet actually performs as part of that narrative: that is, if the lyrics merely interrupt Todd's progress toward revenge, the music proceeds inexorably toward that revenge. Most obviously, its nerve-wracking suspensefulness, which builds with an almost orgasmic drive, provides sinister accompaniment to the duet's lyrics. Its resistance to conventional resolution intensifies that suspense; listeners know that the musical progressions can only cease with a violent interruption of some sort—presumably Todd slicing the Judge's throat, this silencing his voice permanently. Moreover, as Stephen Banfield points out, the minuet from the rape scene is suggested in the "hum" that accompanies Todd's query, "As pretty as her mother?"—a musical overlap that symphonically links this song to the revenge plot.[7] Both music and lyric create an almost masturbatory episode, each man fantasizing about his particular desire: for the Judge, marriage; for Sweeney, murder. At first, as if to prolong the pleasure, Todd himself repeatedly disrupts the momentum of the song, as it starts to build to a climax . . .

Puccio:

. . . a form of *duet interruptus* . . .

Stoddart:

... but this interruption ultimately gives way to the central lyric, which reduces gender to a series of gerunds:

> TODD:
> > Pretty women ...
> > Fascinating ...
> > Sipping coffee,
> > Dancing ...
> > . . . .
> > Sitting in the window or
> > Standing on the stair,
> > Something in them
> > Cheers the air.
> > Pretty women ...
> JUDGE:
> > Silhouetted ...
> TODD:
> > Stay within you . .
> JUDGE:
> > Glancing ...
> TODD:
> > Stay forever . .
> JUDGE:
> > Breathing lightly . .
> TODD:
> > Pretty women ... (97-8)

Stoddart:

Woman here is nothing more than the object of the male gaze; indeed, the litany of images is especially licentious in light of the Judge's flagellation song, during which he peers through a keyhole at Johanna's body, silhouetted through her dress as she stands before a window. Todd, now seeking revenge at any price, in effect prostitutes his daughter's image for the sake of keeping the Judge in his control. As the two men sing, the tempo quickens, just as the pulse quickens both in moments of impending violence and sexual release. Of course, fulfillment, sexual or otherwise, is postponed once again as Anthony bursts in singing Johanna's patter song, announcing their clandestine plans to marry.

Puccio:

"A Little Priest" also has a subtextual sexuality, located, that is, in Mrs. Lovett's hankering after Todd. The waltz tempo of this duet reminds us that we are indeed watching a kind of romance unfold in front of us—even if the lovers do resemble Lady Macbeth and Othello more than Ginger Rogers and Fred Astaire. If this is a dance, it is a *danse macabre*. Of course, Sondheim idiosyncratically deploys the waltz in other unlikely places: in "Could I Leave You" (*Follies*), which depicts the emptiness of a marriage; in "A Bowler Hat" (*Pacific Overtures*), which depicts the disintegration of traditional Japanese culture; in "Last Midnight" (*Into the Woods*), which depicts the devastation of the world.[8] In "A Little Priest," the waltz serves at least two functions: as a *dance-à-deux*, the waltz re-presents the synergy and synchronicity that we see emerge over the course of the duet between Todd and Mrs. Lovett; as a "romantic" dance, it implies Mrs. Lovett's matrimonial scheme, which she hopes to effect through the business partnership she proposes to Todd. In the middle (and longest) section of the song, Todd and Mrs. Lovett engage in a contest of *double entendres*—a kind of "Any pun you can do I can do better." They appraise their potential customers, who come from all levels in the social hierarchy: public servants (lawyers, clergymen, politicians, military personnel), middle-class figures (bank cashiers, financiers, fops, poets, actors), and the laboring classes (potters, butlers, clerks, sweeps, locksmiths). But, while Todd is bent on revenge and entertains a metaphysical view of their enterprise, Mrs. Lovett is merely an opportunist:

> TODD:
> The history of the world, my love—
> MRS. LOVETT:
> Save a lot of graves,
> Do a lot of relatives favors . . .
> TODD:
> —is those below serving those up above.
> MRS. LOVETT:
> Everybody shaves,
> So there should be plenty of flavors . . .
> TODD:
> How gratifying for once to know—
> BOTH:
> —that those above will serve those down below! (108)

These two discourses, however, ultimately harmonize in a single ideology, mirroring not only the metaphorical cannibalism of the English class system, but also the literal cannibalism of the revenge plot. Madness and capitalism are shown to be compatible, even congenial, bedfellows. By the end of the duet, Todd and Mrs. Lovett are no longer competing for the cleverest puns, they are setting one another up, playing the straight man for each other's jokes, revealing a promising partnership. Here, the waltz serves its traditional purpose by bringing together the two protagonists; it is the musical motif that represents their coupling, and later, ironically underscores their uncoupling—its only reprise occurring when Todd dissolves the relationship by tossing Mrs. Lovett into the bake-house oven.

Stoddart:

Both of these duets have quintessential Sondheim qualities: they are dramatic songs in that they give their singers something to act. Todd may sing about "Pretty Women," but he is thinking about slitting the Judge's throat; Mrs. Lovett may sing about chopping up poets and lawyers, but she is thinking of marriage with Todd. With subtexts conveyed largely through music, these duets have both explicit and implicit layers that create the fictive structure of the play—what we might refer to as "what is really happening." The duet forces us to experience simultaneously two motivational trajectories which entwine around one another creating a third theatrical effect.

Puccio:

This entwining gets a bit complicated in *Follies*, where there are *two explicit* fictive layers: the present moment and the remembered (or misremembered) past, for example, in the duet "Too Many Mornings," in which Ben sings to his memory of what Sally (his old flame) was, and Sally sings to her fantasy of what Ben can never be. The play's stage directions describe what we cannot know by merely listening to the song. As Ben describes the emptiness of his marriage with Phyllis, the ghosts of Young Ben and Young Sally appear; Ben addresses Young Sally asking, "Did I love you, Sally? Was it real?" (62). Sally and Young Sally speak in unison of their . . .

Stoddart:

. . . her . . .

Puccio:

. . . love for Ben. The stage directions tell us:

> BEN *opens his arms.* YOUNG SALLY *slips into them. He sings the song and plays the scene to her.* SALLY, *too, although she stands alone, is in* BEN*'s arms. She moves precisely as* YOUNG SALLY *does, as if the two of them were one.* (62)

"Too Many Mornings" is a love song with lyrics in the conditional mood: it speaks of the things that Ben and Sally *would* do if only they could. The soaring Puccini-esque music, on the other hand, much more indicative in mood, expresses the romantic ideal that Ben and Sally are mentally constructing out of their memories and wishes. The collision of the conditional and the indicative, of their desires and their realities, constitutes Ben and Sally's tragedy.

Stoddart:

But Sondheim sometimes complicates this method, taking the duet one step further by multiplying it—not merely by adding to the number of voices (which would actually amount to nothing more than writing trios, quartets, quintets), but by placing two or more duets together within a single musical construct. These double- and quadruple-duets dramatize additional layers of conflicts, ironies, and parallels in their narratives. "Kiss Me / Ladies in Their Sensitivities" from *Sweeney Todd*, for instance, while it begins as a conventional patter song that highlights the charged romantic moment between Anthony and Johanna, quickly gets more complicated. With the contrapuntal appearance of the Judge and the Beadle, this double-duet soon forwards the plot by exposing the counterschemes of the two pairs: the lovers engineer Johanna's escape, while the two men plot her ensnarement. Moreover, the song demonstrates the insidious romanticizing of women in Victorian society: the sexually ambiguous (countertenor) Beadle praises the "sensitivities" of "ladies" while Johanna, however flustered, takes the initiative in her rendezvous with the young sailor.

Puccio:

While this double-duet in *Sweeney Todd* explodes Victorian gender stereotypes, the double-duet "You're Gonna Love Tomorrow" and "Love Will See Us Through" in the *Follies* "Loveland" sequence, dismantles the facade of romantic illusion generated and perpetuated by traditional musical theatre. This duet highlights the self-reflexivity of the show through a hyperromantic pastiche. While Stephen Banfield refers to the duet as woefully "insipid," we believe that just this quality plays into an effective, if cynical, subtext: the middle-aged foursome watch as their young counterparts blithely sing in a now "colorized" version of their past narrative.[9] What Banfield criticizes as "insipid" is intentionally so, as the lyric and music line combine to antagonize the aging vaudevillians with a vacuous cheerfulness that is certainly undercut by the grim reality of the present tense. First, Young Ben and Young Phyllis sing optimistically about their life together:

> YOUNG BEN:
> I'll have our future suit your whim,
> Blue chip preferred.

YOUNG PHYLLIS:
    Putting it in a synonym,
    Perfect's the word. (88)

Then Young Buddy and Young Sally cheerfully confront the possibility of marital malaise with an upbeat cynicism:

YOUNG BUDDY:
    I've some traits, I warn you,
    To which you'll have objections.
YOUNG SALLY:
    I, too, have a cornu-
    Copia of imperfections. (90)

The real duet here is not between Young Ben and Young Phyllis, or between Young Buddy and Young Sally, or even in the counterpoint between the two songs: the real duet occurs, instead, between the saccharine pastiche and the sour reality of their present lives.

Stoddart:

The two time frames intersect in "Waiting for the Girls Upstairs," a double-duet in which the four principals reminisce about the typical night "after the curtain came down" (24). It begins as a duet between Ben and Buddy who, like Todd and the Judge, sing of the women in their lives. A counterduet between Phyllis and Sally follows, recounting their memories of "waiting around for the boys downstairs." As these two duets enter into counterpoint, the stage directions indicate that *"the force of their collective memories"* summons the ghosts of their younger selves (27). The middle-aged Ben, Phyllis, Buddy, and Sally watch their young counterparts continue the double-duet, replaying the banal courtship that their older selves were just idealizing.

Puccio:

But they don't just watch. The play text indicates that the principals *"now one and now another sings a phrase, a word or two along with the memories"* (28). This postmodern ventriloquism succeeds in entangling the past with the present, thereby displaying to the present that the past was actually a good deal more vapid than their romanticized recollections suggest. As Ben sings toward the end of the number, their experiences were "Very young and very old hat" (31). The musical structure of this contrapuntal duet reproduces the theatrical and dramatic structure of the play itself. It not only splits the past and the present, it *unsplits* them—dramatizing that the binary system that insists on an irreversible separation between the past and the present does not and cannot account for the power of memory so compelling that it recreates the past. When the past becomes recollected in *this* duet-system, there is a brief overlap of both time frames, which illustrates how both the past and the present construct a single text—how any rigid oppositional rhetoric is artificial and inadequate. Even while the play forces us to separate the principals and their younger selves, it simultaneously warns us that any attempt to do so is mistaken.

Stoddart:

Or, in the words of another Sondheim song, "If only this once, you wouldn't think twice."[10] The genuinely deconstructive mission of all of these duets, however, is revealed in the maddeningly paradoxical fact that you cannot arrive at any such unitary perception without first witnessing the double, even oppositional, nature of these narratives and characters. The very ontologies of these songs dismantle if you attempt to ignore, disentangle, or erase their doubleness. While the duet may allow for the interlocution or collision of *two* voices, it simultaneously dramatizes a *single* musical moment. In other words, "it takes two," to understand the richness and complexity of . . .

Both:

. . . one.

NOTES

[1] An earlier version of this essay was presented as a dialogue between the authors, at a special session on Sondheim at the annual convention of the Modern Language Association, in Chicago, December 1995.

[2] Sondheim and Wheeler 1991.

[3] Goldman and Sondheim 1971, 72. Diegetic songs are ones that the characters recognize as songs as well as the audience. See Banfield 1993, 184-87.

[4] Laurents and Sondheim 1965; Lapine and Sondheim 1991.

[5] Furth and Sondheim 1970.

[6] Sondheim and Wheeler 1991a.

[7] Banfield 1993, 295-96.

[8] Sondheim and Weidman 1991a; Lapine and Sondheim 1992.

[9] Banfield 1993, 193.

[10] See *Gypsy* in Laurents et al. 1973.

PART 2

PLAYS

CHAPTER 7

Enchantment on the Manicured Lawns
The Shakespearean "Green World" in
A Little Night Music
Paul M. Puccio

A Little Night Music (1973) might be said to begin where Ingmar Bergman's *Smiles of a Summer Night* (1955) ends, for that film finishes *with a song*.[1] After a night of lovemaking with Petra, Frid is so moved by "the sight of her rounded thighs . . . that he begins to sing."[2] Frid's lusty singing echoes across these two texts, and while he has no song in the official version of the musical play, the impulse toward music, which Frid's song represents, survives in the very act of musicalizing this Bergman film.[3]

While *A Little Night Music* has this explicit and unarguable source, I believe that we can usefully identify and explore the echoes of another text in this Stephen Sondheim–Hugh Wheeler–Harold Prince collaboration, namely Shakespeare's *A Midsummer Night's Dream*. This essay does *not* presume to suggest that Sondheim, Wheeler, or Prince (or Bergman, for that matter) consciously or deliberately adapted Shakespeare's play, nor is it in any way concerned with hypothesizing about their *unconscious* motivations. Rather, my approach is *intertextual*, perhaps in a more purely Kristevan sense; that is, I am interested in how certain signs (in this case, elements of Shakespeare's play) come to be transposed and rearticulated in these later texts—reinscriptions that do not reflect authorial intention so much as the inevitable presence of these signs within the textual systems of the romantic comedy.

As we will see, the parallels among the three texts are compelling enough to invite a semiotic approach, which decenters questions of adaptational intention and inquires, instead, into the (re)deployment of narrative and linguistic codes that occur within the stretches of intertextual space. Or, put more simply, the striking similarities that we can trace across Shakespeare's romantic comedy, Bergman's film, and the Sondheim–Wheeler musical play demonstrate that the relationships between and among texts within literary (dramatic) history cannot be reduced to relatively simplistic questions of conscious attribution.[4] Writing and composing within aligned, if not exactly identical, textual traditions, Shakespeare, Bergman, Sondheim and Wheeler all utilize narrative and thematic conventions that manifest themselves with a startling coherence.

While all three texts share hallmarks of the romantic comedy (mismatched pairs of lovers, the contrast of city and country, generational conflicts, magic potions and a supernatural aura, and a happy resolution with marriage as the successful narrative goal), Shakespeare's play, for Anglo-American audiences certainly, is a prototype for the genre. Exploring the modes of filmic adaptation, Dudley Andrew proposes that very familiar texts—"the many adaptations of Shakespeare come readily to mind" (98)—can assume "a certain pre-established presence" in later "borrowings":

> To study this mode of adaptation, the analyst needs to probe the source of power in the original by examining the use made of it in adaptation. Here the main concern is the generality of the original, its potential for wide and varied appeal; in short, its existence as a continuing form or archetype in culture. This is especially true of that adapted material which, because of its frequent reappearance, claims the status of myth: *Tristan and Isolde* for certain, and *A Midsummer Night's Dream* possibly. The success of adaptations of this sort rests on the issue of their fertility not their fidelity.[5]

Andrew theorizes that in such "borrowings," one text is "assimilated" into another, and so the relationship between the two is not strictly linear but, to some degree, coalescent. In this way, we might say that *A Little Night Music* is not another "adaptation" of *A Midsummer Night's Dream*, but another "rendering" of the play.

This essay acknowledges the "fertility" of *Night Music*, by acknowledging the dynamic relationship that exists intertextually between it and Shakespeare's "mythic" romantic comedy, and by interrogating how both plays participate in sign systems that cross boundaries of genre, history, and authorship. I will map out these boundary crossings in three categories: character and narrative development; supernatural framework; and self-reflexive theatricality. While I am primarily interested in examining the coalescence of *A Midsummer Night's Dream* and *A Little Night Music*, I will also describe and analyze *Smiles of a Summer Night* for its own assimilation of Shakespeare, and for the source material it offered to Sondheim, Wheeler, and Prince for their theatrical project.

I

LYSANDER: *The course of true love never did run smooth.*

—*A MIDSUMMER NIGHT'S DREAM*, 1.1.134

> DESIRÉE: *Darling, how would you feel if we had a*
> *home of our very own with me only acting when*
> *I felt like it—and a man who would make you a*
> *spectacular father?*
> FREDRIKA: *Oh, I see. The lawyer! Mr. Egerman!*
> . . . .
> DESIRÉE: *However, there is one tiny snag.*
> FREDRIKA: *A snag?*
> DESIRÉE: *Lawyer Egerman is married.*
> FREDRIKA: *That could be considered a snag.*
>   —*A LITTLE NIGHT MUSIC*, 91; 100-01

Without actually retelling the story of Shakespeare's play, *A Little Night Music* shares many of the basic plot intrigues and developments, as well as character types and thematics, that we find in *A Midsummer Night's Dream*. Perhaps the most obvious comic conventions cluster around the lovers' narratives and their flights into the "green world," a comic paradigm famously delineated by Northrop Frye:

> Shakespeare's type of romantic comedy follows a tradition established by [George] Peele and developed by [Robert] Greene and [John] Lyly, which has affinities with the medieval tradition of the seasonal ritual-play. We may call it the drama of the green world, its plot being assimilated to the ritual theme of the triumph of life and love over the waste land. . . . the action of the comedy beings in a world represented as a normal world, moves into the green world, goes into a metamorphosis there in which the comic resolution is achieved, and returns to the normal world. The forest in this play is the embryonic form of the fairy world of *A Midsummer Night's Dream*, the Forest of Arden in *As You Like It*, Windsor Forest in *The Merry Wives of Windsor*, and the pastoral world of the mythical sea-coasted Bohemia in *The Winter's Tale*.[6]

Night Music establishes a similar pattern of dichotomies: the "normal world" of the city is associated with interior scenes and daytime, while the "green world" of the Armfeldt country estate is associated with exterior scenes and nighttime.[7] In this way, the quotidian world of commerce and domestic life is contrasted with a mysterious nocturnal reality that is, furthermore, in touch with nature. The city, moreover, is a site of various forms of disarray and turmoil: Fredrik and Anne and Henrik's misdirected family affections; Carl-Magnus and Charlotte's marital disquiet; and Desirée's pursuit of "the glamorous life," as well as her affair with Carl-Magnus, an indiscretion that demonstrates that Shakespeare's Titania is not the only woman in drama who has been "enamored of an ass."

In opposition to the city, and these manifestations of subjective and intersubjective chaos, the lawns and gardens of the Armfeldt estate prove to be a place where characters come to greater self-knowledge, where submerged emotions surface, and where lovers ultimately discover, or rediscover, one another. When first discussing the possibility of joining the weekend party, Charlotte quips "We'll go masked" (97); in fact, that is the condition in which all of the lovers appear when they first arrive in the country. The events of the weekend constitute a painful and elaborate unmasking for them all. As Fredrik himself acknowledges, "If I never had come / To the country, / Matters might have stayed / As they were" (147). Entering the "green world" of the country estate, however, assures that matters will *not* stay as they are; indeed, the closing line of act 1 ("A weekend in the country / Where . . . / We're twice as upset as in . . . town" [102-03]) refers to this very transformation—especially once we read "upset" to mean "overturned" or "unsettled," rather than merely "anxious" or "worried."

This transformation is precisely what we see in the narrative of the young lovers in *A Midsummer Night's Dream*: Hermia and Lysander flee the court of Athens because Egeus, Hermia's father, insists that she marry Demetrius instead of Lysander, whom she truly loves. The lovers head for the woods, initially setting out to secure asylum with Lysander's widowed aunt.[8] Instead, Demetrius follows them, and Helena (Hermia's childhood friend who loves Demetrius herself) follows as well. While in the woods, all four lovers get caught in a web of enchantment, spun by the resident fairies Oberon and Puck: the eyes of the two men are first anointed with a fairy "love juice," which causes them to redirect their affections from Hermia to Helena; after a series of chaotic exchanges between and among the lovers, Oberon administers an antidote to Demetrius. This antidote results in Demetrius returning Helena's affection and surrendering his claim to Hermia, leaving her free to marry Lysander.

While the lovers in *Night Music* are not all of them young, and their plot complications are quite different, there is yet one pattern of interlocking triangles that corresponds to the relational dynamics in *Midsummer*. The following diagram provides an affectional flow-chart for the characters' initial muddles, with arrows indicating amorous preferences:[9]

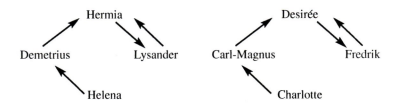

Just as Helena dotes on Demetrius who claims Hermia as his own, Charlotte dotes on Carl-Magnus, who claims Desirée as his own; just as Lysander and Hermia love one another, but are prevented from marrying by the law of her father, Fredrik and Desirée love another, but are prevented from marrying because he is already married (another manifestation of the law).

We can trace further parallels in the resolutions of these tangled situations. In an effort to gain his affection, Helena alerts Demetrius of Hermia and Lysander's flight into the country, thereby causing Demetrius to pursue the pair, with Helena in tow. With similar motivation, Charlotte informs Carl-Magnus of Desirée and Fredrik's imminent meeting at the Armfeldt country estate—a revelation that results in his following them, with Charlotte in tow.[10] Once both couples are in the country, there is *specious* lovemaking between Lysander and Helena, just as there is between Fredrik and Charlotte. In *Midsummer*, Puck accidentally applies the "love juice" to Lysander's eyes, and when he wakes to see Helena beside him, he declares, "Not Hermia, but Helena I love" (2.2.113). Charlotte, on the other hand, initiates the flirtation between herself and Fredrik in order to inspire Carl-Magnus's jealousy, which, she rightly assumes, will reanimate the passion in their marriage. While the relations between both pairs are inauthentic, the situations result in analogous contests between the two men in the equations: Lysander demands that Demetrius fight him (3.2.252-56), and Carl-Magnus challenges Fredrik to a game of Russian Roulette.[11]

In both cases, however, blood is spared, the couples are righted, and Charlotte/Helena and Carl-Magnus/Demetrius are ultimately united.[12] These unions represent a restoration of authentic pairings: Demetrius himself admits that he had loved Helena before Hermia:

> And all the faith, the virtue of my heart,
> The object and the pleasure of mine eye,
> Is only Helena. To her, my lord,
> Was I betrothed ere I saw Hermia;
> But like a sickness, did I loathe this food;
> But, as in health, come to my natural taste,
> Now I do wish it, love it, long for it,
> And will for evermore be true to it. (4.1.169-76)

Eternal faithfulness is, perhaps, too much to ask of Carl-Magnus, but he and Charlotte *were* married before he met Desirée, which at least grants their relationship the virtue of precedence; moreover, Carl-Magnus and Charlotte share a certain grim compatibility, which is evident despite Hugh Wheeler's decision to emphasize Carl-Magnus's fatuity against Charlotte's brittle poise.

The sadomasochistic edge of their relationship is decidedly more pronounced in Bergman's film, however, in which Charlotte first appears in riding clothes and with a riding crop in hand. She engages in target practice during her conversation with Malcolm [Carl-Magnus]:

She fires her third shot.

MALCOLM: Look at that—a bulls-eye.

He hands her the newly loaded pistol.

CHARLOTTE: Just think if I shot you instead. What would you say then?
MALCOLM: What do you intend to do today?
CHARLOTTE: It'll be a boring day, as usual.
MALCOLM: Perhaps you can pay a visit to your friend, Anne Egerman.
CHARLOTTE: That's an idea.

Malcolm puts on his tunic and fastens its many buttons; his monocle glistens.

MALCOLM: She's probably totally ignorant of her husband's escapades.
CHARLOTTE: Poor Malcolm, are you so jealous?

Malcolm touches his elegant mustache with his forefinger. Charlotte has lowered the weapon and keeps it cocked in both hands. He takes his cap and walks toward the door. He is suddenly furious, but his large eyes are calm.

MALCOLM: I can tolerate my wife's infidelity, but if anyone touches my mistress, I become a tiger. Good morning!

He kisses her fingers and closes the door behind him. Charlotte raises the pistol and fires at the mirror on the door, splintering it into a thousand pieces. (79-80)

Commenting on the songs that he wrote early on for the play, Sondheim identifies their tonal alliance with *Smiles of a Summer Night*: "I had already written six songs that were much bleaker, more reflective, almost out of Strindberg . . . I was writing for Bergman's film, not Hugh Wheeler's play."[13] This subdued quality is evident in the jettisoned song "My Husband the Pig," in which Charlotte announces:

> My swain is a swine
> Or, to further refine
> It, a pig!
> It's ghastly and vastly ironical,
> A cynical, clinical chronicle:
> "The woman who married a monocle." (208)[14]

Also in this song, Charlotte asks, "Does he think a duet is a duel" (208), a question that we might say is answered by "Bang," the rejected duet/duel between Carl-Magnus and Desirée.[15]

CARL-MAGNUS:	DESIRÉE:
Whatever ground I gain	
I fortify remorselessly.	
	Bang! Bang!
The foe engages	
	Bang!
By shifting the terrain—	
How pitiful to be a woman.	
	Bang!
Attack,	
	Bang!
Retreat,	
	Bang!
Lay back,	
	Bang!
Reform.	
	Bang! Bang!
Outflank,	
	Bang!
Deplete,	
	Bang!
Move up and then restorm.	
	Bang! Bang! Bang! Bang!
The siege succeeding,	
	Bang!
The time grows shorter,	
	Bang!
She lies there pleading,	
	Bang!
I give no quarter . . .	
Bang!	Bang! (204)[16]

The "bleakness" and "reflectiveness" of these early songs are still evident in the final version of *Night Music*.[17] The imbrication of violence and sexuality continues to characterize Carl-Magnus in the standard version of the play, although this dimension of his character is more submerged; it finds expression in the military musical flourishes identified with his appearances, in his martial braggadocio, and in such lines as his instructions to Charlotte, "Pack everything I own / That shoots" (99), discreetly tucked in amidst several other fragments of conversation in "A Weekend in the Country."

Wheeler translates the more farouche elements of Bergman's characterization of Charlotte into her refined verbal ripostes, yet *both* Charlottes resemble Shakespeare's Helena. All three women are aware of (and articulate about) their foolish but incurable attachments to men who are arrogant, unfaithful, vain, and stupid. Indeed, Charlotte in *Night Music* admits, "As a man, my husband could be rated as a louse, a bastard, a conceited, puffed-up, adulterous egomaniac" (81). The language of both Bergman's Charlotte and Sondheim and Wheeler's Charlotte echoes Helena's, especially in its conscious depiction of willing self-debasement. Describing her "devotion" to Demetrius, Helena proclaims:

> I am your spaniel; and, Demetrius,
> The more you beat me, I will fawn on you.
> Use me but as your spaniel; spurn me, strike me,
> Neglect me, lose me; only give me leave,
> Unworthy as I am, to follow you.
> What worser place can I beg in your love
> (And yet a place of high respect with me)
> Than to be used as you use your dog? (2.1.203-10)

In a rare moment of vulnerability, Charlotte in *Smiles of a Summer Night* reveals the confusion and hopelessness of her emotions:

> I hate him, I hate him, I hate him, I hate him . . . . Men are beastly! They are silly and vain and have hair all over their bodies . . . . He smiles at me, he kisses me, he comes to me at night, he makes me lose my reason, he caresses me, talks kindly to me, gives me flowers, always yellow roses, talks about his horses, his women, his duels, his soldiers, his hunting—talks, talks, talks . . . . Love is a disgusting business! . . . In spite of everything, I love him. I would do anything for him. Do you understand that? Anything. Just so that he'll pat me and say: That's a good little dog. (89-90)

Sondheim's version of this speech captures the same enslavement, as well as suggesting the intelligence of the woman speaking:

> I'm before him
> On my knees
> And he kisses me.
> He assumes I'll lose my reason,
> And I do.
> Men are stupid, men are vain,

> Love's disgusting, love's insane,
> A humiliating business! (83)

Closer to the animal metaphors that Helena uses are the sentiments in "My Husband the Pig":

> My husband, the pig,
> The swaggering bore
> I'll do anything for,
> What a pig!
> The air of disdain is appalling,
> The level of decency nil.
> If he thinks that I'll always come crawling,
> Ha! I will.
> My husband, the pig.
> I worship the ground
> That he kicks me around
> On, the pig. (206)

Yet, like Helena, Charlotte is content when "the pig" recognizes his love for her. Demetrius, we have seen, satisfactorily pledges his love and fidelity, while Carl-Magnus makes the best offer he can. At the end of *Smiles of a Summer Night*, Charlotte complacently accepts him:

> *He falls on his knees laughing. She falls on her knees opposite him. She is still serious.*
>
> CHARLOTTE: Swear to be faithful to me for at least—
> MALCOLM: I'll be faithful to you for at least seven eternities of pleasure, eighteen false smiles and fifty-seven loving whispers without meaning. I'll be faithful to you until the last gasp separates us. In short, I'll be faithful to you in my way. (120)

In *Night Music*, these characters achieve a similar *rapprochement*. Carl-Magnus "forgives" Charlotte for her flirtation with Fredrik, once the lawyer's failure at Russian roulette diminishes his masculinity in the dragoon's estimation:

> CARL-MAGNUS: . . . I feel this house is no longer a suitable place for us.
> CHARLOTTE: Oh yes, my darling, I agree!
> CARL-MAGNUS: You will pack my things and meet me in the stables. I will have the car ready.
> CHARLOTTE: Yes, dear. Oh, Carl-Magnus! You became a tiger for me!

> *(They kiss)* (181-82)

Two members of the Quintet appear and comment on this marital "harmony," suggesting the cost at which it is accomplished:

MRS. ANDERSSEN (*Sings*):
   Men are stupid, men are vain,
   Love's disgusting, love's insane,
   A humiliating business . . .
MRS. SEGSTROM:
   Oh, how true!

(CARL-MAGNUS *and* CHARLOTTE *break the kiss.* CARL-MAGNUS *exits.*
CHARLOTTE *runs up to the house*)

MRS. ANDERSSEN:
   Aaaah,

(*When* CHARLOTTE *closes the house doors*)

   Well . . . (182)

This reprise of "Every Day a Little Death" suggests that while Carl-Magnus's entanglement with Desirée has ended, Charlotte's life will not likely change much. This particular episode in their marriage has been resolved; more than that the text cannot say.

The other couples who have entered the "green world" reach more decisive conclusions. Rather neatly conforming to a Freudian paradigm, Anne and Henrik defy the law of the father and run off together.[18] Presumably they will consummate their relationship more successfully than Anne and Fredrik ever did, and Henrik's rejection of Martin Luther might ease his need to play the cello quite so ferociously.

Yet the loss of Anne does not represent the desolation of Fredrik's world so much as it liberates him from a relationship that never completely satisfied him. He exclaims to Desirée, "How unlikely life is! To lose one's son, one's wife, and practically one's life within an hour and yet to feel—relieved. Relieved, and, what's more, considerably less ancient" (183). The sense of rightness he confronts in his life moves Fredrik to propose a new life with Desirée: "A coherent existence after so many years of muddle[.] You and me, and of course, Fredrika . . . " (183). This arrangement represents the final recoupling in the narrative, musically indicated by Fredrik and Desirée singing together for the first time in the play:

FREDRIK:

(*They kiss. The music swells. Sings*)

Make way for the clowns.
DESIRÉE:
Applause for the clowns.
BOTH:
They're finally here. (184)

Without sacrificing character complexity or damaging narrative coherence, *Night Music* manages to meet the terms of Puck's formula for a happy ending:

Jack shall have Jill;
Nought shall go ill:
The man shall have his mare again,
and all shall be well. (3.2.461-63)

The text even addresses Fredrik's mildly suspicious observation regarding these outcomes, "How unlikely life is"; we ought to recall that in the act 1 Prologue, Madame Armfeldt states, with her accustomed certainty, "Everything is unlikely" (25). Sylvan Barnet, hazarding a generalization about Shakespearean comedy, observes that this restoration of harmony is central to the form:

If we look at Shakespearean comedy as a whole . . . we see that generally speaking it is a comedy of young lovers who encounter difficulties but who are ultimately united; the plays follow the Renaissance formula for comedy, according to which, in the words of Shakespeare's fellow playwright Thomas Heywood, "comedies begin in trouble and end in peace."[19]

Despite the fact that Fredrik and Desirée are not young, their narrative conforms to the pattern Barnet proposes, and the "unlikelihood" of this "peaceful" resolution is perhaps less important than its structural inevitability.

Although the traditional romantic comedy further depicts the return of the lovers to the city—a sign that the lessons learned in the country can be assimilated and exported back to the world of day light and routine—the fantasy of *Night Music* allows its lovers to remain in that magical and transformative "green world."[20] Here they finally waltz with their proper partners, implying that, having journeyed into the woods, they have achieved not only a knowledge of one another but also a knowledge of themselves.[21] And while this waltz (like all of the dances in the play) is not diegetic, it nevertheless evokes the wedding dances that mark the conclusions to many of Shakespeare's comedies. *A Midsummer Night's Dream* does not end with such a wedding dance performed by the lovers themselves, but we last glimpse the couples in that play (including Theseus and Hippolyta, who have also achieved serene relations) walking off hopefully to their marriage beds. The harmony of movement embodied in *Night Music*'s final waltz represents a similar resolution, as well as promising the "coherent existence" that Fredrik and Desirée identify as their own cherished desire.

II

OBERON:
   How now, mad Spirit?
   What night-rule now about this haunted grove?
      —*A MIDSUMMER NIGHT'S DREAM*, 3.2.4–5

FREDRIKA: *But how does* [the summer night]
   smile? . . . how does it happen?
MADAME ARMFELDT: *You get a feeling. Suddenly the*
   jasmine starts to smell stronger, then a frog
   croaks—then all the stars in Orion wink.
      —*A LITTLE NIGHT MUSIC*, 26

If we allow Heywood's claim that "comedies begin in trouble," we might note that trouble is revealed early in both *Smiles of a Summer Night* and *A Little Night Music* in dreams. Both texts depict Fredrik's afternoon nap and the trace of his evidently erotic dream of Desirée. In Bergman, the still-sleeping Fredrik amorously caresses Anne and murmurs, "Desirée . . . how I have longed for you" (42 ellipsis in original); in *Night Music*, Fredrik "does a kiss" (41) before singing Desirée's name at the end of "Now / Soon / Later," and most performers settle for the pillow as their substitute love object. In both scenes, Fredrik's desires are revealed to Anne, and his dreams alter her sense of (waking) reality. In other words, she begins to see her married life more clearly because of what Fredrik says and does with his eyes closed. Moreover, in both *Summer Night* and *Night Music*, Fredrik remembers his dream of Desirée, so he, too, sees his life more clearly because of his dream. Peter Holland's summary remark concerning education-by-dreams in *Midsummer* proves valid here: "Living with one's dreams is never an easy process."[22]

Rather inevitably, dreams perform a similar illuminating, though unsettling, role throughout *A Midsummer Night's Dream*. Marjorie Garber observes that sleep in this play "is the gateway, not to folly, but to revelation and reordering."[23] Dreams provide access to another (less obvious, more mysterious) condition of being, another state of consciousness, another means of perception. "The title of the play," as Michael Mangan points out, "signals the importance of dreams and its associated modes of knowing: fantasy, imagination, magic."[24] In *Midsummer* these elements enter the diegesis explicitly in the characters of the fairies, whose interference causes chaos at first, and harmony at last. The magic, after all, is wrought by them, and they constitute the play's fantasy-narrative.

But the play also yokes together the experience of fairy intervention with dreams themselves: Puck administers the "love juice" to Lysander and Demetrius (and Oberon administers it to Titania) while they sleep, so that the alterations in their perceptions and desires occur as if they resulted from their dreams. And to resolve the muddles caused by these alterations, Oberon leads the four lovers to sleep before correcting their misperceptions and setting all right for them:

> When they next wake, all this derision
> Shall seem a dream and fruitless vision,
> And back to Athens shall the lovers wend
> With league whose date till death shall never end. (3.2.370-73)

Moreover, all of those affected by the fairies' magic (even Titania) regard *as a dream* its influence and the events that transpired because of it. Once Oberon applies the antidote to Titania's eyes, she awakes not only from a sleep but from her enchantment with Bottom; she exclaims, "what visions have I seen!" (4.1.77)—and, like Adam, she wakes to find that her dream has become flesh. As the lovers depart from the transformative "green world," amazed by the changes in their relations with one another, Demetrius suggests, "let us recount our dreams" (4.1.199). And Bottom, waking from his sleep (and returned to his wonted form), repeats the sentiments expressed by the other dreamers: "I have had a most rare vision. I have had a dream, past the wit of man to say what dream it was" (4.1.204-06).

While all of these "dreams," in fact, happened (Titania *was* infatuated with an ass; the lovers *did* play musical partners for the better part of an evening; and Bottom *was* subject to a considerable, if appropriate, physical metamorphosis), these characters can best account for the extraordinary nature of their "visions" by locating those visions within the realm of dream.[25] After all, how else could they reasonably explain the transformations at the center of their visions? Garber proposes, more broadly:

> It is . . . transposition or transformation which is the special prerogative of the dream state and the center of interest of the whole of *A Midsummer Night's Dream*. Dream is truer than reality because it has this transforming power; it is part of the fertile, unbounded world of the imagination.[26]

Transcending reason, magic and dreams have ever-expanding fields of possibility; they can be the agents of any otherwise unbelievable (or to use Fredrik's and Madame Armfeldt's word, "unlikely") occurrence. And it is the imagination that allows characters (and audiences) to accept, if not perfectly understand, the ways of magic and dreams.

The tension between reason and imagination plays out most openly in *Midsummer* in an exchange between Theseus and Hippolyta. After the lovers have returned from the "green world" and presumably recounted their dreams not only to one another but also to the figures of authority in the court, Hippolyta remarks " 'Tis strange, my Theseus, that these lovers speak of" (5.1.1). Theseus responds with a now-famous speech:

> More strange than true. I never may believe
> These antique fables, nor these fairy toys.
> Lovers and madmen have such seething brains,
> Such shaping fantasies, that apprehend
> More than cool reason ever comprehends.
> The lunatic, the lover, and the poet
> Are of imagination all compact.
> . . . .
> And as imagination bodies forth
> The forms of things unknown, the poet's pen
> Turns them to shapes, and gives to aery nothing
> A local habitation and a name.
> Such tricks hath strong imagination,
> That if it would but apprehend some joy,
> It comprehends some bringer of that joy;
> Or in the night, imagining some fear,
> How easy is a bush supposed a bear! (5.1.2-8; 14-22)

So speaks the voice of "cool reason," for Theseus is hardly endorsing a belief in "antique fables" or "fairy toys," nor is he celebrating those "seething brains" that mistake a bush for a bear. While he admits to the power of the imagination, he does not applaud it so much as mistrust it; in this speech, Theseus merely concedes to the capacity that some people have to be mightily and everlastingly deluded.

Hippolyta reveals a far greater openness to the possible actuality of the lovers' dreams. Unlike Theseus, she does not dismiss their unlikelihood:

> But all the story of the night told over,
> And all their minds transfigur'd so together,
> More witnesseth than fancy's images,
> And grows to something of great constancy;
> But, howsoever, strange and admirable. (5.1.23-27)

Hippolyta is no less rational than Theseus in arguing that when four people report the same curious events, there is likely some truth to their reports, however "strange and admirable" they may at first appear to be. Her willingness to accept Truth in "the story of the night" moreover implies her own affinity with the mysterious nighttime and "green world" realities constructed in the dreams and magic of the play. (Theseus never replies to Hip-

polyta's statement regarding the lovers' narrative—a sign that their relationship may continue to be marked with a certain degree of discord.)

I've included this protracted discussion of *A Midsummer Night's Dream*
in order to map out some of the ways in which the tension between reason and
imagination functions within the other system of oppositions I've established
in all three texts—namely, that between daytime/city and nighttime/country.
While the reason/imagination opposition is not so neatly and consistently
performed by two characters in *Summer Night* or *Night Music* (as it is in *Midsummer*, by Theseus and Hippolyta), the tension, nevertheless, survives in the
later texts. On the side of reason, Fredrik is the most obvious representative: a
lawyer, he embodies social norms, making a profession of determining and
maintaining order. Although he experiences a great deal of chaos (both mentally and externally) throughout the narrative before redirecting his own life
to satisfy his needs and desires, his initial appearances in both texts over-de-
termine the orderliness of his mind and the restraint of his behavior.
Bergman's film opens with Fredrik in his law office, presenting to us the effi-
cient and fastidious public self:

> *Fredrik Egerman, attorney, closes his large ledger with a bang so that the*
> *dust flies, places it on the shelf behind his desk, takes off his pince-nez, puts*
> *it away in its case, looks at his watch, winds it several times, sets his desk in*
> *order—pens, inkwell, ruler, writing paper and books—combs his beard*
> *quickly with a small comb, rises resolutely and begins to whistle as he walks*
> *into the next room . . . (35).*[27]

Sondheim recreates this aspect of his character immediately in Fredrik's
first song, "Now," in which the lawyerly mind rationally considers how best
to approach an unconsummated marriage:

> Now, there are two possibilities:
> A, I could ravish her,
> B, I could nap . . .
> Say it's the ravishment, then we see
> The option
> That follows, of course: . . .
> A, the deployment of charm, or B,
> The adoption
> Of physical force. (32)

And Fredrik is himself aware of this aspect of his character, as he admits
to Desirée that Anne "bursts with a kind of madness / *My well-ordered ways*"
(60; my emphasis). As we have already seen, Fredrik and the power of reason
more generally meet their match in the "green world" of the Armfeldt country
estate, the site of mystical forces aligned with the tender passions. But then,

all of the guests predict that the weekend will be "*enchanting* / On the mani-cured lawns" (102; my emphasis).

Early in act 2, members of the Quintet alert us to the changes in conditions that will work their magic, so to speak, on the characters gathered together for the weekend:

> MR. LINDQUIST:
> The atmosphere's becoming heady,
> The ambiance thrilling,
> MRS. SEGSTROM:
> The spirit unsteady,
> The flesh far too willing. (143)

These shifts in mood reflect part of the original concept for the play—what Sondheim calls "a fantasy-ridden musical":

It was to take place over a weekend during which, in almost gamelike fashion, Desirée would have been the prime mover and would work the characters into different situations. The first time, everybody would get mixed up, and through farcical situations, would end up with the wrong partner. Then, magically, the weekend would start again. The next time everything worked out, but Henrik committed suicide. The third time, Desirée arranged everything right but this time when she was left alone with Fredrik, he put on his gloves and started to walk off the stage because she hadn't done anything to make him want her.

The way all this worked was that Madame Armfeldt, who was like a witch figure, would reshuffle the pack of cards and time would revert and we'd be back at the beginning of the weekend again. The characters would then re-form, waltz again, and start over. It was all to be presented like a court masque with a music-box quality. But Hugh Wheeler finally gave up on it. He just couldn't make it work to his satisfaction.[28]

This concept would have kept the dreamlike magical elements much closer to the surface; certainly, the merging of the lovers' narrative (with its patterns of rearrangements) and the explicit deployment of enchantments would have resulted in a text startlingly similar to *A Midsummer Night's Dream*.

As Joanne Gordon indicates, however, traces of the play's original concept remain in the surreal dance sequences, the Quintet, the masquelike dinner scene, Madame Armfeldt's speeches, and the "perpetual sunset" of the Swedish white night.[29] These elements not only help to define the style and produce the tone of the play, they create an analogue to the fairy atmosphere of *Midsummer*, with its spiritual lookers-on, manipulating human wills and acutely comprehending human muddles.

Harold Prince writes of his own rather metaphysical take on the role of the Quintet in the play: "I got the idea that they might represent the positive spirits in a negative household. Everyone in *Night Music* is frustrated, humiliated by sexual role-playing. The five Liebeslieder people are secure."[30] Their importance is suggested by the fact that they open the play, and their liminal identity implied by their appearing before the houselights are down—as if they originate someplace other than the framework (let alone the diegesis) of the play. Their first utterances (vocal scales) resolve into coherent melodies, microcosmically representing how the narrative itself will unite a nearly random collection of people and bring coherence to their lives. In the Overture, they introduce fragments of three songs that have crucial thematic importance in the play: "Remember," conjuring memories of the past into the consciousness of the present; "Soon," with its longing for what is just out of reach; and "The Glamorous Life," with its evocation of the theater, a theme relevant not only to Desirée but (as we will see in Section Three) also to the self-conscious theatricality of the play itself.

Just as they cross the boundary between the daytime world (reproduced inside a theater by a lit house) and the nighttime world (of the play that occurs after the houselights come down), the Quintet magically violate boundaries throughout the play. When Desirée spies Fredrik in the theater, members of the Quintet, who are doubling as audience members for the play within the play, begin to sing "Remember," as if they shared the memories of the principal characters, or could read their minds and are free to express what Fredrik and Desirée cannot:

MRS. NORDSTROM:
 That dilapidated inn—
 Remember, darling?
MR. LINDQUIST:
 The proprietress's grin,
 Also her glare . . .
MRS. NORDSTROM:
 Yellow gingham on the bed—
 Remember, darling?
MR. LINDQUIST:
 And the canopy in red,
 Needing repair? (47-8; ellipsis in original)

In act 2, they both comment on the events taking place in the country and serve as projections of the principal characters. Like the fairies in *Midsummer*, they are the resident spirits, observing the events as outsiders, but also endowed with an intimate knowledge of the lovers' emotions.

When the three women in the Quintet sing "Perpetual Anticipation," introducing one of the play's most explicitly magical scenes, we cannot be sure if they are describing the emotional condition of the scene or creating it:

> Perpetual anticipation is
> Good for the soul
> But it's bad for the heart.
> It's very good for practicing
> Self-control.
> It's very good for
> Morals,
> But bad for morale. (154)

Are these three singers doubles for Desirée, Anne, and Charlotte—verbalizing what those women are suppressing? Are they the Three Fates, musically weaving the destinies of Madame Armfeldt's guests? Are they spirits who have seen these confusions and sorrows before, and are now sharing their wisdom?

We might ask similar questions of the Quintet's various appearances in the play's final scene, which is set throughout the Armfeldt house and garden. Here, members of the Quintet reprise *for characters* their signature songs in the play. Only once in this scene do characters sing of their own emotional state: when Fredrik and Desirée achieve their union at the very end. Other emotional climaxes are channelled through the Quintet; for instance, when Fredrik watches Anne and Henrik run off together, it is Mr. Erlanson who expresses his bittersweet response:

> MR. ERLANSON (*Leans, looking onstage, sings*):
> She lightens my sadness,
> She livens my days,
> She bursts with a kind of madness
> My well-ordered ways.
> The happiest mistake,
> The ache of my life . . . (177)

While the Quintet certainly are, as Prince claims, "optimistic, extroverted observers," their self-composure grants them a kind of superiority that evokes Oberon and Puck's distance from the lovers in *Midsummer*; their (sometimes literally) marginal relationship to the events of the narrative suggests both the sentiment and the perspective of Puck's observation: "Shall we their fond pageant see? / Lord, what fools these mortals be!" (3.2.114-15).[31] However literally mortal the members of the Quintet are, the affect that their stage presence creates is often more spiritlike than human.

The other characters in *Night Music* who are extrinsic to the lovers' narratives—Petra, Frid, Fredrika, and Madame Armfeldt—also, though in different ways, share an understanding of the night and its mysteries. Like the Quintet, they possess from the start a clear-sightedness that the lovers themselves do not attain until the end of the play. While there is nothing especially spiritual about either Petra or Frid, their particular perspectives on lovemaking dissociate them from the other lovers in the play, and provide them with shrewd insights on the human heart.[32] Petra's panegyric to exuberance and self-expression not only contrasts with the reticence of the other couples, it also comments on the sacrifices that propriety demands:

> There are mouths to be kissed
> Before mouths to be fed,
> And there's many a tryst
> And there's many a bed.
> There's a lot I'll have missed
> But I'll not have been dead when I die!
> And a person should celebrate everything
> Passing by. (174)[33]

In Sondheim's original plan for the play, Frid would have expressed, even more scornfully, a censure of the lovers:

> Let them float in their words
> Till they slowly drown.
> Don't they know, don't they,
> What they want?
> Silly, silly people!
> Patient and polite,
> Crying in their teacups,
> Shying from the night—(200)[34]

Frid (and Petra presumably) needn't shy from the night, perhaps because it is a more native element for them; they enjoy an affiliation with "nature," knowing "what they want," and not allowing refined manners to prevent them from grabbing hold of it. In the standard production Frid may not appear as an element of the mystical night, but his earlier incarnation apparently was to evince an understanding of it and of its power over lovers. This would have linked him more closely to Bergman's Frid, who articulates the mythology of the smiling night: "The summer night has three smiles, and this is the first—between midnight and daybreak—when young lovers open their hearts and bodies. Can you see it back there at the horizon, a smile so soft that one has to be very quiet and watchful to see it at all" (109). Frid may not be able to perform magic, but he does have the wisdom to comprehend it.

Fredrika's role as an observer is established from the opening of the play: during the "Night Waltz," "FREDRIKA *wanders through the waltz . . . watching*" (22). We soon discover that her grandmother encourages a certain kind of attentiveness in her:

FREDRIKA: You said I should watch.
MADAME ARMFELDT: Watch—what?
FREDRIKA: It sounds very unlikely to me, but you said I should watch for the
   night to smile. (25)

At once Madame Armfeldt's protégée and yet suspicious of her, Fredrika
watches everyone, which allows her to judge keenly though unassumingly.
Even during the act 2 dinner scene, Fredrika, the stage directions tell us, is
"*seated at the piano,* [and] '*accompanies' the scene*" (156). However,
Fredrika is hardly a disinterested observer; she knows that the events transpir-
ing around her might very well change her life significantly.[35] When Desirée
informs her of the plan she cherishes, Fredrika demonstrates that, like her
grandmother, she is astute and blunt:

DESIRÉE: . . . Darling, how would you feel if we had a home of our very
   own with me only acting when I felt like it—and a man who would
   make you a spectacular father?
FREDRIKA: Oh I see. The lawyer! Mr. Egerman!
DESIRÉE: Dear child, you're uncanny. (91)

"Uncanny" is a provocative word choice, as it refers to an unsettling ac-
curacy that is supernatural or occult in its quality if not its source. Fredrika is
neither witch nor fairy, but her quiet watchfulness and her tutelage with
Madame Armfeldt make her a not altogether typical child; we might say that
the events of this narrative actually constitute her education in the ways of the
night, that her being sent off to practice her piano (at the end of the act 1 Prologue) suggests that she is learning "a little night music."[36]
   The most magical character in both *Smiles of a Summer Night* and *A Little Night Music*, however, is Madame Armfeldt.[37] Originally conceptualized
as a "witch figure," she was to control the fates of the other characters, especially the lovers, for each time she reshuffled her cards the lovers' narrative
would start again and play itself out differently.[38] Even in the official version
of the play, she possesses, like Oberon, powers of magic and vision. Gordon
aligns her character with a different Shakespeare play: "Madame Armfeldt
assumes a Prospero-like power as she evokes the magic of the traditional
masque."[39] Of course, Prospero and Oberon are worth comparing, as both of
them are enchanters who function as stage managers, and both magically
bring off romances between young lovers. Enid Welsford further argues that
the two plays in which these characters figure represent Shakespeare's ab-
sorption of the court masque tradition, with its music, its stylized dances, and
its nighttime revels.[40] Madame Armfeldt, as we will see, is associated, from
the act 1 Prologue, with the summer night, and it is at her country estate that
the most masquelike scene will occur.

In the Prologue, she not only presents the mystical theory of the "smiles of a summer night," but also reveals her capacity to interpret those smiles, and to identify the signs of their appearance: "the jasmine starts to smell stronger, then a frog croaks—then all the stars in Orion wink" (26). While establishing her character, this Prologue also sets the tone for the narrative to follow: like Fredrika, we now know to watch the different behaviors of the young, the fools, and the old; we also might attend to the vaguely supernatural aura, which not only enhances the play tonally but also enters its narrative through Madame Armfeldt.

The dinner scene is one of the most densely (and ethereally) stylized sequences in the play. In it, Madame Armfeldt sits "in solitary splendor" (155-56), facing the other characters and the audience. She speaks little, but evidently watches closely. The actions of the various lovers are choreographed, which exaggerates their couplings and recouplings; because the waltzing in this scene needn't be presented as part of the diegesis, these episodes of dance might appear especially surreal—interrupting or commenting on the scene's dialogue, rather than figuring as part of the party's entertainment.[41] Observing the misdirected desires and suffocated emotions of her guests, Madame Armfeldt offers them a magical remedy:

> Ladies and gentlemen, tonight I am serving you a very special dessert wine. It is from the cellars of the King of the Belgians who—during a period of intense intimacy—presented me with all the bottles then in existence. The secret of its unique quality is unknown, but it is said to possess the power to open the eyes of even the blindest among us . . . (159; ellipsis in original)

This magical wine appears in *Summer Night*, as well, though Bergman is less reticent about identifying the "secret of its unique power":

> *She raises her glass. Out of the twilight, out of nowhere, a melody is heard. It seems to have been born out of the night, out of the bouquet of the wine, out of the secret life of the walls and the objects around them.*
>
> OLD LADY [MADAME ARMFELDT]: A story is told that this wine is pressed from grapes whose juice wells forth like drops of blood on the white skin of the peel. It is also said that to every cask filled with this wine a drop of milk from the swelling breasts of a woman who has just given birth to her first child and a drop of seed from a young stallion are added. This gives the wine a mysterious, stimulating power, and whoever drinks of it does so at his own risk. (100)

Both scenes vibrate with hints of the supernatural, as if a spiritual presence were about to penetrate into the narrative. No fairies appear, but, like

Oberon, Madame Armfeldt intervenes in the sad lives of the muddled lovers who surround her, providing them with a mysterious cure for their confusions.[42]

It is after this scene that they begin to cast off their restraints and reveal their suppressed feelings: Henrik speaks defiantly to Fredrik and later admits to his love for Anne; Anne realizes that she returns Henrik's love and runs off with him; Charlotte comes clean of her plot to "seduce" Fredrik; Carl-Magnus "becomes a tiger" for Charlotte; and, of course, Fredrik and Desirée discover a shared harmony. Less apparent is Madame Armfeldt's own vulnerability to the wine's "power to open the eyes of even the blindest among us," for she too admits to a secret: she tells Fredrika of the Croatian Count, her first lover, who gave her a wooden ring:

> It had been in his family for centuries, it seemed, but I said to myself: a wooden ring? What sort of man would give you a wooden ring, so I tossed him out right there and then. And now—who knows? He might have been the love of my life. (179)

This admission that she might have made a mistake is as unwonted in Madame Armfeldt's character as any of the other reverses we see occurring at various locations in her country house and gardens. Her own behavior may be the most compelling evidence that the dessert wine is, indeed, magical.

A Midsummer Night's Dream ends with the promise of continued magical influence on the lives of humans, as Oberon instructs the fairies to bless the unions of the three couples:

> With this field-dew consecrate,
> Every fairy take his gait,
> And each several chamber bless,
> Through this palace, with sweet peace,
> And the owner of it blest
> Ever shall in safety rest. (5.1.415-20)

At the conclusion of *Night Music*, however, the enchantress dies, leaving the couples to live on without her.[43] Of course, the shadow of Madame Armfeldt's death stretches across the narrative, as she speaks of its eventuality throughout the play, predicting the hilarity at her wake and the fine wine that will be served for the occasion. The timing of her death, however, serves a more poetic purpose in the text, for she dies only after she has given to the young all that she had to offer: the virtues of honesty, the graciousness of the past, and the magic of intuition.[44] Once they learn what they can from her, she has nothing more to give them—and so the night recalls her.[45]

One of the most compelling intersections between *A Midsummer Night's Dream* and both *Smiles of a Summer Night* and *A Little Night Music* is the reference to midsummer itself. Both *Summer Night* and *Night Music* are actually set at midsummer (Midsummer Day, the longest day of the year, is 24 June), when the days are at their longest, and the sun remains above the horizon for a startlingly long time. *A Midsummer Night's Dream*, on the other hand, is set around May Day, for when Theseus discovers the lovers asleep in the wood, he comments, "No doubt they rose up early to observe / The rite of May" (4.1.132-33). Numerous scholars have interrogated the ostensible confusion between the play's title and its calendar setting, typically explaining that the play's title likely refers to the occasion of its first performance (a court event, such as a wedding, that was celebrated at midsummer). More recent criticism, however, tends to decenter these concerns, and, instead, to explore the similarities between May Day and Midsummer.

François Laroque provides a historical framework for this critical approach:

> In England, as in most of the countries of mainland Europe, the advent of summer and the triumph of light over darkness was greeted with a show of bonfires. These bonfires were the focus for all kinds of revelries which perpetuated the memory of superstitions and quite a few magic rites, all of which were associated in popular culture with the particular powers of this, the shortest night of the year. . . . As many of [the figures who appeared in Midsummer parades] also appeared in the May game, a certain confusion arose between the rites of May and those of Midsummer Eve.[46]

He further argues that "In *A Midsummer Night's Dream*, Shakespeare played on the similarity between the festivities of May Day and those of Midsummer, deliberately confusing them as if they were more or less equivalent."[47] Providing further grounds for collapsing the two festivals, Joseph Strutt documents May Games that actually extended into the middle of June.[48] And C. L. Barber proposes that the observance of May Day, to which Theseus refers, "can be thought of as happening on a midsummer night, even on Midsummer Eve itself . . . The point of the allusions is not the date, but the *kind* of holiday occasion."[49] Relevant to our consideration of *Summer Night* and *Night Music*, Sir James Frazer, in *The Golden Bough*, explains that this identification of the two festivals also existed in Sweden.[50] Historians indicate that both postwinter festivals celebrate the coming of light, that the nighttime festivities allowed (and perhaps even encouraged) young people to take to the woods for various forms of licentiousness, and that, along with All Hallows' Eve, both May Day and Midsummer were the most likely times for the appearances of fairies.[51]

As we have already seen, all of these aspects resonate throughout the three texts. The only point I'd like to explore further is the inescapability of the light. Caroline Spurgeon helpfully informs us that "moon" appears twenty-eight times in *A Midsummer Night's Dream*, three-and-a-half times more than in any other of Shakespeare's plays, and "moonlight" is referenced six times (out of the eight references in all of Shakespeare); this moonlit background, she suggests, "supplies the dreaming and enchanted quality in the play."[52] In Bergman, bright light bathes all of the evening scenes at the country house, and it is often difficult to know if the white disk in the sky is the sun or the moon. This perpetually lit night refuses to allow any of the lovers to escape from seeing; they cannot hide from one another or from themselves. This effect is repeated in *Night Music*, where the Quintet keeps us posted on the status of the summer night:

MRS. ANDERSSEN:
> The sun sits low,
> Diffusing its usual glow.
> Five o'clock . . .
> Twilight . . .
> Vespers sound,
> And it's six o'clock . . .
> Twilight
> All around, (133; ellipses in original)

"Perpetual sunset / Is rather an unset- / Tling thing" (134) not only because it prevents people from hiding, but because it mirrors a world out of joint. Sun and moon are not in their rightful places, night resembles day, and the movements of the clock are meaningless. The atmospheric conditions mirror the human muddles at the center of the narrative:[53]

MRS. NORDSTROM:
> The sun sits low
> And the vespers ring,
MR. ERLANSON:
> And the shadows grow
> And the crickets sing,
> And it's . . .
MRS. NORDSTROM:
> Look! Is that the moon?
MR. ERLANSON:
> Yes.
> What a lovely afternoon! . . .
> The evening air
> Doesn't feel quite right
MRS. NORDSTROM:
> In the not-quite glare
> Of the not-quite night. (140-41)

That these disruptions threaten to disturb characters' mental states aligns them with the folk-belief in "midsummer madness"; because the woods exist outside the rational world, one must expect one's reason to come under attack there. The old English word "wood," in fact, means "mad," thus Demetrius's remark, "And here am I, wode within this wood, / Because I cannot meet my Hermia" (2.1.192-93). The midsummer setting of *A Little Night Music* evokes that traditionally enchanted time of the year when the spirit world and the visible world mingle, when irrational powers gain ascendency, and when the munificence of the light can grant vision to misguided lovers.

III

THESEUS:
Come now; what masques, what dances shall we
*   have,*
To wear away this long age of three hours
Between our after-supper and bed-time?
Where is our usual manager of mirth?
What revels are in hand? Is there no play,
To ease the anguish of a torturing hour?
                    —*A MIDSUMMER NIGHT'S DREAM*, 5.1.32-37

DESIRÉE:
Isn't it rich?
Isn't it queer?
Losing my timing this late
In my career?
And where are the clowns?
There ought to be clowns.
Well, maybe next year . . .
                    —*A LITTLE NIGHT MUSIC*, 170

Both *A Midsummer Night's Dream* and *A Little Night Music* are self-con-sciously theatrical: their embedded play scenes (the Mechanicals' perfor-mance of "Pyramus and Thisby" in *Midsummer*, and the scene from *Woman of the World* in *Night Music*) not only mirror the larger narratives which they serve but also remind us of the theatrical nature of those narratives. Watching an audience watching a play, we can hardly forget that we too are an audience watching a play. This self-reflexiveness specifically queries the boundaries between reality and art, between reality and dream, and between art and dream.

Dreams, we have already seen, provide characters in these texts with ac-cess to truths that might otherwise remain submerged in their (daytime) consciousnesses. In this way, they are more real than reality, because they are often more truthful. Art (in this case, theatrical art) similarly offers uncomfortable truths, and, in its artifice, calls attention to the posturing and "masking" (as Charlotte suggests) that are perpetrated offstage. Yet, the highly controlled and formally shaped artifice of drama can also envision the coherence lacking in people's muddled lives, and so art might be said to have an educative quality—revealing truths that reality can prevent us from seeing. These somewhat heady implications are not delivered pedantically in these texts, however; rather, they are evident in the tensions between the frame plays and their interior dramatic presentations.[54]

However primitive and unintentionally farcical the Mechanicals' performance of "Pyramus and Thisbe," the plot of that narrative mirrors Hermia and Lysander's own situation: violating parental wishes, two lovers flee from home and meet in the night. Of course, the original "Pyramus and Thisbe" ends tragically, which contrasts, of course, with the comic resolution of Hermia and Lysander's narrative. But the Mechanicals' *comical* rendering of "Pyramus and Thisbe" twists its function within the larger play: instead of opposing the happy outcome of Hermia and Lysander's efforts, it actually underlines it, reminding us that were it not for the fairies' intervention, Hermia and Lysander could well have been discovered and returned to Athens, their story perhaps ending as tragically as Pyramus and Thisbe's.[55] In other words, the Mechanicals' corruption of tragedy into comedy reflects the same transformation effected in the magical "green world." In that way, not only are reality (Hermia and Lysander) and drama (Pyramus and Thisbe) imbricated, so too are the realms of dream and theatrical representation, for in both of these realms tragedy can unsuspectedly turn to comedy.

When Lysander and Demetrius laugh derisively throughout the performance of the Mechanicals' play, we see to what extent they are unaware of these narrative and thematic equivalences. Whatever the intensity of their experiences in the woods, they seem to have returned unscathed. On the other hand, neither Hermia nor Helena speaks at all during the (lovers') play—perhaps implying that they are more sensitive to the resonances of the narrative they are observing, however ridiculous its trappings.

In *Night Music*, the embedded scene from *Woman of the World* similarly confutes the boundaries between reality and drama. Of course, the character of the Countess, with her wily charms and her collection of lovers ("as many as the pearls in the necklace which she always wears" [46]) is an exaggerated version of Desirée herself—perhaps Desirée as Charlotte and Anne see her. But even the particulars revealed in this interior dramatic scene correspond to the characters and plot of *Night Music*. The Second Lady (Mrs. Anderssen) declares that her husband "fell in love with the Countess on sight. She took him as a lover for three months and after that I had him back. . . . My husband had become a tender, devoted, admirable lover, a faithful husband" (46);

this summarizes, tolerably well, the course of Charlotte and Carl-Magnus's story—as Desirée does briefly take the dragoon for a lover, before he returns to his wife. On the other hand, the First Lady (Mrs. Segstrom) resembles Anne; a less worldly woman and less experienced lover, she knows the Countess only by her reputation. Her speech might easily be spoken by Anne to Desirée: "you are all but a legend to me. I implore you to reveal to me the secret of your success with the hardier sex!" (48).

The structure of the dialogue in this scene further produces the interplay between this embedded French farce and the main play.[56] The frame scene begins with Anne inquiring about Desirée, "Does she look like her pictures" (45), and the interior scene begins with the First Lady inquiring about the Countess, "Tell me something about this remarkable Countess" (46). The responses of the Second Lady, therefore, address both the First Lady (in the interior scene) and Anne (in the frame). The two scenes continue to play in tandem, with Fredrik and Anne practically interacting with the stage performers:

> FIRST LADY: . . . I implore you to reveal to me the secret of your success with the hardier sex!
> ANNE: She smiled at us!
>
> . . . .
> DESIRÉE: Dear Madame, that can be summed up in a single word—
> ANNE: She's ravishingly beautiful.
> FREDRIK: Make-up.
> DESIRÉE: —dignity. (48-49)

The two dramatic levels comment on one another, the rudimentary plot foretells some of the tensions we will see enacted later in the play, and the characterization of the Countess presents Desirée's public persona—though the Second Lady's caveat ("the personality of the Countess . . . is too rich in mysterious contradictions to be described in a few short moments" [46]) should prepare us for the complexities of Desirée's character, as they are developed throughout the play.

As soon as the Countess/Desirée appears, she recognizes Fredrik in the audience, and the boundaries between interior and frame plays further dissolve. In a highly stylized fashion, the action freezes, and members of the Quintet (doubling as audience members) begin singing "Remember." We recognize that a line has just been crossed: members of an audience disregard their passive roles and become active parts of a scene, presuming to know the intimate details of other characters' lives. And just as we observe this dismantling of boundaries, Anne observes another: she exclaims, fiercely, to Fredrik, "She looked at us. Why did she look at us" (48). While we may laugh at Anne's naivete, she is merely calling attention to a transgression that we are already aware of: just as the two members of the audience/Quintet look through and not at Fredrik and Desirée, Desirée looks through and not at the fourth wall of the stage.

While this is the only explicitly "theatrical" scene in *Night Music*, other structural and stylistic elements call attention to the play's highly wrought theatricality. To begin at the beginning, the play's vocal Overture calls attention to itself as a construct composed for the stage. I have already discussed the thematic resonances of the songs introduced in the Overture; Foster Hirsch describes the Quintet themselves as pointedly self-reflexive:

> A quintet of wry musical commentators weaves in and out of the action, puncturing romantic reveries, introducing and reprising fragments of songs, providing transitions, and above all reminding the audience of the show's essential theatricality, the fact that a musical is *not* just like a play.[57]

This is especially true of the Overture—an immediate indication that *Night Music* makes no claim to realism. Before the houselights are down, we have before us five singers; with no apparent connection to the play's diegesis, the Quintet perform as if in a lieder concert, aware only of their own singing. This creates an initial impression of performative self-consciousness, while also postponing any apprehension of narrative or character. And while we could say much the same thing of conventional overtures (performed by stage orchestras), the startling fact of a *vocal* overture draws attention to itself as a metatheatrical construct.

Dance in *A Little Night Music* is masquelike, not only because of its high stylization, but because of its integral importance to the thematics and narrative of the play. Welsford's arguments for the masque dimensions in *Midsummer* might all be repeated in this analysis of *Night Music*:

> The real soul of the masque . . . was the rhythmic movement of living bodies . . . In *A Midsummer Night's Dream* most—not all—of the dances are vitally connected with the plot. . . . The influence of the dance has affected not merely isolated songs and speeches, but the whole structure of [the play]. . . . The plot is a pattern, a figure rather than a series of events occasioned by human character and passion, and this pattern, especially in the moonlight parts of the play, is the pattern of a dance.[58]

The opening Night Waltz functions, as Gordon has pointed out, like an Elizabethan dumb show, wordlessly presenting the primary tensions of the plot, while also establishing the sometimes surreal elegance of the play's tone.[59] Its detachment from the diegesis not only gives it a dreamlike quality, but also a self-consciously theatrical one; if the Overture presents us with five singers, then the Night Waltz presents us with nine dancers.[60] Because we do not yet know who these people are, we focus on their movements and on the *mise-en-scène* of which they are a part. This visual waltz teaches us to watch for the *patterns* of coupling in the play, while the musical waltz hints at the three-part figures (love triangles) that will dominate the plot.[61] Stephen Banfield reminds us that the waltz further evokes the "bourgeois social and sexual coupling" of *fin-de-siècle* Europe.[62]

In the final moments of the play, the companion waltz not only represents narrative closure (showing us all of the couples, *"at last with their proper partners"* [185]), it also produces structural balance by closing the play with its opening melody. Likewise, the reappearance of Mr. Lindquist at the piano, striking a piano key, just as he did at the start of the Overture, executes a neat formal symmetry; the final words of the text, *"And the play is over"* (185), similarly draw attention to the theatrical structure. Gordon reads these closing gestures as constitutive of the text's "artifice, the sense that we're watching a play-within-a-play," and she maintains that this artifice demonstrates that "happily-ever-after romances can occur only in the unreal environ of operetta."[63] This analysis is useful, as it recognizes that form creates meaning, and that the self-consciousness of *Night Music*'s theatrical construct reflects crucial thematic concerns.

But it is here where *A Midsummer Night's Dream* might suggest further interpretive possibilities. Puck's closing speech, after all, similarly insists that an audience acknowledge the play *as a play*, calling attention to himself and the others who share the stage with him as actors:

> If we shadows have offended,
> Think but this, and all is mended,
> That you have but slumb'red here
> While these visions did appear.
> And this weak and idle theme,
> No more yielding but a dream,
> Gentles, do not reprehend.
> If you pardon, we will mend. (5.1.423-30)

But this speech goes one step further, and conflates acting and dreaming: Puck also invites his audience to consider the possibility that, like the lovers in the woods, they have merely dreamt all that they have seen—that, in other words, the "midsummer night's dream" is theirs. This would imply that the audience share the imaginative capacities of the lunatic, lover, and poet—for is there any significant difference between dreaming about fairies and believing in them? Puck is hardly allowing his audience to disregard or dismiss the magical events they have seen; he is merely shifting the source of those events from the pen of the poet to the minds of the audience themselves.

Just as Puck offers his audience the chance to believe in dreams, and not to belittle them as delusions, as Theseus might, the very dreamlike conclusion of *A Little Night Music* allows its audience an extended sojourn in the "green world" itself. While its closing moments may remind us that *Night Music* is but a play, the Shakespearean resonances across the text suggest that its very stature as a play gives it access to that "night-rule" that enchants the woods outside Athens as well as Madame Armfeldt's country estate. Enchantment, as we have seen in both plays, does not mean transformation so much as revelation; "magic" is another name for "insight," and what one sees with one's eyes closed may be nearer the truth than what daylight shows.

NOTES

[1] Sondheim and Wheeler 1991; Bergman 1960. Desirée is also moved to sing in Bergman's film—while walking with Fredrik from the theater back to her digs, and during the weekend party. Bergman's Henrik is also musical. He plays the piano excitedly while Fredrik and Anne nap; he plays "some stormy bars from Chopin's Fantasy-Impromptu" (106) after fleeing the dinner party at Madame Armfeldt's; and he woos Petra with a guitar.

[2] Bergman 1960, 124.

[3] Frid's song, "Silly People," was cut during the Boston tryouts because, Sondheim explains, "it was felt that . . . Frid wasn't important enough to spend some four minutes with" (Sondheim and Wheeler 1991, 200). David van Leer remarks that "the Bergman of *Night Music* is not the murky Freudian of *Virgin Spring* or *Cries and Whispers* but a lighthearted sentimentalist, strongly influenced by Viennese operetta (which in fact Bergman had been directing shortly before filming *Smiles of a Summer Night* . . .)" (van Leer 1987, 115-16). While *Smiles of a Summer Night* is for Bergman a lighthearted and sentimental comedy, it is not without a darkness characteristic of its *auteur*. Frank Gado observes, "Perverse as it may sound, Bergman's best comedy reads the human condition as dismally as his most pessimistic films. Its motto could be the 'one lesson' Mrs. Armfeldt says her many years have taught her: 'You can never protect a single human being from suffering'" (Gado 1986, 184). And Bergman's comment upon seeing *A Little Night Music* in 1993 confirms his own sense of the darkness of *Summer Night*: "I was surprised that it was possible to eliminate the shadows of desperation, eroticism, and caprice without the whole story collapsing. At the moment I forgot that this entertaining and witty musical had anything to do with my picture" (Prince 1974, 178).

[4] Throughout this essay I will refer to Bergman's published screenplay of *Smiles of a Summer Night*; unless I indicate otherwise, that screenplay closely represents the film as produced. Harold Prince explains that he, Sondheim, and Wheeler began the project by screening the film and reading the screenplay, and my analysis suggests that *A Little Night Music* is inspired by both sources, which do occasionally differ (Prince 1974, 172). For Shakespeare, see Shakespeare 1997.

[5] Andrew 1984, 98-9.

[6] Frye 1957, 182.

[7] The shift from the Shakespearean world of the court to the bourgeois world of the town—the shift, that is, from the lives of the nobility to the lives of the middle-classes—is described wistfully by Madame Armfeldt: "In a world where the kings are employers . . . In a world where the princes are lawyers" (68). This accurately captures the difference between the social milieus of *A Midsummer Night's Dream* and *A Little Night Music.*

[8] Michael Mangan argues that the lovers are seeking to escape a male-dominated world (the court where Egeus maintains power) through their flight to a female-dominated one (the aunt's home) (Mangan 1996, 155). In *Night Music*, we can trace a similar trajectory: the lovers leave homes where fathers and husbands rule, and weekend at a country house where a conspicuously matriarchal figure reigns.

[9] Mathematical or diagrammatic precision is repeatedly associated with all three texts. Writing of the lovers in Shakespeare's comedy, David P. Young remarks, "almost any discussion of them is apt to resort to diagrammatic figures" (Young 1966, 94). Similarly, Bergman initially conceived of *Smiles of a Summer Night* as a project in narrative cartography: "I thought of it as a technical challenge to write a comedy with a mathematical relationship: man—woman, man—woman . . . four pairs. Scramble them and then solve the equation" (Gado 1986, 181). And, both Stephen Banfield and Jonathan Tunick provide different diagrams for the affectional trajectories in *A Little Night Music*. See Banfield 1993, 227. For Tunick see Sondheim and Wheeler 1991, 2.

[10] In Bergman's film, Carl-Magnus and Charlotte are legitimately invited.

[11] Furthermore, Demetrius/Carl-Magnus is assumed dangerous to the health of Lysander/Fredrik by Hermia/Desirée: Hermia declares to Demetrius, "If thou hast slain Lysander in his sleep, / Being o'er shoes in blood, plunge in the deep, / And kill me too" (3.2.47-9); Desirée, seeing Carl-Magnus carry Fredrik over his shoulder, exclaims, "You lunatic! You've killed him" (181).

[12] By sheer coincidence, actress Diana Rigg played both roles on film: Helena in Peter Hall's *A Midsummer Night's Dream* (1968), and Charlotte in Harold Prince's *A Little Night Music* (1978).

[13] Zadan 1987, 182.

[14] The lyrics to all songs not included in the standard text of *A Little Night Music* are published as addenda to the Applause (1991) edition of the play, which I cite throughout this essay.

[15] This song finds its textual source in a dinner-scene speech of Malcolm's, which appears in the published screenplay but not in the film: "Here comes the man, marches up, shoots his broadside. Bang. The enemy retreats, takes new positions. New offensive. The positions are ripped up. Bang. Bang. Then the chase goes over stock and stone until the game—I mean the enemy—lays down his arms in front of superior forces, but I give no quarter. I raise my weapon and there she lies bleeding with love and devotion—I mean the enemy. Then I secure my position and make a wonderful meal, the feast of truce; passions rage, intoxication mounts, and the morning sun finds

the soldier in the arms of the enemy, slumbering sweetly. After a little while he gets up, girds his loins and starts out to do new deeds of bravery . . . New games—I mean enemies . . . (99, ellipses in original).

[16] This agonistic lovemaking evokes Theseus's depiction of his relations with Hippolyta: "Hippolyta, I woo'd thee with my sword, / And won thy love doing thee injuries" (1.1.16-17). Indeed, *A Midsummer Night's Dream* begins with precisely this metaphor of love as a battleground: Theseus has captured Hippolyta upon conquering the Amazons, of whom she was Queen—a scenario that establishes a thematic of patriarchal control that will play out in other narratives in the play (including the struggle between Oberon and Titania, and that between Egeus and Hermia). Peter Holland remarks, "Hippolyta has been conquered, defeated into marriage. Theseus is well aware that his courtship has been entirely military but his language leaves unclear whether she has simply agreed through defeat or whether she is now in love with him" (51).

[17] The distinctions between draft versions of this play and the final or official version are dismantled (usefully, I think) in the 1995 production for the Royal National Theatre (directed by Sean Mathias). This production incorporates "My Husband the Pig" into the montage number "In Praise of Women," and it folds the film version of "The Glamorous Life" into the standard stage version. Such reconstructions of the text suggest that we might consider *A Little Night Music* not so much a stable entity (the artefact of its original production) as an ever-shifting theatrical and narrative whole that includes all of the songs Sondheim ever wrote for it. Theorizing about the "four last songs" that Sondheim wrote for *Company*, Banfield proposes that we might "decline the scriptural authority of *Company*'s original production, its decisions and solutions, and collaborations . . . [and] paradoxically be able to grasp more facets of the conceptual truth by allowing the alternative endings equal validity, to suggest that all four songs ought to be in the score" (Banfield 1993, 164). Allowing such postmodern plenitude to shape our understanding of the text(s) of *A Little Night Music* would resist any traditionalist attempts to privilege a hierarchical analysis, in which trunk songs, for instance, are not regarded as valid or integral pieces of the whole.

[18] Leo Salinger identifies a relevant comic plot paradigm that is performed in *A Midsummer Night's Dream*: the "daughter's flight from an angry father to the woods, where by the aid of chance she is both united with her lover and reconciled with her father" (Salinger 1974, 28). It takes little distortion to see how this paradigm relates to Anne, Henrik, and Fredrik. Anne's regard for Fredrik is decidedly more daughterly than wifely, and both *Smiles of a Summer Night* and *A Little Night Music* suggest that Anne and Henrik are at least half-way in love with one another before they enter the "green world." In Bergman, after Anne and Fredrik return home from the theater, she asks, "Would you be jealous . . . if Henrik began courting me? Or if I became a little infatuated with him? I say this only as an example" (49). In *Night Music*, when she confronts Henrik's declaration of love, Anne responds, "Oh how scatterbrained I was never to have realized. Not Fredrik . . . not poor old Fredrik . . . not Fredrik at all" (172; ellipses in original).

[19] Shakespeare 1972, 31.

[20] In Kay Young's reading of the play, this ending suggests that by resisting any depiction of Fredrik and Desirée's married life, *Night Music* implies yet another Sondheim critique of marriage, conforming to the antisentimental romance narratives in musical plays such as *Company* (1970), *Follies* (1971), and *Sunday in the Park with George* (1984). Young reminds us that while Fredrik and Desirée sing "together a final line which is about their achieving at last a mutual presence to one another," they do so *before* they marry (Young 1994, 73). Stephen Banfield also reads the ending of the play as dark and portentous: "Henrik betrays his seminary puritanism, Anne loses her virginity and her position and wealth as Fredrik's wife, Fredrik, as he admits, loses his family and must surely lose his clients as a result of being prepared to "sit through all eight performances" of *Hedda Gabler* at Helsingborg [*sic*] for Desirée's sake prior to holidaying in Malmo, and with the breakup of his household Petra may well lose her job, as Frid must presumably lose his with the death of Mme. Armfeldt. . . . Their world is falling around them as they lie in the grass together; the waltz is a symbol of comic destruction" (Banfield 1993, 246-47). I'm not entirely sure that everything Banfield identifies as signs of destruction are quite that: Henrik's puritanism is a sad and blighting influence on his life; Anne's virginity results from her marrying the wrong man; there is no particular reason to assume that Fredrik will lose clients merely because he's gone on holiday; and the conclusion of the narrative brings Fredrik, Desirée, and Fredrika together, creating a legitimate family for Fredrika.

[21] Describing the (re)arrangements of partners in *A Midsummer Night's Dream*, G. K. Hunter suggests how the dance can function as a metaphor for the romance plot: "The pattern of the dance is what matters, and the pattern is one which works through an alternation of errors, trying out all possible combinations of persons: Helena in love with Demetrius, Demetrius in love with Hermia, Hermia in love with Lysander, and then (change partners) Hermia in love with Lysander, Lysander in love with Helena, Helena in love with Demetrius, Demetrius in love with Hermia—but this is worse, so change again: Hermia in love with Lysander, Lysander in love with Helena, Helena in love with Demetrius, but completely at a loss when Demetrius seems to be pretending to return her love; finally we settle on the only stable arrangement, where no-one is left out" (Hunter 1962, 10). The lyrics for "Love Takes Time," the opening waltz in the film version of *A Little Night Music* (1978), similarly captures this pattern of errors and recuperation: "Curious, love is, / Self-tormenting, / Embarrassing, love is, / Unrelenting, / A labyrinth, love is. / Just resenting / The time love takes / Compounds the confusion it makes. / One muddles the facts with the fakes. / And love is a lecture / On how to correct your / Mistakes" (209).

[22] Holland 1994, 110.

[23] Garber 1974 59-60.

[24] Mangan 1996, 157.

[25] As Holland points out, there is but one literal dream in *A Midsummer Night's Dream*: Hermia's nightmare of being attacked by a serpent (2.2.146-150) (Holland 1994, 4). This might, indeed, be read as a phallic threat, as "Lysander has presented

Hermia with the problem of his sexual desire, and her dream enacts her anxiety about it" (13). The serpent might also evoke a less particularly sexual threat to the Edenic "green world" where the lovers find themselves. Both readings, however, grant to dreams a power to re-present (indeed, to envision) what is not immediately apparent to the conscious mind. For a useful discussion of the roots of English Renaissance dream-analysis, see Holland 1994, 3-16.

[26] Garber 1974, 62.

[27] Like Henrik's piano-playing and Desirée's singing, Fredrik's whistling expresses the less restrained part of his character.

[28] Zadan 1987, 182.

[29] Gordon 1990, 124.

[30] Prince 1974, 174-75. Prince also notes that "Each is a personality, each has a response to the events of the evening. No two are alike" (175). They are named throughout the text (Mr. Lindquist, Mrs. Nordstrom, Mrs. Anderssen, Mr. Erlanson, and Mrs. Segstrom), and two of them have names referenced in the narrative itself. While Fredrik sings "Now," Anne complains about "that grumpy old Mrs. Nordstrom from next door" (32), and Fredrik identifies one of his "typists and things" as "Mrs. Amalia Lindquist" (45).

[31] Prince 1974, 175.

[32] Much of this characterization is adapted pretty directly from Bergman. In *Summer Night*, for instance, Petra and Frid even have the film's final lines—celebrating their own lusty appreciation of life, acknowledging those who cannot share it, and wryly commenting on those who allow life to pass them by: "FRID: There isn't a better life than this. / PETRA: And then the summer night smiled for the third time. / FRID: For the sad, the depressed, the sleepless, the confused, the frightened, the lonely. / PETRA: But the clowns will have a cup of coffee in the kitchen (124).

[33] In Bergman, this sentiment is even more conspicuously framed as a statement of *carpe diem*: when Petra discovers that the statue of a "magnificently shaped woman" represents the youthful Madame Armfeldt, she exclaims, "My God, what life does to us"; Frid responds in a line that is obviously one of the direct inspirations for "The Miller's Son," "Take advantage of every moment" (92-3).

[34] Frid has few significant spoken lines in the standard version of the play, though the sentiments of "Silly People" can be traced in his comments to Petra about his mistress's weekend guests: "You saw them all at dinner, dressed up like waxworks, jabbering away to prove how clever they are. And never knowing what they miss. . . . Catch one of them having the sense to grab the first pretty girl that comes along—and do her on the soft grass with the summer night smiling down" (166).

[35] This sense is very movingly evoked in the New York City Opera production (1990), directed by Scott Ellis; during Desirée and Fredrik's final reconciliation, Fredrika is visible behind a window of the facade of the country house, watching her mother and (putative) father reunite.

[36] This reading of Fredrika corresponds to the characterization of Desirée's child in *Smiles of a Summer Night*. Here, the child is a four-year-old boy, who never speaks,

and his initial appearance (during Fredrik's visit to Desirée's rooms) is practically occult: "The door to another room is slowly opened and both of them turn around. Nothing is seen at first; then a boy about four years old appears, dressed in a long nightshirt. He marches through the room and marches out through another door without taking notice of Fredrik and Desirée" (64). Fredrik's initial response, "*What* was that" (64; my emphasis), hints at the spectral or fairylike quality that the boy possesses. He appears in the film infrequently, typically under the care of either Desirée or Madame Armfeldt. While he and Fredrika serve the same function narratively (to suggest that Fredrik and Desirée have had a child and that their ultimate union represents the consolidation of a family), Wheeler and Sondheim obviously develop a more resonant and complex character.

[37] Bergman apparently sees her in this light: when the dinner guests are walking out to the yellow pavilion for coffee and liqueurs, he tells us that "Frid walks in front, carrying the old lady like an ikon" (105).

[38] She would not have been unlike the postmodern narrator–author of John Fowles's *The French Lieutenant's Woman* (1969), who, by setting his pocket-watch back a quarter of an hour, effects a revised replay of the novel's final scene. Even Fowles cannot resist comparing such supernatural command over the lives of others to theatrical directing or stage managing: his narrator stares at the scene of his influence "with an almost proprietory air, as if it is some new theater he has just bought and is pretty confident he can fill. . . . he very evidently regards the world as his to possess and use as he likes." Fowles 1969, 475.

[39] Gordon 1990, 147.

[40] Welsford 1962, 324-35.

[41] The stage directions describe the dances as "stylized" (158), suggesting that these movements merely represent interior states of mind and are not "really" happening during the dinner. The New York City Opera production, on the other hand, opted for more "realism," and staged the waltzes as after-dinner dancing.

[42] In *Summer Night*, the camera lingers on each guest as he or she partakes of the wine: Desirée "drinks deeply"; Malcolm "finishes his glass in one draught and then allows the top of his tongue to play over his lips"; Anne drinks to "my love," Charlotte to "My success," Fredrik to Anne; Henrik, after a moment's indecision, empties "the whole glass and [puts] it down so violently that he cracks its fragile stem" (100-01). In *Night Music*, the stage directions state that "*Only* MADAME ARMFELDT *and* CHARLOTTE *drink*" (159). We may take this to mean that the other characters are not even self-aware enough to know that they are blind and in need of the magical wine, or that they are afraid of what the wine will reveal to others and to themselves. That the wine is not directly responsible for the attacks of honesty that shape the remaining events of the evening does not mean that it serves no purpose as a catalyst, however; we might say that the wine contributes to the "heady" atmosphere and "thrilling" ambiance, which Mr. Lindquist sings of (143), and which is surely experienced by all of Madame Armfeldt's guests.

[43] This is presumably Wheeler's creative decision; in Bergman's film, Madame Armfeldt does not die.

[44] A more political reading of the play would likely propose that, representing an outmoded aristocratic order, Madame Armfeldt must die before the middle classes can assume ascendency. Given the play's *fin-de-siècle* context, such an overthrow of the established order would anticipate the social and economic disruptions that would accompany World War I.

[45] Like the aliens to mirth in so many of Shakespeare's comedies, there is no place for her at the weddings that will close this narrative. In *A Midsummer Night's Dream*, Egeus does not appear as part of the act 5 wedding party; from the beginning of the play opposed to the desires of the young lovers, Egeus cannot celebrate the consummation of those desires.

[46] Laroque 1991, 140-41.

[47] Laroque 1991, 217.

[48] Strutt 1876, 458.

[49] Barber 1959, 120.

[50] Frazer 1959, 81-2; 87.

[51] Frazer 1959, 90; Strutt 1876, 464; Laroque 1991, 25-6.

[52] Spurgeon 1935, 260-61.

[53] Titania describes an analogous correspondence between the discord in her relationship with Oberon and disturbances in nature: "The seasons alter: hoary-headed frosts / Fall in the fresh lap of the crimson rose, / And on old Hiems' thin and icy crown / An odorous chaplet of sweet summer buds / Is, as in mockery, set; the spring, the summer, / The childing autumn, angry winter, change / Their wonted liveries; and the mazed world, / By their increase, now knows not which is which. / And this same progeny of evils comes / From our debate, from our dissension . . . " (2.1.107-16).

[54] This section of my essay will focus almost exclusively on the two plays, and reference Bergman's film only occasionally.

[55] In such a case, *A Midsummer Night's Dream* might have ended more like *Romeo and Juliet*, the play that Shakespeare wrote within the same three year period during which he wrote *Midsummer*.

[56] The corresponding scene in Bergman's film does not create the same sense of interplay between theatrical scene and frame scene; while many of the screenplay's lines are reproduced exactly in *Night Music*, the two dramatic levels do not work in tandem, as they do in the musical play.

[57] Hirsch 1989, 106.

[58] Welsford 1962, 330-31.

[59] Gordon 1990, 128. James Goldman finds these two openings ineffective: "I never thought that the lieder singers singing the opening was an overture. . . . I thought it was the start of the show" (quoted in Zadan 1994, 191). I hardly want to dispute the observations of an accomplished writer for the stage and screen, but I wonder what else a medley of songs presented at the start of a musical play could be other than an overture. Goldman continues, "Then there was that dance. . . . unless you knew

the show, you wouldn't have a clue that those people who were dancing were characters in the show. The things they did in the dance had application to what came later but you didn't know that in the beginning" (Zadan 1994, 192). This confusion must have occurred frequently in the Renaissance and pre-Renaissance theater, where dumb-shows typically introduced plays, but whose audiences, we may assume, were able to recall later in the plays the images presented in the opening dumb-shows.

[60] The film version of *Night Music* makes this self-conscious theatricality much more conspicuous, by actually filming the opening and closing waltzes on the stage of a theater. With camera shots of the backs of stage flats and the manual movement of stage machinery, this version of the opening dance foregrounds the thematics of acting as pretence—the public masks that hide actual feeling. The shift toward the close of the dance from the stage to a realistic woods setting is perhaps meant to evoke the magic of theater (its ability to transport audiences to other places), but only serves to remind me, at least, of how much complexity is lost by removing the theatrical frame from *A Little Night Music.*

[61] Tunick explores the extent to which this symmetry of form is evident in the play: "Sondheim tends here toward trios with the characters separated ('Now,' 'Later,' 'Soon') and duets regarding a third person ('You Must Meet My Wife,' 'It Would Have Been Wonderful,' 'Every Day a Little Death')." These songs of alienation and yearning for cohesion and balance all represent the unstable number three drawn to the stable two—the triangle yearning to be reconciled to the proper couple (Sondheim and Wheeler 1991, 3).

[62] Banfield 1993, 227.

[63] Gordon 1990, 152.

CHAPTER 8

Arresting Development
Law, Love, and the Name-of-the-Father
in *Sweeney Todd*

Joseph Marchesani

In January 1996, I took one of my undergraduate arts classes to see *Sweeney Todd* at Pittsburgh's Public Theater, my first experience with a live performance of Sondheim's musical. Featuring Len Cariou in the title role he had originated, the performance, I felt, realized most of the show's aims: its trajectory through dark comedy and horrific melodrama proved at once arresting and disturbing. Subsequent discussion with my students suggested that they, too, had been caught up in this artfully dissonant reenactment of Todd's murderous career.

Some months later, I found myself trying to explain—for a conference in Cortland, New York—the arresting grip and disturbing pull that Sondheim's musical seemed to exert on me, on my students, and on many others who have been fascinated by this work. As I developed my explanation, I focused increasingly on the psychodynamics that seem to transform Todd from the nearly eradicated Benjamin Barker into the mythically inscribed "Demon Barber of Fleet Street."[1] And as I focused on this climactic transformation of Todd, I relied—with increasing interest—on Jacques Lacan's psychoanalytic theories.

Todd remains, of course, a literary creation. But Lacan himself has made use of literary figures in developing his theories. In his famous *Seminar*, for example, he turns to *Oedipus at Colonus* and *Amphitryon* to explain key ideas.[2] What will interest me in the explication of Sondheim's musical that follows are the ways in which the psychodynamics of a fictional creation like Todd align themselves with the terms used to describe real human beings in a theory as complex and tantalizing as Lacan's. Todd's psychodynamics are so clear and artfully constructed that Lacanian concepts seem at times tailored to the task.

In explicating Todd's psychodynamics, then, I will use Lacan's theory—particularly his notions of the Imaginary, the Symbolic, and the Real registers in which for him human psychodynamics function—to do the following: (1) to describe Todd's disturbed mentality as a multistage process that transforms him from the "naive" Benjamin Barker to the psychotic "Demon Barber of Fleet Street;" and (2) to consider how those registers resonate through Todd's interaction with other principal characters in the play, with Mrs. Lovett and Judge Turpin, with Anthony and Johanna, and with the Beggar Woman (Lucy) and Tobias Ragg.

Lacan's reworking of psychoanalytic theory replaces Freud's biological model with a verbal model indebted to Ferdinand de Saussure. In Lacan's threefold system, the Imaginary, the Symbolic, and the Real orders are registers that redesign the psychoanalytic map. Lacan's three registers provide sites in which the subject's psychological experiences exist as processes of signification. In Saussure, signification is discussed as a theory of signs, which is to say, the separability of a signifier from a signified. In these processes as Lacan uses them, the subject does not apprehend the signified directly; the signified is present only through its signifiers. At the same time, the relationship between signifier and signified remains a dynamic and unstable one, a process that is always incomplete and subject to reinterpretation.[3]

In each of Lacan's three registers, the relationship between signifier and signified varies characteristically. In the Imaginary, the subject (as ego) tries to construct itself from its identification with the "other" as an entity that is complete and autonomous. In aiming at a fixed and static identity, however, it contradicts the dynamic instability between the signifiers and the signified, denying what makes the other something else, as if it could absorb the other into itself.[4] In *Sweeney Todd*, perhaps the most direct example of this illusory quality in the Imaginary occurs as Todd identifies with Judge Turpin, seeking to counter the eradication of Barker by assuming the Judge's autonomy and illicit power for himself.

In Lacan's Symbolic register (which is also for him the register of the unconscious), the subject operates through a reticulated chain of signifiers—cross-linked and looping back on themselves—in a dynamic system that is always in the process of becoming, in which the subject is always driven to pursue the unapprehendable signified.[5] In *Sweeney Todd*, the most direct example of this elusive and restless dynamic probably lies in the concept of the law and capitalistic enterprise. Both operate as systems of signifiers, but what they signify has been corrupted and dehumanized. Within these systems, Barker tries—and fails—to make his living and support his family. After Barker's failure, Todd interprets the systems as misdirected desire and misallocated power in his pursuit of Judge Turpin. And when Todd fails at first to kill the Judge, the Demon Barber tries to become these systems, making the desire they evoke and their power his own.

Operating within both the Imaginary and the Symbolic registers at once, the subject experiences these register as conflicting arenas. The conflict is further complicated by the subject's experience of Lacan's Real as anything, mental or material, that the Imaginary and the Symbolic cannot assimilate.[6] In one sense, this Real exists as the shards of experience that can be neither woven into the Symbolic's chains of signifiers nor absorbed within the Imaginary as the illusory elements of the other. When the unassimilated elements experienced in the Real are psychologically damaging, they become the basis for the trauma that can trigger psychosis. In this sense, *Sweeney Todd* offers its most direct examples at two crisis points. The first is the series of events that eradicate Benjamin Barker's identity, and the second is Todd's initial failure to kill Judge Turpin. In both instances, we may say that the generation of signifiers fails for these events: in Lacan's sense, they are beyond imagining, and the Symbolic cannot integrate them into the chains of signification where the subject operates.

We can summarize the personal trajectory of Todd's catastrophic and ultimately self-destructive career by saying it is defined by the reconstruction of his ego at these two critical points. The first point, which transforms him into a criminal (Sweeney Todd), occurs after Judge Turpin effectively destroys Benjamin Barker, Todd's earlier "naive" identity, by falsely convicting Benjamin in order to debauch Lucy Barker, his "beautiful" wife. In Lacanian terms, we can describe this transformation into the criminal (from Barker into Todd) as the transgression of his Symbolic register by his Imaginary one. Between Todd's return to London and his initial failure to kill the Judge, his mission of vengeance remains personal: revenge on the Judge for the wrongs done to Benjamin Barker.

As Alfred Mollin has noted, however, Todd's initial failure to kill the Judge provokes an escalation in the intensity with which he experiences the desire for vengeance, an escalation that transforms his more personal revenge into a mission of universal vengeance. The wronged barber metamorphoses into the world's avenger.[7] Once this metamorphosis has taken place, all humanity becomes Todd's target. Thus, the second reconstruction, which transforms Todd into a psychopath (the "Demon Barber of Fleet Street"), occurs when he fails to kill the Judge after returning to London expressly to do so. In Lacanian terms, we can describe Todd's transformation into the psychotic, into the Demon Barber, as the subsuming of his Symbolic register completely by his Imaginary one.

Within the dramatic action of Sondheim's musical, Todd's interaction with the other principal characters articulates these two critical points of transformation. Throughout the musical, Todd's interactions with these characters provide the telling moments that spell out how these transformations occur and the consequences that they have for all involved. What makes these interactions integral to a Lacanian analysis of Todd is the way that they frame the dynamic in which the Imaginary subsumes the Symbolic within the greater context of Lacan's three registers.

As we prepare for a more detailed explication of the psychodynamics of Todd's character, we can outline this framing articulation by saying that the action of the musical incorporates each of Lacan's registers through a pair of characters. Through Todd's interaction with each pair, they articulate the significance that the Lacanian registers have for Todd. In this scheme, Anthony and Johanna articulate the Imaginary, Judge Turpin and Mrs. Lovett articulate the Symbolic, and the Beggar Woman (Lucy) and Tobias Ragg articulate the Real. For Todd's psychodynamics, this scheme enacts the dialectical counteraction as Todd's mentality transforms into psychosis. As Todd's Imaginary turns psychotic and subsumes his Symbolic, the self-confounding conflict unleashes the Real, the register in which the "death instinct" operates. For a time, the Demon Barber aspires to be death, but in the greater scheme, the Demon Barber, too, must die.

I

Our understanding of Todd begins with Benjamin Barker, the identity Todd assumed before he was falsely convicted and transported to Australia by Judge Turpin. Most of our information about Barker comes through three scenes: (1) the song with which Todd inverts Anthony's innocent perception of London at the opening of act 1 by telling Anthony about an unnamed "barber and his wife" (32-3); (2) Mrs. Lovett's sequel in the next scene, which not only amplifies the details of Todd's song, but also enables her to identify Todd as Benjamin Barker (37-40); and (3) the subsequent scene in which Pirelli also identifies Todd as Barker, having seen Todd's razors and his barbering skills (78).

These scenes tell us who Barker was and what has happened to him. As Barker, Todd had the ego of an ordinary adult male, one whose sexuality would seem to have been realized in taking a wife, Lucy, who bore him a daughter, Johanna. In retrospect, however, Todd bitterly faults the barber for being "foolish" and "naive," failings that Mrs. Lovett later amplifies by adding that such "foolishness" was a "crime." Pirelli's effort to blackmail Todd by threatening to expose him as Barker also amplifies this concept of naïveté: Pirelli believes that Todd is identical to the naive Barker, who could not protect himself or his family, and Pirelli's mistake exemplifies a folly of his own that will prove no less dire than Barker's had been.

In Lacanian terms, Barker's naïveté characterizes the illusory quality within his ego. Operating in the Imaginary register, the ego is constructed by identifying with what is outside itself, its experience of the "other."[8] This construction, as we pointed out above, aims at stabilizing its identity, at giving it a fixed value; what it finds desirable in the other, it wants to incorporate within itself. The process is unidirectional. It wants to be autonomous and empowered. But for Lacan, the identity it achieves is a virtual construction, like the image in a mirror: it is decipherable but not there.[9]

For Barker, this means that the stability of the world and the role he envisions for himself in it are insubstantial. In his naïveté, what he imagines for himself and his family cannot stand up to the forces arrayed against them. That illusory world is summed up by the "London" of which Anthony sings, the London of city bells that call to him of desirable possibilities (29).[10] For Todd, who has been forcibly disabused of such illusions, that London cannot exist. His London can only be a "hole in the world / Like a great black pit" (32) where that London that others imagined had seemed to be.[11]

The London that Todd imagines after his return is more congruent than that of Barker or Anthony with the Symbolic register, especially as that register is displayed in the dehumanizing systems of commerce and the law that define the social milieu for this musical drama. While these systems do not seem to have been significant for Barker previously and operated outside his naive awareness, they exist as powerful operators for Todd. In eradicating Barker's naive imagining, though, the law develops as a powerful system of signifiers for Todd, interconnecting his much darker conceptions of human nature, its corrupted desires and self-serving power.

In Lacan, as we noted above, the Symbolic is the register through which the unconscious makes its appearance, operating as a system of interlinking signifiers or the "Other," a dynamic network through which one's identity is always in the process of becoming, always being reformulated.[12] In *Sweeney Todd*, this system of signifiers operates as a judicial system that has been corrupted and an economic system that rewards only ruthless pragmatism. Amid this system, Barker's foolishness is criminal in at least two senses: it victimizes him and it victimizes those who depended on him.

Mrs. Lovett's amplification of Todd's song recounts this victimization for us. Lustful, corrupt, and powerful, Judge Turpin has Barker arrested falsely and then sentences him to be transported to Botany Bay, the penal colony of Australia. With Barker removed, the Judge rapes the unprotected Lucy. The rape is mimed for us as Mrs. Lovett sings, reinforcing her verbal account with visual force. When Todd's reaction to that account confirms for her his previous identity as Benjamin Barker, she tells him that Lucy has poisoned herself and that Judge Turpin has taken the infant Johanna to rear as his ward. Desiring Todd for herself, however, she reaffirms the destruction of Barker's naive ego by withholding the crucial information that Lucy survived the poison, albeit as the lewd and pathetic Beggar Woman.

Obviously the stuff of stagy melodrama, Mrs. Lovett's account nevertheless suggests the multiple ways in which the eradication of Todd's identity as Barker has also demasculinized him. The process by which he is arrested, convicted, and exiled strips him of the markers for the others that he had used to construct his identity as an adult male: his livelihood, his home, and his family. His roles as husband and father are eradicated by the separation that denies him further social and sexual congress with his wife, that removes him as the protector for her and their daughter, and that destroys his ability to provide for them by working as a barber. Exacerbating these traumatic insults to Barker's masculinity, Judge Turpin himself illicitly usurps Barker's marital and paternal rights by raping Lucy and seizing custody of Johanna.

To understand in Lacanian terms how this process demasculinizes Barker, we need to introduce Lacan's concepts of the Phallus and the Name-of-the-Father, concepts which he identifies as preeminent signifiers in the Symbolic register.[13] Lacan's concept of the Phallus includes at least three attributes that are of use here. Distinguished from the penis because it is figured as always erect, it is linked to the Real because it can produce other beings. As the first object of pleasure, it becomes the signifier for the impelling force of desire in human nature. Subsequently associated by the imagination with either the penis or the clitoris, however, it can generate the castration anxiety that is connected to another key Lacanian concept, the Name-of-the-Father, which signifies all agencies that would restrict desire or threaten to punish transgressions.[14]

We can see how these concepts help to explicate Barker's demasculinization. Although Mrs. Lovett's account depicts Barker as Johanna's biological father, Judge Turpin's adoption of her makes him her legal parent; in *Sweeney Todd*, it is the Judge and not Todd whom she addresses as "father" (49 and 72). As we noted above, the judicial system in *Sweeney Todd* is corrupt, but we can see now as well that this corrupt judicial system also operates as the Name-of-the-Father. As it demasculinizes Barker by depriving him of his wife and his work, it certainly restricts his desire, and it punishes his naïveté with a trumped up conviction and a life sentence to Botany Bay.

Moreover, the power of these concepts resonates symbolically in the barber's razors that are lost to Barker until he can return to Fleet Street as Todd. Not only are the razors, as the very tools of his trade, essential to his ability to provide for himself and his family, but they also signify the crucial ambivalence in the nature of sexual identity. On the one hand, they evoke the power of sexual desire, the erotic allure that their grooming is meant to enhance. In the musical, we can observe this allure in action when the Beadle sings "Ladies in Their Sensitivities" to persuade Judge Turpin to visit Todd the first time to make a more presentable appearance for Johanna (86-7). On the other hand, the razors also operate as a negative Phallus, evoking the threat of emasculation, the castration anxiety of a thwarted or lost sexuality.

By eradicating Barker's oppressors, the razors—especially when Todd raises them over his head—suggest that Todd's penchant for slitting throats turns the demasculinizing process that had victimized Benjamin Barker back against other men. *Sweeney Todd* highlights this reversal quite powerfully, by presenting, first, Todd's metaphoric description of the Judge as a "vulture" with a "claw" (32) and, then, Todd's metonymic self-description as he lofts his largest razor at the end of "My Friends" with the exultant exclamation, "My right arm is complete again!" (43).

Throughout the musical, Todd demasculinizes his victims. His first victim, Pirelli, who reveals himself as a protégé of Barker, the professional equivalent of a son, has taken on his own professional dependent, Tobias Ragg. In their first encounter after Todd returns to London, Todd bests Pirelli professionally, but his skill and Pirelli's observation of Todd's distinctive razors enable Pirelli to identify Todd as Barker. Unfortunately for Pirelli, Todd is not the naive fool that Barker was. When Pirelli threatens to expose him, Todd first chokes him and then slashes his throat. Parallel to Judge Turpin's adoption of Johanna after Barker was transported, Pirelli's death at Todd's hands leaves Tobias to the parental embrace of Mrs. Lovett.

Like the scene depicting the death of Pirelli, the musical's remaining scenes insist on the masculinity of Todd's victims. In the deliciously macabre duet, "A Little Priest," which concludes act 1, all of the victims anticipated by Todd and Mrs. Lovett are male, and the sexual innuendo becomes most explicit when she responds to Todd's request for "general" by asking, "With or without his privates?" (110). With the notable exceptions of Mrs. Lovett (whose throat Todd does not slash) and the Beggar Woman (whom he repeatedly fails to recognize as Lucy), Todd's victims in act 2 are other men (154-58). And when Todd finally does succeed in killing Judge Turpin, he lures the Judge back to his barber chair by promising that Johanna will be there, teases the Judge with hints that she is ready for his advances, and slashes his throat only when he has aroused the Judge's anticipation as fully as possible (194).

Despite the associations linking the Phallus with castration anxiety, Lacan insists on the Phallus' preeminence in the Symbolic order because he also identifies it as the signifier for pleasure, the primary force in human desire.[15] In explaining the concept of desire, he theorizes that desire operates not just from a need requiring some effort from an other to be met, but also from a demand that eroticizes the effort; that is to say, the other's effort to meet the need must include a sense of love. At the same time, Lacan asserts that desire can never be fulfilled because the love demanded would have to be unconditional and absolute; no other has the ability to respond adequately. That such desire can never be fulfilled provides an ongoing intimation of death.[16]

With the traumatic undoing of Barker's naively constructed ego, a large psychic hole gapes where Barker's desire for a mature sexuality and masculine autonomy had been. To experience that hole is to be suspended in an inescapable castration anxiety, an anxiety that provokes the reconstruction of Barker's ego as Sweeney Todd's. We should note here that Barker's new name, Todd, incorporates the German word for death, "Tod." For Todd, the connotations of death will operate in all the Lacanian registers.

When Todd first returns to London, his ego identifies itself with Judge Turpin and the overwhelming power with which the Judge had eradicated Benjamin Barker. Nominally a figure of the law, Judge Turpin, as we have

noted, has corrupted the law to serve his own desires. Paralleling the way in
which Todd's name incorporates the idea of death, his rhyming interpretation
of the Judge, subsumes the "law" within a metaphoric "claw":

> A pious vulture of the law
> Who with a gesture of his claw
> Removed the barber from his plate (32)

In his new guise, Todd will bend the law to serve his desire, and in doing
so, he, too, will operate as a claw, a scavenger-avenger. And Todd's claw is, of
course, razor-sharp, fatally so.

Considered for its psychodynamics, this transformation suggests that
Todd's initial failure to kill the Judge operates like a reenactment of the traumatic events that had transformed Barker into Todd. Now, however, the traumatic assault afflicts Todd himself, so that his ego is impelled to reconstruct
itself in terms that are even more extreme. If the earlier reconstruction enabled the Imaginary to transgress the Symbolic, this new reconstruction enables it to subsume the Symbolic entirely. From this point on, Todd's ego is
reconstructed as that of "the Demon Barber."

To explain psychosis, Lacan distinguishes between that which the mind
would repress and that which it would expel. That which it would expel are
those elements of the Real which profoundly threaten its operation, in other
words, the events of a trauma. In a psychosis, however, the effort to expel
such elements is confounded. Instead, they return, as if from outside the self,
manifesting themselves as the Name-of-the-Father and generating a castration anxiety so acute that the Symbolic is overwhelmed in a proliferation of
delusional signifiers.[17] In *Sweeney Todd*, then, crossing into the delusional
means the creation of an even more megalomaniacal subject, the Demon Barber, in which the Imaginary subsumes the Symbolic, redefining Todd as
death's own agent.

II

We can now extend our explication of Todd in Lacanian terms by observing
how the triad of the Imaginary, the Symbolic, and the Real has also been embodied in the cast of characters surrounding Todd. The redistribution of a protagonist's psychological dynamic among the other dramatis personae has
long been a characteristic of the theater's literary artistry. We need only consider how many aspects of Oedipus, for example, are mirrored in Creon, Tire-
sias, Jocasta, and even the Shepherd to note how this technique enriches the
work's formal coherence even as it enables the essential conflict to resonate
across the entire dramatic action. At the same time, as distributed among
these other characters, the three registers provide a dialectical counter-action

as Todd grows increasingly psychotic. It is this counteraction that enables the musical to shift Todd from death's agent to death's subject, so that the tale can be resolved with Todd's own death.

In the action of *Sweeney Todd*, we can see how Sondheim's dramatic sensibility positions Todd amid three pairs of characters who can signify the workings in Todd of the Imaginary, the Symbolic, and the Real. Each of Lacan's three registers, in fact, is signified by a male and a female character: the Imaginary by Anthony and Johanna, the Symbolic by Judge Turpin and Mrs. Lovett, and the Real by Tobias and the Beggar Woman (Lucy).

As we have noted earlier, in Lacan's Imaginary register the ego aims to fix its identity as complete and autonomous. Through Todd, we can associate this process with Anthony, whose character is most like that of the eradicated Benjamin Barker, and in Johanna, whose character is most like that of the comparably eradicated Lucy. Like Barker, Anthony is fixed on a belief in the absolute power of romantic love and convinced that his desire for it can be fulfilled by Johanna. Like Barker's Lucy, Johanna is beautiful and innocent, and she is almost reckless in the pursuit of her own romantic attachment with Anthony. As Todd observes in his response to Anthony's initial rapture about London, "You are young. / Life has been kind to you. / You will learn." (29).

Even as Anthony and Johanna desire to come together in the unrealizable ideal world that had been the desire of Barker and his Lucy, however, their movement through *Sweeney Todd* suggests how the Imaginary does not allow the subject to prevail within its register. In conceptualizing the Imaginary, Lacan uses the analogy of a mirror: looking in it, the subject believes in the truth of the reflection, but what the subject sees is virtual, not the object itself, but an appearance. Throughout *Sweeney Todd*, Anthony and Johanna seem especially prone to visual mistakes, attributing a truth to appearances that remains unsupported.

The scene in which Anthony first encounters Johanna helps to reveal how this quality of the Imaginary operates at cross-purposes with the realization of their desires. Consider, for example, the songbird that Anthony uses to gain Johanna's attention. Johanna's first song, addressed to all the captive birds, asks how they can sing in captivity when the lark that she keeps will not. As she sings, the audience hears the tender sentimentality of her question and senses the pathos of her confinement as Judge Turpin's ward.

Singing from her second-story window, her attention on the birds, she does not see Anthony in the street below and does not hear him singing for her to look at him. Caught up in the world she is imagining for the birds, a caged world that appears like her own, she neither sees nor hears the attractive young man in front of her. When she finally does notice him, they fall silent, and before they can speak, the Beggar Woman distracts Anthony, and Johanna darts back inside (44-6). Although this part of the scene may seem merely like an ornamental interlude to much of the audience, an expository piece to introduce the ingenue, some audience members still attending to the tale of Sweeney Todd may detect an echo of Benjamin Barker's imprisonment and the obsessive focus that already characterizes his return as Todd.

When Anthony and Johanna resume their tentative tryst, the initial sentimentality and pathos of the songbirds is glossed more darkly. For when Anthony asks why the bird he is buying to lure Johanna out of the house beats its wings against its cage, the seller explains, "We blind 'em, sir . . . and not knowing night from day, they sing and sing without stopping" (48). In all likelihood, this is not the answer that Johanna would imagine to the question in her song. At the very least, it suggests that sentimental imagining can only persist when a world like London cannot be seen for what it is.

What can be seen in a world like London is revealed in the scene's conclusion, when the lovers-to-be are discovered by Judge Turpin and the Beadle. At the Judge's order to drive Anthony away, the Beadle grabs the bird from its cage and wrings its neck. In case Anthony misses the import of this action, the Beadle threatens him: "Next time it'll be *your* neck!" (49). As the Beadle's action and his threat extend the meaning of the bird from Johanna to Anthony, the audience can also extend its meaning to all transgressors of London's law.

If this interpretation suggests a link between the Imaginary register and the illusions of desire, that link is reinforced within the scene by the moments in which Anthony is distracted from Johanna by the Beggar Woman. In their previous encounter, when Anthony had just arrived in London with Todd, his reaction and Todd's reaction to her had provided sharply contrasting expositions for their characters. Todd's almost violent rejection of her sexual solicitation had led to his veiled recounting of his lost past. The irony, of course, is that the "beautiful" Lucy whom Todd recalls has become the lewd Beggar Woman he now rejects. As he reimagines what he has lost, he cannot see what his wife has become. In contrast, Anthony, while deflecting her bawdy invitation more gently than Todd does, sees in her only a half-crazed beggar, deserving of pity and a coin (30-1).

Interrupting Anthony's approach to Johanna, the Beggar Woman's second interaction with Anthony enriches the association between the misperceptions of the Imaginary and the illusions of desire. According to the stage directions, she thrusts "a clawlike hand" from a pile of trash where she has been concealed as she thrusts her begging bowl at him (46). The description, of course, echoes Todd's metaphor for Judge Turpin from the song mentioned in the earlier paragraph. As if she were now endowed with a power like the Judge's, the effect, here, also separates the young couple.

When she has appealed to Anthony as "a miserable woman" for a few more coins, she begins to shuffle off, but before she can disappear again, he calls to her to answer several questions for him. Between the stage direction and the lines which immediately follow, we can infer that the analogy of the songbirds, already attached to other characters in this scene, has applications to her as well: in the metonyme of the claw, in the pathos of her approach to Anthony, and in the interrogation to which she is put. Audience members who have identified her as the ruin of Barker's Lucy, might detect additional parallels in the way she was ensnared by the Judge and in the poison that she took as a kind of blinding for her wits.

Unintentionally invoking that previous trauma, Anthony calls her "mother" (46), and his questions ask her to identify the house as Judge Turpin's and Johanna as the Judge's ward. After identifying Johanna for Anthony, the Beggar Woman warns him not to trespass there with "mischief on his mind" (47), now anticipating what will happen if the Judge should discover the two together. From that warning, she quickly slides into another bawdy solicitation, appalling Anthony by grabbing his crotch and lifting up her skirts.

This turn to the scene offers the sharpest possible contrasts to the romantic idealism that Anthony and Johanna imagine for themselves. The contrasts point us in two directions. One is the guilty lust that characterizes Judge Turpin's desire in his rape of Lucy and obsession with Johanna. The other is the less hypocritical lust that the Beggar Woman tries to satisfy for money. If Johanna is the image of her mother from Barker's illusory London, the Beggar Woman is her mother in the London of Sweeney Todd. The contrast does not imply that this is what Johanna must become, but it does suggest that this image of romance in ruins is more congruent with the Symbolic systems of law and commerce as they exist in Sweeney Todd's London.

As Anthony and Johanna offer us a representation of the Imaginary in Todd, Judge Turpin and Mrs. Lovett offer us an opposing representation of the Symbolic order. Between them, they embody the chains of signifiers through which Todd's mentality is impelled toward the psychotic. Here reside the power and autonomy that Anthony and Johanna would mistakenly attribute to their desire for romantic love. Mrs. Lovett's ruthless entrepreneurial zeal links itself inextricably to Todd's mission of vengeance. Judge Turpin's equally ruthless sexual zeal prompts its murderous equivalent in Todd's insatiable throat slashing. Though the unrestrained course of action by Mrs. Lovett and Judge Turpin prove self-confounding in the end, their careening energy along the way is taken up by Todd as his own course achieves its heady pace.

In reestablishing himself at Mrs. Lovett's after his return to London, Todd re-places himself in what had been the Barker family's home. As a signifier, however, the room on Fleet Street does not recover what had been, but emphasizes, instead, what has been lost. At the same time, Mrs. Lovett's willingness to mislead Todd about his Lucy's fate so that she can further her own romantic desire to become Todd's wife defines even more sharply the dimensions of his loss.

For the audience, Lucy's reappearances at Mrs. Lovett's as the bawdy but pathetic beggar woman strongly highlight the contrasts between the two women. Mrs. Lovett still has her home, and Todd soon becomes the provider whose supplies transform her pie shop into a commercial success. Lucy is homeless, and her husband not only provides for her no longer, he does not even recognize her. Mrs. Lovett's lust for enterprise is matched with a romantic longing for the marital respectability of a middle-class wife. Lucy has fallen into the begging underclass of unmarriageable women for whom lust is the only enterprise available. In the end, of course, their fates converge amid Todd's catastrophe. Failing to recognize Lucy, Todd kills her so that she will not impede his second, successful effort to avenge himself on Judge Turpin. Then, when he does realize who she is, he kills Mrs. Lovett for misleading him about her survival.

Whereas Mrs. Lovett operates as an inverted signifier for Lucy, Judge Turpin operates as an inverted signifier for Barker and a mirroring one for Todd. We have already described Judge Turpin's role in eradicating Barker's presence as provider, husband, and father, so that he could usurp those roles to fulfill his own desires. When Todd returns to London, the Judge becomes the dramatic embodiment of the Name-of-the-Father, the signifier at once for the trauma that Barker had tried to expel from his being and for the power and autonomy with which Todd identifies to accomplish his revenge. The mirroring between Todd and the Judge is rendered musically in their two renditions of "Pretty Women," the show's most harmonious duet. Its reprise in act 2 prompts the Judge to exclaim of Todd, "How seldom it is one meets a fellow spirit!" (194).

As we have noted, too, when Todd's first attempt on the Judge fails, that identification is reinscribed in more grandiose terms: the barber's revenge is now capitalized as the Demon Barber's cosmic vengeance. By the time Todd slashes Judge Turpin's throat, he has amplified the Judge from the corrupt agent of poor Barker's undoing to the most powerful exemplar of London's general corruption that the Demon Barber must excise.

Todd's own fate waits in Lacan's intractable Real, embodied in Lucy-as-Beggar and the simple Tobias Ragg. Like the traumas that reconstruct Barker as Todd and Todd as the Demon Barber, Todd can assimilate neither Lucy-as-Beggar nor Tobias. He cannot see who they are. He cannot hear what they say. Their images and their language do not signify for him.

When Todd returns to London, the Lucy of his imagination is dead. That Lucy died in the sequence of traumatic events that eradicated Barker. The Lucy who remains as the Beggar Woman, is a zombielike creature, an embodiment of death's power. Throughout *Sweeney Todd*, she reminds us how much the living have to lose. Her bawdy sexuality parodies the respectability of romantic desire. Her begging challenges the legitimacy of Mrs. Lovett's zealous enterprise. Her prophetic voice—unheeded—articulates the truth about the corrupted systems of law and commerce that characterize her world. Only the lunatics escaping from Fogg's Asylum heed her cry, "City on fire!" (156). Lucy-as-Beggar is not the beautiful Mrs. Barker, but a noisesome, bawdy impediment to Todd's mission of vengeance. The prophetic inquiry that she thrusts at Todd—"Don't I know you?"—does not register with him until he has killed her (197). Nor does her effort to warn him about Mrs. Lovett—"the devil's wife" with "no pity . . . in her heart" (192)—mean anything to him until he has been shocked by his identification of her corpse.

The spontaneous heedlessness with which he slashes her throat has all of the marks of Lacan's Real, an irredeemable accident, unanticipated in his scheme to kill the Judge. His recognition of her at last has the same accidental quality, coming just when the light from the oven falls on her face as its door is opened to dispose of her body. She is the only female victim of Todd's razor to that point. Todd's realization that he has killed his Lucy prompts him to avenge her death by another, by killing Mrs. Lovett in her own oven (200).

In the symmetry of Todd's catastrophic ending, Mrs. Lovett's death, in turn, is avenged by Tobias Ragg. The other representative of Lacan's real, Tobias enters the action with Pirelli. For Todd, Tobias is a presexual simpleton, excluded from Todd's imagining. When Todd kills Pirelli, Tobias is being mothered by Mrs. Lovett, and Todd leaves Tobias with her to be assimilated as the child into her enterprise and the illusory family life she envisions with Todd. When the pie shop develops into a commercial success, Tobias takes on the promotional and service roles for that enterprise that he previously carried out for Pirelli (141).

Even as Mrs. Lovett's pies become a commercial success, however, Tobias remains mistrustful of Todd and Todd's influence with Mrs. Lovett. Suspicious when Pirelli disappears after his encounter with Todd, Tobias imagines himself as Mrs. Lovett's protector in "Not While I'm Around" (173). Like Lucy's attempts to warn Todd about Mrs. Lovett, Tobias' attempt to warn her about Todd go unheeded.

Unlike Lucy, however, Tobias does not enter the action as an exemplar of death. Although Pirelli's elixir is a fake, Tobias's effort to promote it emphasizes the illusion that it promises for rapid hair restoration. As such, it becomes in his presentation the antithesis of Todd's razors, an elixir for restored virility and vitality rather than Todd's instrument of death and demasculinization. A further contrast exists in their names. Whereas Todd has connotations of the German word for death, Tobias connotes the dutiful Biblical son who was guided by an archangel to restore his father's sight.

During the second act of *Sweeney Todd*, however, Tobias's efforts to act like a dutiful son for Mrs. Lovett and to show her the truth about Todd fail. The concluding events only confirm Tobias' worst fears. Promised the secret of the pie shop's success to distract him from his suspicions about Todd, Tobias finds himself locked in the bakehouse as the Beadle's bleeding corpse slides into view from Todd's deadly tonsorial parlor. Before Tobias can be further traumatized by the bodies of the Beggar Woman and the Judge, he tries desperately to escape from this awful revelation of death by descending into the unused, unlit cellar below the bakehouse (182-83). From the truth of death, of course, he can find no escape.

Like the traumatized Barker and Lucy before him, Tobias cannot assimilate that truth. By the time he climbs back up from the cellar, his hair has turned white, a sign that madness has overtaken him (200). His emergence from the trap door of the cellar parallels Todd's entrance during the opening "Ballad of Sweeney Todd," when the stage directions say "he rises out of the grave" to sing with the rest of the cast (25). Like Todd before him, Tobias is now death's agent. He returns to find Todd, more Benjamin Barker than Demon Barber, distraught as he cradles the body of Lucy, his razor lying on the floor. Wielding the razor, Tobias slashes Todd's throat.

With Todd's death, the contention between the Lacanian registers of the Imaginary and the Symbolic are resolved in the Real. That contention, which pushes Todd into the psychotic, leads him, for a time, to believe that he can be death. In the end, however, the Real intimations of death, which shadow us throughout our lives, are realized as they must be, inevitably and inescapably.

Writing of *Oedipus at Colonus* in his *Seminar*, Lacan focuses on Oedipus's question: "Am I made man in the hour when I cease to be?"[18] Using this question to explicate Freud's *Beyond the Pleasure Principle*, Lacan amplifies it: "When the oracle's Prophecy [*parole*] is entirely fulfilled, when the life of Oedipus has completely passed over into his destiny, what remains of Oedipus?"[19] Lacan then answers his own question: "*Oedipus at Colonus* shows us—the essential drama of destiny, the total absence of charity, of fraternity, of anything whatsoever relating to what one calls human feeling."

Sweeney Todd is not Oedipus, but his fate is reenacted as a tragic tale in our musical theater. Sondheim's dramatic craft encourages us to grant it a mythic resonance. The intimations of tragic destiny that Lacan intuits in Oedipus are not irrelevant to Todd's hold on us.

NOTES

[1] Sondheim and Wheeler 1991.

[2] Lacan 1991.

[3] Bowie 1991, 62-8. For a fuller understanding of Lacanian terms like Imaginary, Symbolic, Real, Phallus, and the Name-of-the-Father and of Lacanian theory in general, see Bowie.

[4] Bowie 1991, 92.

[5] Bowie 1991, 93.

[6] Bowie 1991, 94.

[7] Mollin 1991, 406-07.

[8] Lacan 1991, 112.

[9] Bowie 1991, 23.

[10] Sondheim and Wheeler 1991, 29.

[11] Sondheim and Wheeler 1991, 32.

[12] Bowie 1991, 82.

[13] Bowie 1991, 125-26.

[14] Bowie 1991, 108.

[15] Bowie 1991, 128.

[16] Bowie 1991, 137.

[17] Bowie 1991, 109.

[18] Lacan 1991, 229.

[19] Lacan 1991, 230.

CHAPTER 9

Visions and Re-visions

The Postmodern Challenge
of *Merrily We Roll Along*

S. F. Stoddart

For Sondheim enthusiasts, the most memorable anecdote concerning the staging of *Merrily We Roll Along* (1981) is the fact that it closed after sixteen performances.[1] This is also the most perplexing anecdote concerning this self-reflexive musical. Although characterized as a score of "intellectual depth and emotional passion," one of Sondheim's "most winning" accomplishments, critics generally view the show as a simple experiment in form, adapting through a series of musical "transitions" the Kaufman–Hart fable concerning a Broadway song-writing team *backwards*, the narrative beginning where it ends—the show ending with its start.[2] A 1985 revival, directed by James Lapine at La Jolla, further complicates the history of Sondheim's *Merrily We Roll Along;* in addition to George Furth's revisions to the book, Sondheim revised the score—deleting some songs, adding others, and even reassigning numbers between characters. This reworking created a score Sondheim now calls "definitive."[3]

The metamorphosis of this theatrical morality play should intrigue Sondheim *aficionados* because the revisions enlighten the plot's complex relationships, forming a more coherent narrative that focuses on the rise and fall of the partnership between Franklin Shepard and Charley Kringas. The germ of the saga, George S. Kaufman and Moss Hart's *Merrily We Roll Along* (1934), provides clues as to how to "read" the Furth–Sondheim text. The uncanny parallels in the historical context to each show links them in a more subtextual sense.[4]

For it is within the breakdown of the plot's central partnership that what I call the postmodern challenge arises in *Merrily We Roll Along*. Franklin Shepard's initial vision of the duo's future—together—becomes revised in his personal decision to sell his artistic promise for the benefits of the materialistic American dream. Franklin's greed destroys the partnership, leaving Charley alone and true to his craft. The pair never composes the songs they desire to as young men, songs that would criticize the very American ideology that creates the monstrous "Franklin Shepard, Inc."; he alone only regurgitates his one hit. Sondheim and Furth recreate the fable of Kaufman and Hart to self-reflexively criticize the American ideal and its corruptive effect on the young artist; consequently, the play also succeeds in criticizing the very Broadway tradition that staged it—and that condemned it.

RECONCILING ART AND HISTORY:
RE-VISIONING THE PAST

In order to decipher this project, we need, first, to establish some theoretical groundwork; the tenets of Marxism prove most helpful as its approach to the schism between art and history helps to distill the motives of Kaufman and Hart in telling their initial story backwards, and the motives of Sondheim and Furth in wanting to retell the story backwards. Generally, critics believe that the primary motivation of both artistic treatments rests in a longing for things, persons, or situations not present—a nostalgic desire to examine a man's life through celebration. However, nostalgia is not an historical perspective, but an idealized wish fulfillment—neither play simply tells the story of how one man becomes another through life's little moments. Instead, the self-reflexivity of both pieces focuses primarily on the corrupted artistry of Richard Niles and Franklin Shepard, analyzing their personal alteration through the historic moment. In this light, Sondheim retells the story of the artist Richard Niles as the composer Franklin Shepard, consciously drawing upon the uncanny parallels in the historic moments: Sondheim underscores the cliché that history repeats itself by telling the story of another artist who corrupts himself by selling his integrity to American ideology. Frederic Jameson sums it up best:

> We may therefore conclude this preliminary discussion by emphasizing the two basic characteristics of concreteness in art. First of all, its situations are such as to permit us to feel everything in them in purely human terms, in terms of individual human experience and individual human acts. Second, such works permits life and experience to be felt as a totality: all its events, all its partial facts and elements are immediately grasped as part of a total process, even though this essentially social process may still be understood in metaphysical terms. For the most important aspect of this feeling of totality for us is not at the moment the ideological explanation given it but rather its immediate presence or absence in that particular social life from which the writer draws his raw material . . . . if this feeling of immediate wholeness and inter-relationship is not there in real life to begin with, the artist has no means at his disposal to restore it; at best he can only simulate it.[5]

Jameson's claim underscores the reason Kaufman and Hart, initially, and Sondheim and Furth, secondly, decided to tell the same story in the same manner. It is not important to simply show how the state of art in America has been commodified by the post-industrial ideology—this would only make the story *nostalgic*, a desire for "the way that it was" (to quote Mary's plaintive song from act 1). Instead, the backward structure emphasizes the irony connected to such naive idealism, and the cyclic influence history employs to destroy such honest desire. This correlation of one's social experience with the historical moment underscores the cynicism and sadness we (the audience) feel as the curtain comes down on the "happy ending."

The similarities and parallels between the 1934 play and the 1981 musical, support this reading. Figure 9.1 shows a chronological comparison of the two texts:

Figure 9.1: Chronological Comparison

Merrily (1934)	Scene	Merrily (1981)	Scene
1934	Richard Niles' Home; Long Island, NY	1979	Franklin Shepard's Home: Bel Air, CA
1927	Restaurant Le Coq D'Or Hills Hotel	1975	Polo Lounge, Beverly
1926	Richard Niles' Apartment	1973	Jeffrey Nye's Television Show
1925	Jonathan Crale's Studio	1968	Frank's Central Park West Apartment
1924	Courthouse Corridor, Manhattan	1966	Courthouse Corridor Manhattan
1923	Althea Royce's Apartment	1964	Alvin Theater: "Musical Husbands"
1922	Living Room, the Murneys	1962	Living Room, Gussie and Joe's
1918	Park, Madison Square	1960	Nightclub, Greenwich Village
1959	Charley and Frank's Apartment		
1916	Chapel, Local College	1957	Rooftop, Upper West Side, NY

Additionally, we not only see how one text mirrors the other, in respect to focusing on public places for Frank and Charley's story, but we see that the alterations selected by Sondheim create similar effects, such as the change in locales (from Long Island to Bel Air) and areas (the chapel to the rooftop; the park to the nightclub), each showing a method of updating the staging without losing the overall effect. Franklin and Charley engender these public spheres, a fact that highlights the plot's tragedy as *theirs*. Because these public spaces accord a degree of safety to their relationship, their private moments become public, in their effort to maintain a heterosexual distance—a distance required by the American ideal.

More significantly, Figure 9.1 places the timelines side by side, revealing how these specific contextual points in time create parallel effects. In the original, Richard Niles leaves college in 1916 and enters a world that sees America as a world power. The 1918 park scene occurs toward the end of World War I, a time when conservative values persuaded the American public to turn its back on the world at large, to focus attention on creating an "Age of Prosperity," characterized by historians as an age of automation. However, as Richard's ideals shift from being genuine to being self-serving, his personality also shifts, mirroring once again the attitudes that prevailed within the American psyche of the 1920s, the conservative forces creating a similarly self-serving America. Richard's personal crash, his fall in social stature embodied in his public beating of Jonathan Crale, coincides with America's economic crash and subsequent economic depression. It is this physical blow (similar to Franklin's public blow, which ends his partnership with Charley Kringas on national television) that causes us to ponder his fate, the chaotic party that opens the play mirroring the psychological chaos of the central protagonist.[6]

The parallel created by the Furth–Sondheim text not only coincides with the artistic fate of Richard Niles, but it follows a similar historic cycle. The earliest scene, where Franklin, Charley, and Mary watch the launching of Sputnik from their apartment rooftop, casts the partners in a similar role, as they rise up to meet the forces of a world moving toward further automation, now known as technology. Their lives move through a liberal America, as opposed to Richard's conservative America, but it leads to the same end—to a world whose ideals become self-serving after the horrors of Vietnam. We see the partnership disintegrate on television, in 1973, the same year many lost faith in our American ideals with the televised Watergate hearings and the televised resignation of Richard Nixon. Frank's diseased social position hits its highest as America turns from the liberal agendas of the Carter years to the self-serving era of Reaganomics—a move which would ultimately reveal the pitfalls of self-interest and economic self-preservation.[7]

Most critics obscure the friendship between Franklin and Charley, choosing to place more emphasis on Franklin's marriages to Beth and Gussie (in chronological order) and/or the trio of Mary, Franklin, and Charley.[8] But these readings do not take Sondheim's own reading of the musical into account, nor do they look at the Furth–Sondheim piece in relation to the Kaufman–Hart original.[9] The friendship between the play's principles, Richard Niles (composer) and Jonathan Crale (artist), emerges as the central focus for the original play; Sondheim's experiment goes one step further, making the friendship a partnership, a much more centralizing experience in respect to artistic creativity—a form of marriage—that situates Franklin Shepard and Charley Kringas as the moral core of the musical text. Given the self-reflexive nature of this musical play, it is imperative to see this relationship as the one that grounds Franklin to humanity. The fruits of their collaboration—money—forms a phallic power in the ideological sense of America; it becomes the one "mistress" who succeeds in wooing Frank away from his virtuous partner.[10]

RECONCILING THE PERSONAL AND THE SOCIAL: REVISING THE RE-VISION

The second complexity in discussing *Merrily We Roll Along* rests in the revisions that Sondheim made as the show went into performance in 1985. Figure 9.2 shows a song-by-song comparison of what he altered for the La Jolla production:

Figure 9.2: Revision Comparison

Merrily (1981)	Cast Assignment	Merrily (1985)	Cast Assignment
Overture / Hills of Tomorrow	Company	Overture	Orchestra
Merrily We Roll Along	Company	Merrily We Roll Along	Company
Rich and Happy	Frank and Guests	That Frank	Guests and Frank
Merrily We Roll Along (1979-75)	Company	First Transition	Beth, Joe, Jerome, Scotty, Terry
Old Friends (1) Like It Was	Mary, Charley	Old Friends (1) Like It Was	Mary, Charley
Merrily We Roll Along (1974-73)	Trio: Mary, Charley, Frank	Franklin Shepard, Inc.	Charley
Franklin Shepard, Inc.	Charley	Second Transition	Tyler, Ru, Dory, Meg, Bunker, Scotty
Old Friends (2)	Mary, Frank, Charley	Old Friends (2)	Mary, Frank, Charley

Figure 9.2: (continued)

Merrily (1981)	Cast Assignment	Merrily (1985)	Cast Assignment
		Growing Up (1)	Frank, Gussie
		Third Transition	Meg, Dory, Scotty, Ru, Jerome, Tyler
Not a Day Goes By	Frank	Not a Day Goes By (1)	Beth
Now You Know	Mary, Company	Now You Know	Mary, Company
		Act 2 Opening	Gussie
It's a Hit!	Joe, Frank, Mary, Charley	It's a Hit!	Joe, Frank, Mary, Charley, Beth
		Fourth Transition	Dory, Jerome, Scotty,
		Meg, Tyler	
		The Blob (1)	Gussie, Company
Merrily We Roll Along (1964-62)	Terry, Company	Growing Up (2)	Gussie
Good Thing Going	Charley, Frank, and Company	Good Thing Going	Charley, Frank
Merrily (1981)	Cast Assignment	Merrily (1985)	Cast Assignment
		The Blob (2)	Company
Merrily We Roll Along	Company	Fifth Transition	Dory, Jerome, Scotty
Merrily We Roll Along (1961-60)	Bunker, Meg		
Bobby and Jackie and Jack	Charley, Beth, Frank, and Ted	Bobby and Jackie and Jack	Charley, Frank, Beth, Pianist
		Not a Day Goes By (2)	Beth, Mary, Frank
		Sixth Transition	Jerome, Scotty
Opening Doors	Frank, Charley, Mary, Joe, Beth	Opening Doors	Frank, Charley, Mary, Joe, Beth
Our Time	Frank, Charley, Mary, and Company	Seventh Transition	Frank Jr., Beth, Mrs. Spencer
The Hills of Tomorrow	Company	Our Time	Frank, Charley, Mary, and Company

In examining the revisions made to the musical structure of the show, we can see Sondheim's intentions through the effects of these important alterations. And, these revisions and reassignments further support a textual reading that prioritizes the Franklin–Charley partnership, showing that the budding artistic promise and compromise of artistic integrity still lie at the center of *Merrily We Roll Along*.[11]

The first noticeable deletion is "The Hills of Tomorrow," a mood piece that opened and closed the original show. The song positioned the forty-two-year-old Franklin Shepard as the commencement speaker at the same high school he and Charley Kringas graduated from twenty years before. Originally, this song not only introduced the "Merrily We Roll Along" vamp, but it created a metaphor for the musical—the play represented the mental breakdown of Frank—the musical being a mental depiction of all that transpired in his head during this commencement speech. This move, in essence, created sympathy for Franklin's altered character. Ending the play with a reprise of his graduation speech and this song of celebration reveals that Frank acknowledges his own artistic corruption, and paves the way for him to change during this "mid-life crisis." Removing the song and the staging from the La Jolla production causes the musical to open with the raucous party celebrating Franklin Shepard's co-option of his artistic ideal for the American movie scene. The overture here is more frantic than before, almost becoming cacophonous as it raises the curtain on a scene similar to Kaufman and Hart's original. Here, while the superficial guests swill champagne, Frank placates his second wife, Gussie Carnegie, a washed-up Broadway singer, while wooing a young starlet, who is later blinded when Gussie dashes a vial of iodine in her face. Replacing the original's "Rich and Happy" with "That Frank" here presents a passive Frank, one who lets others extol his virtues. For instance, in this new song, Frank's *guests* sing of his revision, rather than making Frank seemingly brag about himself:

("Rich and Happy")
FRANK:
   Life is swinging,
   Skies are blue and bells are ringing.
   Every day I wake up singing,
   "Look at me, I'm rich and happy!"

   Days are sunny,

   Working hard for lots of money,

   Filled with people smart and funny,
   Filled with people rich and happy. (12)

("That Frank")
ALL:
   That smile—
   He's hot but he's cool.

   What style—
   And what a great pool!
   If you had no idea what charisma
   meant—
   And you just can't be jealous, he's
   such a gent—
   He's the kind of man that you
   can't resent,
   That Frank! (3)

Both songs employ the same refrain, Frank singing "It's my time coming through," but the revision emphasizes that Frank is still singing about "our dreams coming true," rather than "my dreams coming true" as in the original. By altering the tone of the song, Sondheim allows Frank to be a likable, though misguided, protagonist, rather than an obnoxious product of commercialization. This idea is central to the revised plot because the play becomes personal drama, rather than social drama—an important key to understanding that the original musical forced a distasteful interpretation on Frank from the start, while the revision woos the audience into seeing that this is the person corrupted by the very success we all idealize.

Moving directly from "Like It Was" to Charley's manic "memory" of "Franklin Shepard, Inc." rather than separating the piece with the "Merrily" vamp allows this song to capture more directly Charley's desire to bring the condition of which Mary sings in "Old Friends" to fruition. This simple switch intensifies Charley's mania as he pleads for the past. Speeding up the tempo of "Franklin Shepard, Inc." now makes the song resonate as a frantic dirge for Franklin's dehumanized state, and allows us to draw a more obvious parallel between it and act 2's "Opening Doors," another frantic song, this time celebrating the glories of artistic integrity and monetary poverty.

The conscious use of vamps, beginning with the many "Transitions" that now punctuate the musical, helps to highlight the ironies found in the "Old Friends" vamp, first sung by a drunken Mary, and later sung by a naive Frank. Vamps, in this sense, create a symbolic matrix within the structure of the play. In Marxist theory, it is understood that when a writer applies a symbolic touch, that writer is consciously distancing the plot from realism, encouraging the plot to be read moralistically, and somewhat more universally. In this musical, the vamp takes the place of narration or description, working on the spectator's mind in a subconscious fashion, instilling an interpretation of the moment. So, when Mary originally sings "Old Friends," in her drunken present: "Friends this long / Has to mean something's strong, / So if your old friend's wrong, / Shouldn't an old friend come through?" (14), she ironically suggests that the idea of friendship is really the only bond left between Charley, Frank, and her—and that they are each impotent to act on the other's behalf.[12] This gesture conditions Frank's version later in the act, sung ten years earlier, to resonate with the irony of Mary's later version: "Most friends fade / Or they don't make the grade. / New ones are quickly made / And in a pinch, sure, they'll do. / But us, old friend, / What's to discuss, old friend?" (17). Even though the younger Franklin sings of a genuine love for his friends, the repetition of the music stirs something in us since we have heard the tune before. Now, we never believe Frank the way that Charley and Mary once did, because we have seen what he will become.

Sondheim's addition of "Growing Up," another song he repeats twice during the musical, forces a similarly uncomfortable reading of Frank's transition. Sung by Frank toward the end of act 1, the song speaks of his transition from ideal composer to commercial success, all the while justifying his new-found fortune while criticizing the ideals of those closest to him:

> So, old friends,
> Now it's time to start
> Growing up.
> Taking charge,
> Seeing things as they are.
> Facing facts,
> Not escaping them,
> Still with dreams,
> Just reshaping them.
> Growing up.
> Charley is a hothead,
> Charley won't budge.
> Charley is a friend.
> Charley is a screamer,
> Charley won't bend.
> Charley's in your corner. (5)[13]

This poignant moment in the show, followed by a refrain sung by the newly interested Gussie, suggests that the personal ideal has been corrupted by the American ideal—artistic integrity now victimized by the lust for the material. We no longer sympathize with the person Franklin is, because this new number allows us to witness his conscious change of heart.

Reassigning "Not a Day Goes By, " taking it from Frank and giving it to Beth prevents us from feeling too much sympathy for his character early on—Frank is, after all, guilty of adultery with Gussie, and guilty of betrayal, by sleeping with Joe's wife. Holding this sympathy in check is exactly what Sondheim strives for in these revisions to the first act, as they paint a more haunting portrayal of the American dream gone bad. This revision will resonate all the more when we experience the song in act 2 as a duet, sung as Franklin and Beth's wedding vows. This restaging plays in a manner similar to the way multiple versions of "Old Friends" played in this act—hearing the "final" version first, tainted by the cold materialism of Frank's corporate personality, forces the second, "initial" version to sound all the sadder.

The revisions to the second act, beginning with Gussie's bravado performance of Franklin and Charley's one significant "hit," creates a similar effect, as we understand more fully just where Franklin goes wrong. And, it is in this act where we realize that the American dream itself, complete with its promises of materialistic wealth, thwarts the musical marriage of Franklin and Charley. Gussie's interpretation of their one hit, from Franklin and

Charley's fictional "hit" *Musical Husbands,* heard before we experience the "original" version, is loud, brassy, obnoxious. The second version, replicating the song's initial unveiling as part of *Take a Left,* Charley and Franklin's politically idealistic show, is sung first by Charley, then as a duet by Franklin and Charley, just as in the 1981 version. This version of the song is no different from the original, creating an extended analogy of the team's friendship through song:

> It started out like a song.
> We started quiet and slow,
> With no surprise.
> And then one morning I woke
> To realize
> We had a good thing going.
> It's not that nothing went wrong:
> Some angry moments, of course,
> But just a few.
> And only moments, no more,
> Because we knew
> We had this good thing going. (8)[14]

The simile helps us to focus on the real core of Franklin and Charley's relationship—not just that they write songs, but they are *one* song—a love song. The ballad, while foretelling the tragedy of their eventual "going," also spells out the depth of their spiritual connection, the "singer" speaking as if to a lover, recognizing the fragility of a relationship. However, adding Gussie's version, and hearing it first, underscores the lengths that Franklin goes to compromise his artistry for wealth. Her version, now only a "standard," has lost the poignancy of this version, the true original. The "song" comes from the youthful passion of Frank and Charley, and their duet here captures the tragedy of their inevitable separation.

As a matter of course, the original second act played with simply recording Franklin's youth as it wound back toward his realization at the high school commencement that he had lost all his integrity. Now, the songs do remain poignant, but they resonate with a mawkish undertone, seething with the tragedy of Frank's not fully understanding all he has lost. This effect is all the more reenforced with Sondheim's decision to now end the musical with "Our Time," certainly one of Sondheim's most glowing tributes to the potential of youth. The song now takes on a new symbolism; the beautiful ballad, sung first by Franklin and Charley, then joined by Mary and Company, reveals the dangerous naiveté of youth in the face of the prevailing American ideology. Man, with the opportunity for riches, will sell everything he once held precious to obtain material comfort—even his best friend.

The final parallel between Kaufman and Hart's *Merrily We Roll Along* and Furth and Sondheim's version is their reception by the public at large. In 1934, though awarded a space by the editors of *The Best Plays of 1934–1935*, Kaufman and Hart were only applauded by the highbrow critics who found their experiment challenging and provocative.[15] Similarly, Sondheim and Furth's academic critics recognized that the musical represented a significant experiment, both in 1981 and in 1985. In both cases, the theater-going public found the shows too complex and too depressing, with their foci on the trappings of the American ideological scheme.

However, as we begin to survey Sondheim's work more critically we can surmise that the America of the early 1980s was not yet prepared for a musical which enlightened the very course most of the audience then traveled—a road toward personal ruin through greed. And, if we recollect that the 1985 revision of *Merrily We Roll Along* followed the Broadway rejection of *Sunday in the Park with George* (1984), we can, perhaps, surmise that Sondheim himself found more relevance in this story. Certainly, the greed of the 1980s, similar in scope to that of the 1920s, created an America fraught with cynicism and distrust. Reexamining *Merrily We Roll Along* cautions us to recollect the truth behind the cliché that history repeats itself.

NOTES

[1] Furth and Sondheim 1982 and 1994. For the reference to the fact that *Merrily* closed after sixteen performances, see Zadan 1994, 285.

[2] Gordon 1992, 256. Mondello 1995, 27. Both Craig Zadan 1994 and Gottfried 1993 cite many of the contemporary reviews of both the original production of *Merrily* in 1981, and the La Jolla production in 1985.

[3] Mondello 1995, 27.

[4] Cf. Schiff's remarks on Sondheim's relation with Prince and Mary Rodgers in Schiff 1993, 78. It is perhaps not without interest that this is the last musical to date on which Prince and Sondhein collaborate. [SG]

[5] Jameson 1971, 169.

[6] In the 1985 revision, Furth returned to the Kaufman–Hart drama for inspiration. For the initial party at Franklin's Bel Air home, he added a scene where Franklin's wife, Gussie, throws iodine in the face of a captivated starlet. In Kaufman–Hart's original, Althea Royce Niles throws iodine in the face of a starlet who has her eyes set on Richard.

[7] This is only more complicated when we remember that Calvin Coolidge, thirtieth President of the United States, and the main supporter of this laissez-faire form of government, was the political idol of Ronald Reagan, who became the fortieth President after the 1980 elections.

[8] Most significant is Stephen Banfield, who repeatedly suggests that the marriages form "the central plot activity" of the show. See Banfield 1993, 323. As a matter

of record, he disagrees with Sondheim's own idea that the play mainly concerns friendship, and is, instead, about "Frank's private life" (Banfield 1993, 323).

[9] In the liner notes to the 1982 Broadway recording ("Composer's Note"), Sondheim says: Since *Merrily We Roll Along* is about friendship, the score concentrates attention on the friendship of Mary, Frank and Charley by having all their songs interconnected through chunks of melody, rhythm, and accompaniment" (7).

[10] In this light, the musical follows those parameters established by Robin Wood, who believes that artists traditionally use the musical to discuss how the American capitalist ideology conflicts with the notions of pure creativity when the artist lives within the American culture. See Wood 1981, 58-9.

[11] James Lapine also made conscious revisions in his staging of the show by employing more seasoned actors in the main roles; his decision to use slide projections to highlight the passing of years helped to make the whole clearer—but still not clear enough: "To my amazement, people still didn't get that the play was going in reverse, which astounded me. I did everything but have a calendar with pages flying off" (see Zadan 1994, 283). The reviews were markedly better than the originals, but still reflected an attitude that the improved show wasn't much of an improvement (see Zadan 1994, 284-85).

[12] Furth and Sondheim 1982, liner notes.

[13] Furth and Sondheim 1994, liner notes.

[14] Furth and Sondheim 1994, liner notes.

[15] Zadan 1994, 272.

CHAPTER 10

A Cathedral to Art

Frank Olley

It seems amazing in looking back to 1985 when the New York theater was still going through its first responses to the Sondheim-Lapine *Sunday in the Park with George* and struggling with the lack of "story" in the production's book, that this lack was assumed to be the main reason for what many felt as the cold and distant atmosphere of the work as a whole. Fortunately, Frank Rich in a very perceptive article in *The New York Times Magazine* made both reviewers and audiences more clearly aware of what we see now as the brilliant originality of the Sondheim-Lapine achievement:

> As befits a show whose subject is the creation of a landmark modernist painting—Georges Seurat's "Sunday Afternoon on the Island of La Grande Jatte" (1886)—"Sunday" is itself a modernist creation, perhaps the first truly modernist work of musical theater that Broadway has produced. Instead of mimicking reality through a conventional, naturalistic story, the authors of "Sunday" deploy music and language in nonlinear patterns that, like Seurat's tiny brushstrokes, become meaningful only when refracted through a contemplative observer's mind. . . . "Sunday" is a watershed event that demands nothing less than a retrospective, even revisionist, look at the development of . . . the serious Broadway musical.[1]

In the later 1980s when I first experienced *Sunday in the Park with George* in the theater, I was deeply moved by the first act, amused by the satirical elements of the first half of the second act, and then deeply moved again at the latter part of that act. I was reacting not only as a long- standing theatergoer but also as a theater director and a teacher of dramatic literature, or, perhaps, I had already begun the long process of seeing *Sunday* "through a contemplative observer's mind." I simply could not understand why the work's first Broadway reviewers found it cold, even dull. Many of my profes-

sional colleagues added to the confusion, some enthusiastic for the first act or
for the second act, but none for the work as a whole. Through the subsequent
experience of viewing other productions of *Sunday* and a production of the
next collaboration between Stephen Sondheim and James Lapine, *Into the
Woods*, I began to feel an interesting link between their work and the final
plays of William Shakespeare, especially *The Winter's Tale* and *The Tempest*.
The new blend of musical and theatrical elements of the Jacobean stage available to Shakespeare from 1606 to 1613 provides a fascinating parallel to the
musical theater that develops in America from the late 1920's to the present
and in the British and Irish theaters through roughly the same period, a parallel which I now see at its richest in the Sondheim-Lapine collaboration.

The phrase "musical and theatrical elements" can be a misleading one
and requires clarification. I am not thinking here so much of background atmosphere as of a quality much more active and alive in the sense of Jean
Cocteau's notion of "poetry of the theater" in modern drama—a rich fusion
of music, word, movement, and gesture to communicate the text to the audience.[2] These four elements, then, are inseparable one from the other and together their effect upon the audience is deep and powerful. This is what I have
experienced in *The Winter's Tale* and *The Tempest* and in *Sunday*.

I would like now to consider particularly the relationship between *Sunday* and *Winter's Tale* as related to the favorite Shakespearean themes of time
and art. All that has been said thus far has developed from impressions of the
Sondheim-Lapine work that have become increasingly meaningful to me, but
it is still impression rather than supported theory. As with all of my critical
work on individual plays, it is necessary for me to put the theories to work in
the "laboratory" of my university theater productions. *Sunday* is unique for
me in the very practical sense that because of the challenge of staging this
production successfully I had to make the decision to spend a full academic
year in undergraduate student production rather than the customary two
months that is given to each of our productions. Also, I personally needed
more time as producer and director to test my own vision of the work through
the discipline of daily rehearsals of book and score. My music director, Allan
R. Scott, and I had to work together in every rehearsal to realize our shared
vision of this unique musical play. For me individually my strong sense of the
connection between *Sunday* and *Winter's Tale*, and more remotely *Tempest*,
became more specific as we proceeded, and the basis of that certitude was an
increasing conviction of the brilliance of Sondheim and Lapine in exploring
the theme of time in a manner so reminiscent to me of what Shakespeare had
done with his exploration of the theme in his final plays.

I

It has become a truism to see the Jacobean theater of 1606 to 1613 as related
to so much of what has occurred in the modern theater. But Shakespeare's

work in that theater demands particular attention. As with his contemporaries, his use of romantic materials becomes "darker" and more psychologically realistic for all the melodramatic extravagance of the plot materials. The sudden, apparently unmotivated jealousy of Leontes in *The Winter's Tale* is a case in point, but with Leontes, as is also very clear with Iago, the jealousy and hatred become obsessive to the point that the afflicted character is transformed into an artist of evil design, a perverse creator.[3] Leontes' treatment of Hermione and his obsession with accusing her in a public trial is the driving force of the first three acts of the play, culminating in the death of Hermione and the equally swift penitence of Leontes in 3.2. and 3.3, the "seacoast of Bohemia" scene, is filled with equally dark and powerful elements at the opening—the storm and the arrival of Antigonus with the Mariner, both burdened with an ominous sense of doom and portent at the abandonment of the infant Perdita, child of Leontes and Hermione, cast out by Leontes because of his destructive obsession with the imagined adultery of his wife:

> ANTIGONUS: Thou art perfect then, our ship hath touch'd upon
> The deserts of Bohemia?
> MARINER: Ay, my lord, and fear
> We have landed in ill time: the skies look grimly,
> And threaten present blusters. In my conscience,
> The heavens with that we have in hand are angry,
> And frown upon 's.
> ANTIGONUS: Their sacred wills be done! Go get aboard;
> Look to thy bark, I'll not be long before
> I call upon thee.
> MARINER: Make your best haste, and go not
> Too far i' th' land; 'tis like to be loud weather.
> Besides, this place is famous for the creatures
> Of prey that keep upon 't.
> ANTIGONUS: Go thou away,
> I'll follow instantly.
> MARINER: I am glad at heart
> To be so rid o' th' business. *Exit.* (3.3.1-14)

In the terseness of this opening dialogue we are still very much in the tragic mood of the preceding scene. The only hint of things to come is the Mariner's reference to the "creatures of prey" to be made concrete in the famous stage direction that concludes the final lines of Antigonus' next speech:

> I never saw
> The heavens so dim by day. A savage clamor!
> Well may I get aboard! This is the chase;
> I am gone forever. *Exit pursued by a bear.* (3.3.55-8)

In the fascinating production history of the play, many directors have chosen to keep the atmosphere tragic and tense by a climactic theatrical effect of mammoth projections of giant bears or beasts. More recent productions have gone immediately more light and comic by employing a human actor in a bear costume pursuing Antigonus for a laugh. Since the Shepherd has the next entrance, this approach is certainly just as plausible as a way to lighten the atmosphere with a superb piece of satiric realism. The Shepherd will be followed immediately by his son, the Clown, who will offer in vaudeville routine a comic description of the bear devouring Antigonus and the ship sinking, drowning all the mariners. Literary scholars love to describe the strong possibility that this kind of staging is probably much closer to the way the scene might have been played on the Jacobean stage. If so, it strikes me as a brilliant way on Shakespeare's part of moving quickly through the Shepherd's taking up of the abandoned Perdita, telling the Clown, "Now bless thyself: thou met'st with things dying, I with things new-born" (3.3.113-14).

In that beautifully concentrated statement we are made ready for the figure of Time as Chorus to describe the sixteen years that pass before the second major action of the play, the movement from Leontes' winter of penance through those sixteen years into the springtime of the pastoral world of Bohemia where the young shepherdess, Perdita, can be "mistress of the feast" and of the disguised Florizel. The play moves richly to the final events: Leontes' reunion with his restored daughter and his blessing of her betrothal to Florizel; the reconciliation of Leontes and Polixenes with each other as loving friends; and, finally the artful vision of Hermione's statue and the "miracle" of art becoming nature with Hermione's restoration to life through the ministry of Paulina. The final lines of Leontes orchestrate these themes and finally bring all to harmony in the great metaphor of time. These final lines are initially addressed to Hermione and Polixenes:

> . . . Let's from this place.
> What? look upon my brother. Both your pardons,
> That e'er I put between your holy looks
> My ill suspicion. This' your son-in-law,
> And son unto the King, whom heavens directing
> Is troth-plight to your daughter. Good Paulina,
> Lead us from hence, where we may leisurely
> Each one demand, and answer to his part
> Perform'd in this wide gap of time, since first
> We were dissever'd. Hastily lead away. (5.3.146-55)

But what has all this to do with *Sunday in the Park with George*?[4] My basic point here is relatively simple. The first half of *Sunday*, as with *Winter's Tale*, takes place in what at least seems to be real chronological time. George sketches Dot and others in the park and in his studio. He is Dot's lover and fathers their child, but whereas he is primarily obsessed with the painting, Dot's primary concern is his treatment of her. All of this is in obvious contrast to Jules, who is successful as a painter, and to Yvonne who is a successful wife and mother. On the surface at least, both couples are happily married with a growing child. George wants and needs Jules to recognize his painting, but Jules remains detached and patronizing. Yvonne becomes increasingly envious of the passion that Dot and George have at least experienced, but Dot eventually knows she will need Louis to provide a life for her and her child. In the magnificent closing scene Louis and Dot are leaving for America, but the real action is George's creation of the final painting not with canvas and paint but with stage and actors.

Only at the end of this first act do we begin to realize what Lapine and Sondheim have done with book, words, and music. There is chronological realism as I have been describing it, but at the same time from the very beginning of the work, Seurat's painting is the beginning and the end, the basis of the play's structure from the initial white stage and portals to the white canvas at its conclusion. The painting comes together piece by piece in the first act as George sketches, and at the end of the act, literally directs the composition of the total design. In the second act the painting hangs in the museum gallery as another George presents his Chromolume #7 before the assembled spectators—museum directors, reviewers, friends (and enemies) in the arts. Technology fails and Chromolume #7 has qualified success, a success which the critic, Blair Daniels, belittles. In her view, by merely doing a seventh in a continuing series of chromolumes, the present George has ceased doing anything "new."

We might be reminded here of the beautiful moment in act 1 when the present George's great-grandfather and the Old Lady are together on la Grande Jatte and express old and new views about life and art, although the Old Lady is ostensibly oblivious to the world of art itself. The song "Beautiful" is pure Sondheim—ironically contrasting the opposed viewpoints of the characters but beautifully unifying the words and music of the song:

OLD LADY:
    Changing . . .
    . . . .
    It keeps changing.
    . . . .
    I see towers
    Where there were trees.
    Going,
    All the stillness,
    The solitude,
    Georgie.
    Sundays,

> Disappearing
> All the time,
> When things were beautiful . . .

GEORGE:

> All things are beautiful,
> Mother.
> All trees, all towers,
> Beautiful.
> That tower—
> Beautiful, Mother,
> See?

(Gestures)

> A perfect tree.
> Pretty isn't beautiful, Mother,
> Pretty is what changes.
> What the eye arranges
> Is what is beautiful.

OLD LADY:

> Fading . . .

GEORGE:

> I'm changing.
> You're changing.

OLD LADY:

> It keeps fading . . .

GEORGE:

> I'll draw us now before we fade, Mother.

OLD LADY:

> It keeps melting
> Before our eyes.

GEORGE:

> You watch
> While I revise the world.

OLD LADY:

> Changing,
> As we sit here—
> Quick, draw it all,
> Georgie!

OLD LADY AND GEORGE:

> Sundays—

OLD LADY:

> Disappearing.
> As we look—

GEORGE:
Look! . . . Look! . . .
OLD LADY *(Not listening, fondly)*:
You make it beautiful.

(Music continues)

Oh, Georgie, how I long for the old view.

(Music stops . . .) (77-9)

When I say "pure Sondheim" I mean what this song perfectly demonstrates, a complete fusion of words and music that we hear and feel, so totally that it can move one to tears. It happens here, and it happens in act 2 in Marie's "Children and Art." It happens many times in this extraordinary work in such a way that the two acts become subtly and totally unified with each other. Part of that unity lies in what I have examined in *The Winter's Tale*, the unity of time in the seasons of winter and spring. What Leontes calls that "great gap of time since first we were dissever'd" involves only the separation of two generations. Sondheim and Lapine have given us four generations that eventually transcend time in the timelessness of Seurat's great painting, and the Dot that eventually emerges from the painting in the final scene of act 2 sees both the first and second Georges of *Sunday* as the *same* George!

The most complex and lengthy song in act 2 for George and Company is "Putting It Together" which is sung in the museum gallery after the crowd leaves the Chromolume #7 fiasco to adjourn to that gallery for cocktails. The visual staging is brilliant. The Seurat painting hangs in the center of the gallery wall and dominates the stage. The "art isn't easy" phrase with all of its wonderful ambivalence dominates the conversation while the audience is in full view of the painting so powerfully fulfilled at the end of act 1, but the crowd on stage, with the exception of George, Marie, and Elaine, is indifferent to it. This song is perhaps Sondheim's richest parody in act 2 of the whole process of artistic creation at the end of act 1. The artist must rely totally on cut-outs of himself in order to direct the scene which becomes increasingly frenzied and chaotic, the only result of tension in the contemporary world of life and art, now utterly devoid of—order. . . design . . balance . . . harmony . . . . Let the stage direction speak for itself:

GEORGE *frames the successfully completed picture of the guests and cut-outs with his hands, as at the end of act 1. As soon as he exits, however, the cut-outs collapse and disappear.* (158)

The quiet scene between George and Elaine, divorced but still communicating love and respect, is also a perfect dramatic introduction to "Children

and Art." As Marie dozes off toward the end of the song and is wheeled off by
Elaine:

(GEORGE *looks at the painting for a moment*)

GEORGE:
 Connect, George. Connect . . .

(GEORGE *exits; the painting flies out*) (163)

The final scene might be the richest in the musical:

*The island is once again revealed, though barely recognizable as the trees
have been replaced by high-rise buildings. The only tree still visible is the
one in front of which the* OLD LADY *and* NURSE *sat.* (163)

It is a gray, late March kind of world, still waiting for the return of spring.
"George is adrift" (166):

> George looks around.
> George is alone.
> No use denying
> George is aground.
> George has outgrown
> What he can do.
> George would have liked to see
> People out strolling on Sunday . . .

(DOT *appears.* GEORGE *looks up and discovers her. He stands*) (167)

The timeless world of the painting returns, the two Georges become one
and he and Dot are ready to promenade with the other figures of the painting
who bow to the artist, now ready to "Move On." All tension has ceased as creativity is renewed in the reprise-finale of "Sunday."

II

As I have discussed *Winter's Tale* and *Sunday*, I hope I have implied, at least
to some extent, the more timeless world of *The Tempest*. The art of Prospero
has never been far from my imagination in this discussion, which keeps linking that art with Seurat, asking only contemplative observation. The Prospero
of "Our revels now are ended" speech (4.1.148-59) is, like George in the closing scene of *Sunday*, filled with melancholy as he cannot continue the art of
the masque. At this moment Prospero sees his art as illusion that must "fade

and leave not a rack behind" (155-56). Momentarily, as with George trying to find a way to move on to new creation, Prospero must struggle to still his beating mind. Only when Ariel awakens his compassion for Gonzalo and his former enemies in 5.1.15-32 does Prospero awaken to new possibilities of creativity and life, paradoxically through the ending of his magic and art:

> My charms I'll break, their senses I'll restore
> And they shall be themselves . . . (31-32)

But the farewell to his art (33-57) is filled with a sense of his joy in all the life of his "rough magic." As his Epilogue makes clear art the end of the play (1-20) through the Christian reconciliation with his enemies and the blessing of the betrothal of Miranda and Ferdinand, Prospero can return to the world of human action in Milan from which new life and art are possible in a Christian vision.

> Now I want
> Spirit to enforce, art to enchant,
> And my ending is despair,
> Unless I be reliev'd by prayer,
> Which pierces so, that it assaults
> Mercy itself, and frees all faults.
> As you from crimes would pardon'd be,
> Let your indulgence set me free. (13-20)

In *Sunday*, George has received a blessing from Dot and the figures in the painting and can move on to something new:

> Just keep moving on.
> Anything you do,
> Let it come from you.
> Then it will be new.
> Give us more to see . . . (171)

Something new eventually becomes limitless art:

> GEORGE: (*Reading from the book*): "White. A blank page or canvas.
> His favorite. So many possibilities . . ."

> (*He looks up and sees* DOT *disappearing behind the white canvas. Lights fade to black*) (174)

What then began as the illusion of chronological time in *Sunday in the Park with George*, becomes a large dynamically structured synchronic canvas. In Christian terms, God is the artist and we are all in the infinite painting. From this point of view, life has become art.

And so we see the collaborative art of Stephen Sondheim and James Lapine as very much at one with the great collaborators and individual playwrights of the Elizabethan and Jacobean theaters, particularly Thomas Middleton and William Rowley. In great collaborations, two do become one, and Sondheim and Lapine have much in common with these playwrights, and particularly William Shakespeare, in a Jacobean theater so fascinated with the art of dramatic romance. As Sondheim put it himself in the 1992 "Sondheim: A Celebration at Carnegie Hall," the concert was ostensibly to celebrate the words and music of Stephen Sondheim, but was in fact convened to celebrate the restoration of Carnegie Hall, a "cathedral to art." The concert *also* linked, I have tried to suggest with Sondheim and Lapine (who, in our time, are also reaching, like their predecessors in the English Renaissance, for the mystery of the link between the worlds of nature and art), art and nature.[5]

NOTES

[1] Rich 1984, 53.
[2] Bentley 1955, 193.
[3] Shakespeare 1997.
[4] Lapine and Sondheim 1991.
[5] Thompson 1993.

CHAPTER 11

"Happily . . . Ever . . ." NEVER
The Antithetical Romance of *Into the Woods*
S. F. Stoddart

Since 1866 the American musical comedy has illustrated the romantic, nor-mative values of American culture.[1] Broadway has appropriated the tradi-tional values of this folk art to form an American paradigm in which the communal world of stage actors (the fictive) celebrates and mirrors the real world of the audience (the authentic) by recognizing their heterosexual, mid-dle-class values.[2] Therefore, the American musical comedy generally con-cludes with a romantic melody, promising eternal love in the bliss of an appropriately managed marriage. As the curtain comes down, one can almost hear the audience reciting the cliché which expresses their collective desire: "And they lived happily ever after."

Stephen Sondheim and James Lapine manipulate the basic form of the American musical to defy the traditional values embodied in the romantic musical comedy. *Into the Woods* (1987) negates the conservative goal and virtue of marriage by challenging the audience's assumptions about both marriage and the ideology of the romantic musical narrative.[3] To do this, Sondheim and Lapine interweave four familiar folk tales which combine the quest motif and the marriage motif to explore the ramifications of "Happily Ever After" creating a restyled genre that offers a liberated romance, elevat-ing the philosophy of true community over the restricted artifice of fairy tale coupling.

The folktale's morphology, as defined by Vladimir Propp, allows Sond-heim and Lapine to interconnect the four tales in recognizable and coherent ways.[4] According to Propp, the quest tale paradigm speaks of protagonists in situations where obtaining goals results in episodic perils; as they achieve their wishes, they routinely remove the antagonistic forces. Ultimately, the reader measures the achievement of each goal through the resolution: in most cases, a celebratory wedding feast.[5] This privileging of a heterosexist dis-course becomes the paradigm from which most readers, initially children themselves, begin to realize the ground rules of society. *Into the Woods* criticizes the "bourgeois-Capitalist" ideology of patriarchal heterosexism which restricts definition throughout the culture; thus, the musical places accepted norms under suspicion.[6] And while this particular musical does not blanketly reject the fundamentals of the Capitalist–heterosexist ideology, especially in respect to romance and marriage, the staged tales become the basis for the audience to examine the processes and effects of these normative values.

To achieve this end, Sondheim and Lapine select three of the most popular tales from the Brothers Grimm, "Cinderella," "Little Red Ridinghood," and "Rapunzel," as well as the popular English folk tale "Jack and the Beanstalk."[7] And they then proceed to undercut the "timeless moralities" of these tales by constructing an original one of their own, "The Baker and His Wife," to give thematic unity to the entire narrative construct.[8] The couple are childless. In order to produce progeny, the couple must interact with their fantastic folk community. By following their interaction, we may come to understand more clearly how the musical predisposes the audience to unthinkingly accept marriage as a form of closure, and by that means offer a unified critique of such a structuring device.

In an effort to focus my discussion, I limit myself to dealing with "Cinderella" and "The Baker and His Wife," as their stories operate to deconstruct the romance of wedded bliss.

ACT 1: JOURNEYING TO "HAPPILY EVER AFTER"

The opening sequence of the musical, "Prologue: Into the Woods," complicates the narrative from the start, becoming, according to Nina Mankin, "an exercise in narrative logistics and staging devices."[9] A cleverly detailed backdrop divides the acting area into three dwellings: the home of the dreamy-eyed Cinderella, her stepmother, and two "ugly" stepsisters; the home of the gleefully simple Jack and his overprotective mother; the home of the childless, yet optimistic Baker and his Wife. Cinderella opens the song with the plaintive "I wish" (3), which begins a round that entangles the other characters' wishes, all of which, based in individual desire as they are, show a lack of forethought in their simplicity, and reveal, in turn, the self-centered nature of each character. Cinderella, for instance, believes that marriage will remove her from the drudgery of her existence; the Baker and his Wife desire progeny to solve the complexities of their marital malaise. In this light, one begins to realize that the fairy tale stage mirrors the complexities of our own capitalist desires for individual fulfillment, without respect to others, regardless of the possible consequences to the society at large.

Ideologically speaking, the entire first act, which follows the pursuit of each character's goal, confirms the selfish, yet simplistic, motives of each storybook figure. The attitude here plainly permits act 1 to mirror the assumptions Robin Wood places on the musical as social criticism: the total *lack* of awareness on the part of the characters for one another challenges the notions of individual pursuits for selfish gains, particularly on the part of the childless couple.[10] In order to break the spell of sterility, the Baker and his Wife compromise their values by stealing, lying, and cheating the other characters out of the possessions they need.[11] In their first duet, "Maybe They're Magic," they justify swindling the simple-minded Jack by trading him "beans" for his "Milky-White" cow:

> When the end's in sight,
> You'll realize:
> If the end is right,
> It justifies
> The beans! (30-1)

Their obsessive, compulsive behavior, and the cavalier, selfish attitude toward the possessions of others, reflects the ideological commentary desired by Lapine himself:

> In the fairy tale world, the individual is liberated by his own choices and behavior; in the real world we are more dependent on each other. If you read Bettelheim, or even the Jungians, they say that the issues presented in fairy tales are about individual or collective psychic development. It seems to me that the real world is about being part of the whole and what makes up the stories are your varied parts.[12]

The actions of the childless couple illustrate the problems and entanglements that occur when the ideology of community does not figure into the actions of each individual. Their duet "It Takes Two" illustrates this point one step further, for the Baker and his Wife acknowledge the changes each has undergone for the betterment of their union: "You're not the man who started, / And much more open-hearted / Than I knew / You to be" (54). They find within one another the very things they believed no longer existed, and they jointly sing of their rejuvenated love:

> We've changed.
> We're strangers.
> I'm meeting you in the woods.
> Who minds
> What dangers?
> I know we'll get past the woods.
> And once we're past,
> Let's hope the changes last. (55)

However, the results ring false to the audience, as they achieve these virtues at the expense of the other members of the community.

A second example of this selfish attitude, which questions the heterosexist value system, lies with Cinderella's "straight" path to happiness through marital bliss. Upon visiting the grave of her mother, Cinderella wishes for the material frippery which will masquerade her true identity at the Prince's festival; even though her mother's spirit cautions her ("Are you certain what you wish / Is what you want?" [22]), Cinderella eagerly sees the "silver and gold" thrown down on her as the solution to her unhappy existence—in this light, marriage to the Prince will remove her from a trying domestic situation *and* serve to make her respectable in the eyes of those who demean her in public.[13]

However, the audience does not witness her "triumph" at the Festival; instead, we experience the immediate aftermath when she encounters the Baker's Wife in the woods. In the duet "A Very Nice Prince," the Baker's Wife interrogates the beautifully coiffed Cinderella, who begins to experience reservations concerning the romance paradigm. Acknowledging his "charm for a Prince," she hesitates to develop her responses to the Baker's Wife's questions concerning the romance of this first meeting:

WIFE:
   And—?
   The Prince—?
CINDERELLA:
   Oh, the Prince . . .
WIFE:
   Yes, the Prince!
CINDERELLA:
   Well, he's tall.
WIFE:
   Is that all?
   Did you dance?
   Is he charming? They say that he's charming.
CINDERELLA:
   We did nothing *but* dance. (38)

While the song takes on the tone of two girlfriends gossiping about a first date, the fragmented replies of Cinderella underscore her growing awareness concerning the inadequacy of marriage and its inability to live up to its romantic expectations.

This maturing hesitation underscores the end of act 1 in Cinderella's solo "On the Steps of the Palace," her song of wish fulfillment.[14] She enters limping, having lost one of her gold slippers: "Knowing this time I'd run from him, / He spread pitch on the stairs. / I was caught unawares" (62). While "stuck" on the stairs, Cinderella uses the time to contemplate the reality of her goal, now that her "wish" appears closer to reality with the Prince's obvious infatuation. However, her song does not act as a typical musical number to extol his clever, masculine virtues; the music, light operetta-like in tone, employs lyrics which ironically undercut the romantic expectations of the original fairy tale. Instead, it becomes a point for reflecting upon her condition; Cinderella, literally, finds herself stuck between two worlds, neither of which offer her the independence for which she truly yearns. Here, she understands the consequences of realizing one's goals through the masks of feminine deception:

> You think, what do you want?
> You think, make a decision.
> Why not stay and be caught?
> You think, well, it's a thought,
> What would be his response?
> But then what if he knew
> Who you were when you know
> That you're not what he thinks
> That he wants? (62-3)

Cinderella understands that her masquerade contributes to her ambivalent feelings and she knows that the accepted normality of her goal will have long-reaching implications for her. Maria Tatar sees this realization as allowing us to understand a singular rule of all fairy tales: "It may seem pedantic to demand logic from a genre that traffics in the supernatural, but even fairy tales have their ground rules, and those rules assure a degree of predictability in the plot."[15] In stereotypical fashion, Cinderella resigns control over the situation to the Prince:

> Then from out of the blue,
> And without any guide,
> You know what your decision is,
> Which is not to decide,
> You'll just leave him a clue:
> For example, a shoe.
> And then see what he'll do. (64)

Cinderella's "tale" in act 1 does end with her marriage, an ending that is "happy" in the same way as that of the tale of "The Baker and his Wife"; at the end of act 1, the Baker's Wife is pregnant. But with the Narrator's shout of "To be continued . . . " (78) as the cast sings "Ever After!" we understand that these marriages will undergo new tests in act 2.

ACT 2: UNITING FOR "EVER AFTER"

Act 1 closes with "Ever After," a song that celebrates the joys of attaining individual goals. Its final chorus, however, presents new ironies, with increasing trepidation, as the lyrics note:

> When you know your wish,
> If you want your wish,
> You can have your wish,
> But you can't just wish—
> No, to get your wish
> You go into the woods,
> Where nothing's clear,
> Where witches, ghosts
> And wolves appear.
> Into the woods
> And through the fear,
> You have to take the journey. (77)

The irony here derives from what each character has not yet realized; consequences accrue when one selfishly pursues one's goal. And the newly formed "bliss" of the married couples quickly reveals the ideological foundations of Lapine and Sondheim's narrative.

Act 2 begins with a reprise of "Prologue: Into the Woods" that reveals the collective unhappiness each goal brings to each household. While Cinderella sings "I'm going to be a perfect wife! I'm going to see that he / Is so happy!" (86-7) in a bored tone, the Wife sings "I wish we had more room . . ." (85), and the Baker sings "I'm going to be a perfect father!" (87) while their child cries. Pairing these rounds with Jack's lament, "I miss my kingdom up in the sky" (85), we understand fully what the narrator cynically implies when he remarks, "But despite some minor inconveniences, they were all content . . ." (85). When the consequences of Jack's selfishness materialize in the form of a female Giant who desires revenge for the death of her husband, the situation provides each group of singers with a collective focus: to defend their lands.

WIFE:
> Into the woods,
> It's not so late,
> It's just another journey . . .

CINDERELLA:
> Into the woods,
> But not too long:

> The skies are strange,
> The winds are strong.
> Into the woods to see what's wrong . . .
> JACK:
> Into the woods to slay the giant!
> WIFE:
> Into the woods to shield the child . . .
> LITTLE RED RIDINGHOOD:
> To flee the winds . . .
> BAKER:
> To find a future . . .
> WIFE:
> To shield . . .
> JACK:
> To slay . . .
> LITTLE RED RIDINGHOOD:
> To flee . . .
> BAKER:
> To find . . .
> CINDERELLA:
> To fix . . . (94)

The song ends abruptly indicating the significant tonal difference act 2 creates as it negates the "happiness" of the previous act.

Critics readily acknowledge the tonal distinction between acts 1 and 2, but they do so under the pretense that the surface function of the musical theater form (to entertain) is antielitist. Joanne Gordon notes:

> This communal threat, which has been interpreted by various critics to represent forces of evil as diverse as nuclear proliferation, AIDS, and the deranged individualism of Reaganomics, is a handy device that serves to reunite the characters.[16]

This hypothetical and contextual current neglects the ideological conflict implicit in the narrative. As act 2 continues, the audience senses the chaos and confusion of these now "perfect" lives, which serve to deconstruct the harmony found in the "bourgeois" materiality of their initial goals. The newly organized effort—to save the kingdom—permits the central characters to examine the implications of their supposed rewards, some with more positive results, others with further ramifications.

We learn of dissatisfaction within the walls of the castle, not only from Cinderella's initial chorus, but in the Princes' duet "Agony." Here, we listen to Cinderella's Prince sing of finding another maiden "High in a tower—/ Like

yours was, but higher—/ A beauty asleep" (96), and Rapunzel's Prince sing
of finding yet another maiden: "I've found a casket / Entirely of glass—/ No,
it's unbreakable./ Inside—don't ask it—/ A maiden, alas, / Just as unwake-
able" (96). Despite the humor of the joint lament of the Princes for Sleeping
Beauty and Snow White respectively, the audience cannot deny the shallow
egoism of these beastly brothers.[17] The song ends with the Princes collabora-
tively resigning themselves, "Ah, well, back to my wife . . . " (98), and we further comprehend the ideological order: Cinderella and Rapunzel serve the
occupation of "Princess" adequately, until they behave as individuals; once
they, especially Cinderella, find the routine of daily life boring, the blissful
state of marriage becomes another form of entrapment—another tower for
Rapunzel, and another domestic dirge for Cinderella.

The place of woman in the newfound order further complicates the narrative when the Baker's Wife encounters Cinderella's Prince in the woods.
With his "charming" expressions ("Any Moment") he seduces her; while the
song, and the subsequent actions, humorously capture the fleeting affair—especially in the Prince's quick decision to leave, the "affair" has touched the
Baker's Wife in a truly unique way. Her solo "Moments in the Woods" speaks
of the angst she experiences as a result of her futile protestations:

> Was it wrong?
> Am I mad?
> Is that all?
> Does he miss me?
> . . . .
> There are vows, there are ties,
> There are needs, there are standards,
> There are shouldn'ts and shoulds.
> Why not both instead?
> There's the answer, if you're clever:
> Have a child for warmth,
> And a baker for bread,
> And a Prince for whatever—
> Never!
> . . . .
> Just remembering you've had an "and,"
> When you're back to "or,"
> Makes the "or" mean more
> Than it did before. (111-13)

However, more important to the ideological discussion, the Baker's Wife
realizes the double-standard established by heterosexual coupling. The
Prince blithely leaves the situation he perpetrates without guilt, only the
shammed "Agony" of appearing responsible in public. The Baker's Wife, on

the other hand, wrestles with her conscience, knowing she has wronged her dutiful husband, and realizing that her clandestine memories will influence her marital attitude. The action of the affair and her subsequent response to it confirm that the Baker's Wife is not a simple "object image" but a complex entity in her own right. Her sensitive response reveals her own complex character briefly, as she falls to her death soon thereafter, another victim of the spiteful female Giant.

This action further validates the ideological structure of Sondheim and Lapine's narrative, creating the antithesis of the narrowly pointed moral for each adventure. The surviving characters, Jack, the Baker, Cinderella, Red Ridinghood, and the Witch, begin to argue as they meet to plot a strategy for ridding the land of the female Giant. The discord apparent in "Your Fault" shows the ugly result of individual competition. As the song turns to shouts of blame and accusation, we sense the frustration in a lack of common goal and common spirit; the Witch breaks into her final number, the apocalyptic "Last Midnight," which bluntly shows each character how selfish they continue to be in the face of possible annihilation:

> It's the last midnight.
> It's the last wish.
>
> . . . .
> Told a little lie,
> Stole a little gold,
> Broke a little vow,
>
> . . . .
> Had to get your Prince,
> Had to get your cow,
> Have to get your wish,
> Doesn't matter how—
>
> . . . .
> You're all liars and thieves,
> Like his father,
> Like his son will be, too—
>
> . . . .
> Now, before it's past midnight,
> I'm leaving you my last curse:
> I'm leaving you alone.
> You can tend the garden, it's yours.
> Separate and alone,
> Everybody down on all fours. (120-22)

That these pointed, honest, remarks come from the Witch, the traditionally accepted symbol of evil and duplicity, further indicate Lapine and Sondheim's effort to question the normative role of women in the culture. The final curse attests to the end result of individual selfishness—by simply accepting the patriarchal, heterosexual paradigm, humanity succumbs to the mediocrity of the social system.

However, the four survivors are not "alone" (128-29) but together, and this position certainly politicizes the end result of the musical narrative. While Cinderella begins "No One Is Alone," the others—the Baker, Red Ridinghood, and Jack—soon join her and the song underscores the necessity of working together for the common good:

> Sometimes people leave you,
> Halfway through the wood.
> Others may deceive you.
> You decide what's good.
> You decide alone.
> But no one is alone. (128-29)

After Jack and the Baker succeed in killing the Giant with the assistance of the women, they all return and complete the song, demonstrating once again that individual decisions have implications for the common good. This action settles the chaos to a degree. In "Finale: Children Will Listen," the characters revise their individual plans to redesign the traditional paradigm, bringing Jack, Cinderella, Red Ridinghood, and the Baker into a newly articulated familial plan. Here, Cinderella takes leave of her Prince, Jack and Red Ridinghood decide to look after one another, and the Baker, joined by the spirit of his lamenting Wife, decides he will work at being both "father and mother" (135) to his son. At the Baker's invitation, these remaining four characters agree to reside together, forming a nontraditional family unit center stage, which, given the lessons each member has learned over the course of his or her journeys undoubtedly will survive in spite of the conventional values system which deconstructed the normative unions of the first act.

In a seminal essay on musicals, "Entertainment and Utopia," Richard Dyer finds that "while entertainment is responding to needs that are real, at the same time it is also defining and delimiting what constitute the legitimate needs of people in this society."[18] *Into the Woods* serves a similar capacity as it deconstructs the traditional notions of musical comedy, entertaining while questioning the conventional values of society. In negating marriage as a form of closure, Sondheim and Lapine articulate the need for new definitions by which this newly formed family can exist and operate harmoniously within the world at large. Indeed, this narrative calls into question the very methods by which we raise our children, insofar as fairy tales continue to form the basis for childhood socialization. Using conventional romantic musical forms, the writers highlight their dissatisfaction with these easy prescriptions; their new ideology redefines the paradigm through a more honest, and more complex, notion of communal harmony.

NOTES

[1] Green 1980, 1.

[2] This claim becomes evident in the parallel structures of Broadway and Hollywood, as Jane Feuer notes, "The audience feels a tremendous sense of participation in the team effort, canceling out the alienation inherent in the viewing situation." See Feuer 1982, 17.

[3] Lapine and Sondheim 1992.

[4] Propp 1958.

[5] Propp 1958, 26-63.

[6] I have adopted the method of Robin Wood, who suspects the Hollywood musical of very blatantly criticizing the accepted values of middle-class America. His reading of *Silk Stockings*, in Wood 1975, 28-31 (Rouben Mamoulian's musical version of *Ninotchka*, 1951 [28]), specifies the premise that song (and in his case, dance) contribute covertly to the criticism leveled against normative thinking.

[7] Stephen Banfield incorrectly notes that the tales are appropriated from the Perrault tales in addition to the Grimm Brothers (Banfield 1993, 384); in a televised interview, both Sondheim and Lapine distinguish the Perrault tales (and Andersen's) as legitimate fairy tales, ones which use magic as a solution to the problem, as opposed to the individual spirit. It seems that neither Sondheim nor Lapine wanted "magic" to rule their revisionist fantasy, but a form of "darker, bloodier" realism.

[8] "The Baker and His Wife" provide the thematic link in much the way that Propp details the commonalities of traditional folk tales, the childless couple being a staple of many quest tales (7).

[9] Mankin 1991, 52.

[10] Wood 1975, 28-31.

[11] It is interesting to note that in detailing the theft of her vegetables by the Baker's father, the Witch condemns his procuring the produce by describing it in quite violent terms: " 'Cause I caught him in the autumn / In my garden one night! / He was robbing me, / Raping me, / Rooting through my rutabaga, / Raiding my arugula and / Ripping up the rampion / (My champion! My favorite!)" (12-3). In essence, she forces the couple to employ similar tactics to avenge her own honor—even though she procured Rapunzel as payment for the initial nocturnal rampage.

[12] Mankin 1991, 55.

[13] Florinda, Lucinda, and their mother (Cinderella's stepmother) all ridicule Cinderella's request to attend the ball in the opening number; the stepmother further humiliates Cinderella with a strange request: "I have emptied a pot of lentils into the ashes for you. If you have picked them out again in two hours' time, you shall go to the ball with us" (7). After Cinderella calls on her "little birds" to assist her, the stepmother cancels out her original offer with another humiliating response: "The Festi-

val—! / Darling, those nails! / Darling, those clothes! / Lentils are one thing but / Darling, with those, / You'd make us the fools of the Festival / And mortify the Prince!" (17). In this light, Cinderella's domestic space does not offer her a safe space for her own peace of mind; it becomes natural for her, in her limited experience, to envision marriage as a haven.

[14] One of the narrative intricacies of *Into the Woods* is the way Sondheim allows each major character a song which articulates their wish, and the lesson they learned in its pursuit. For instance, Red Ridinghood sings in "I Know Things Now" of the complexities of innocence: "Isn't it nice to know a lot! / . . . and a little bit not . . ." (36) after her rescue from the Wolf's belly; Jack sings in "Giants in the Sky" what one wish brings—more wishes: "And you think of all the things you've seen, / And you wish that you could live in between, / And you're back again, / Only different than before, / After the sky" (44). The Princes' song "Agony" certainly speaks of the ironic nature of finding perfection in women, only to meet obstacles in obtaining them; The Witch's lament, "Stay With Me" returns her to her former self, a young, beautiful woman—but Rapunzel leaves her to marry her Prince, leaving the Witch to comprehend the pain in wanting too much.

[15] Tatar 1992, 36.

[16] Gordon 1990, 311.

[17] This attitude resounds further when we recognize that the actor who portrays Cinderella's Prince routinely plays the part of the Wolf in Red Ridinghood's adventure.

[18] Dyer 1992, 25.

tween the romantic young soldier and his carefree (and disrobed) mistress was one of the most memorable I've witnessed. Jane Greenwood's costumes, Adrianne Lobel's sets, Beverly Emmons' lighting, Otts Munderloh's sound, Jonathan Tunick's orchestrations, and Paul Gemignani's musical direction combined to produce as subtle and shrewdly supportive a context for Sondheim's work as by now we have come to expect of these individuals with their multifarious talents.

And yet the first responses were largely negative. The first reports, for example, to reach those of us who were working at the time on the first issue of *The Sondheim Review* were that the play was "DOA."[4] Early audiences, moreover, were said to have expressed their disdain vocally. Apparently during one performance when Fosca's death was announced, an audience member yelled "Good!" and others began applauding. And if subsequent audiences found it more palatable—after several revisions and the addition of some new songs—the reaction remained mixed.[5] "Ravishing, Daring, Spellbinding!" screamed one New York newspaper headline.[6] Yet one of the most positive reviewers, who praised Sondheim as "the most gifted composer and lyricist of his generation," nonetheless concluded with the suggestion that "the aftertaste [of the play] is vaguely sour."[7] And one of the most negative reviewers suggested that Sondheim's "perverse brilliance" and "intellectual ambition" has "brought the American musical" to a "dead end."[8]

What is the difficulty? Reduced to its basic terms, the problem is simply the plot. Based upon a movie, *Passione d'Amore*, directed by Ettore Scola in 1981 (in turn based upon a nineteenth-century epistolary novel, *Fosca*, by Iginio Tarchetti in 1869, from which Sondheim and Lapine have also drawn material), the story focuses almost exclusively upon the decision by a young Italian army captain (Giorgio) to relinquish a relationship with the attractive blond-haired, light-hearted, and free-spirited Clara (for whom "love is happiness") for a relationship with the unattractive, dark-featured, possessive, and melancholy Fosca (for whom love is clearly unhappiness), the cousin of the commanding officer who happens to be living at the remote army barracks where Giorgio comes to be garrisoned.

The decision seems singularly unmotivated. Ensconced in Clara's loving arms, Giorgio receives notification of his transfer. He removes himself to the barracks, meets the romantic and self-pitying Fosca, rejects her unilateral and unwelcome advances, and continues his relationship with Clara via letter and occasional visits. Fosca pursues him relentlessly, clinging to him all the more intensely as he rebuffs her increasingly histrionic efforts. In a fever and on the point of exhaustion—having confronted Fosca with her outlandish behavior and then rescued her from an attempted self-destruction—Giorgio departs for Milan on a forty-day sick leave. Fosca follows him onto the train with the expressed intention of remaining nearby during his convalescence. Weakened by his illness, he challenges her plan, and then does a curious thing: he reverses himself. He returns to the outpost with her, and now travels to Milan only long enough to redefine his relationship with his former and understandably baffled mistress.

The gesture nearly costs him his life. The doctor, who earlier encouraged the young soldier's attentions to his dying patient, now arranges for his transfer away from the barracks, and the commanding officer—who is also Fosca's cousin—believes the soldier has misled Fosca in a manner in which she has been misled once before in her life. His discovery in Fosca's bedroom of a love letter in Giorgio's hand—a letter that in fact Fosca had dictated—only confirms his suspicions. He challenges Giorgio to a duel and Giorgio, instead of explaining that while the letter was written by Fosca, his love for her is now genuine, and his transfer is not an abandonment, accepts the challenge. The duel takes place and both are wounded in the exchange of pistol fire, although neither mortally. Having triumphed over her rival, attained the love of the handsome young captain, and revived sufficiently to accompany him to Milan for a forty-day convalescence just a day before, Fosca now dies. Alone in the hospital, recovering from injuries received in the duel, Giorgio reads aloud Fosca's final letter to him, and ponders this strange history which has brought him to his present state.

Why does Giorgio behave as he does? There seems little to redeem his choice. There are virtually no plot complications upon which an audience may blame this decision. The kinds of misunderstandings and sudden twists of fate that are present—for example, regarding the letter or Giorgio's transfer—serve only to heighten the strangeness of his behavior rather than to alleviate it. Clara, for example, is married. But that fact does not seem to bother Giorgio who rather thrives on the romantic and clandestine nature of their interludes.

Nor are there any qualities in either Clara or Fosca which may sufficiently explain his change of heart. Sondheim and Lapine, in fact, seem to have taken pains to make the union as improbable as possible. Clara is presented as demand-free and lusciously attractive, while Fosca is presented as an emotional child—given to hysterical outbursts, sulking, obsessional behaviors of all sorts, and a poisonous self-pity that leaves her at times physically incapacitated. Giorgio seems to have little difficulty obtaining leaves to visit his mistress when he wishes and is, in fact, on the verge of a quite lengthy one when his change of heart occurs. Clara seems available to him virtually whenever he is available to her.

The authors seem even to have altered their sources in this direction. In Tarchetti, for example, Clara breaks off the relationship with Giorgio to return to her husband, a fact which could allow Giorgio's embracing of Fosca to be understood as compensatory—making the best of a bad situation. In *Passion* by contrast Clara would like the relationship to continue, a fact which allows Giorgio's choice of Fosca to seem considerably more free and deliberate.[9]

Nor, finally, are there any qualities in Giorgio that would explain his behavior. These are, after all, consenting adults, we may be tempted to say to ourselves. Giorgio is away from Milan on an assignment of undetermined duration and communicates with Clara largely by letter. Fosca is living alone in an army barracks populated with bored and boorish soldiers. She is the cousin of the garrison commander and has his ready attention. Moreover, Clara is married and has a family of her own quite apart from Giorgio. Is it really so outlandish, we might ask ourselves, that in this remote rustic setting the romantically inclined captain—who writes letters, keeps a journal, reads Rousseau, and is given to rescuing helpless victims—should declare his attraction to this young woman who similarly writes, reads, and fantasizes herself in need of rescue? Is he not merely making the best of adverse conditions whether he is aware of such strategies or not? The soldiers, who act as something of a Greek Chorus to their involvement, certainly think as much. And a similar assumption founds the misunderstanding of Giorgio's intentions by the garrison commander, and perhaps as well by the military doctor who first arranges the match and then apparently arranges Giorgio's transfer.

But Giorgio's character is presented as utterly without the kinds of opportunistic drives that the above scenario supposes, qualities that by contrast seem a part of the garish and insensitive reaction of the soldiers, and that might very well motivate Fosca's former husband. Giorgio is presented as open and boyish with Clara, pitying and compassionate with Fosca in the initial scenes, and when he realizes that Fosca has attached herself to him too easily, he quickly clarifies things for her, explaining fully his relationship to (and love for) Clara, and specifically refusing to mislead her in the manner for which he is later charged.

As a consequence, when he turns away from his sexually open, mature, easygoing lover for this clinically depressed, childlike, self-tormented, woman, the audience is understandably puzzled. Is it possible that Sondheim is simply following his sources? To some extent, of course, Sondheim inherits the differences in appearance and behavior between the two women. But Sondheim has also built his career on precisely his readiness to reject or qualify such dutiful emulation of musical, literary, or dramatic sources—consider his treatment of the myths of Ziegfeld's *Follies*. To say that Sondheim represents his characters one way or another because the sources tell him to do so is like saying Shakespeare in *Hamlet* emulates Saxo Grammaticus because he has to do so, a condition that may shape Saxo's relationship to Aeschylus, but hardly Shakespeare's to Saxo. Sondheim borrows when he wants to and distances himself from his sources when he wants to, and we have indicated above some of the ways in which in fact Sondheim and Lapine alter the source material in the present instance. To read otherwise is to read Sondheim as Fosca reads (or perhaps more precisely "reads to") Giorgio in the central bedroom scene. It is to retrieve from the mirror only the projected clarifying image of ourselves we inscribed there in the first place.

Why then does Giorgio do it? Or perhaps more appropriately, what is Sondheim up to in presenting him as he does? This is a legitimate question for us to ask, of course, because *Passion* shares with *Sweeney Todd* among Sondheim's works the distinction of being undertaken at Sondheim's initiative. Not unlike the barber of the earlier play, who returns from Botany Bay a changed man—who now, for example, sings lyrics intended as a love song to his knives—the young army captain in *Passion* seems drawn to Fosca by a lure that is no longer a matter of the carefree "happiness" with which the play opens, but rather in a more troubled way of his "soul."

However the play is advertised, in other words, the conclusion to which we would seem to be inevitably drawn is that this is not a play about romantic love but about obsession and depression.[10] The turning point comes when Fosca tells Giorgio that she would 'happily' give up her life for him (101). "Would Clara give her life for yours?" she asks (101). And then she answers for herself. "I would. Happily." And at that moment, as he moves to cover her, to shelter her from the elements with his clothing, we have the sense that pity has now quickly turned to something else, perhaps not to the romantic love that the lovers in the opening number tunefully imagine, but something darker and more ominous. "Why is it that the violets and daisies blossom now?" Fosca asks Giorgio when she confronts him on the mountainside and he replies, "They mistake Autumn's warmth for April" (90). We have the sense that a fundamental mistake has been made here, a mistake on Giorgio's part in thinking that Fosca could ever satisfy the expectations that he has of her (and that she has encouraged him to have), and perhaps as well a mistake on Sondheim's part.

To what has Giorgio's pity turned? Giorgio offers us his own account. No one else ever said that to me before, he remarks. "No one has ever loved me / As deeply as you. / No one has truly loved me / As you have, Fosca" (122). What enables the transition from his own point of view is that he moves not from one love relationship to another (which is how theater audiences and critics have for the most part viewed it), but from one level of relating to another, a movement considerably more difficult to examine and visible only upon a careful reading of the text and careful listening to the lyrics and music. It is a movement from the lush erotic comfort of Clara's bed (from which perspective Fosca's unattractiveness and clothedness is paramount) to the soul-searching ominous underworld of Fosca's (from which Clara may seem considerably more superficial and clothed).

Such a transition on Giorgio's part may be good therapy, we may be prepared to concede, but is it good theater? Moreover, even if we accept such terms, does Giorgio not recognize, we may be prompted to object, that Fosca is projecting? Does he not notice that she would say the same to any man to whom she had attached herself, that there is nothing "personal" about it for her, that she hasn't the foggiest idea what Giorgio is like or what his life has been like, only that he fills the bill of resembling the heroes in the romantic novellas she has been reading? "I read to live" (22), she sings.

He does, of course, recognize as much up to a point. He recognizes the difficulties with which he is working at least up to the scene in the train (which is already fairly late in the play), and the observations he makes on their basis prove the occasion for some of Sondheim's most penetrating insights about love and possessiveness (in the storm scene, for example). Moreover, he may recognize as much even later, when he answers the doctor who finds his plan to forgo his leave and stay at the garrison with Fosca foolhardy, and says "I feel it my duty to help her" (104), and even in the next scene when Clara asks "Do you love her?" (108) and he replies "The idea is laughable" and continues to propose to Clara that they "have a life together" (108).

On the other hand, at some point he crosses the line. He breaks off his relation to Clara (in language reminiscent of Fosca's words to him), tells Fosca directly "Yes, I love you" (123), and screams in the duel scene in a manner that the script itself describes as *"a cry that is clearly reminiscent of Fosca's"* (125). And once he crosses that line, once he gives up his former perspective for hers and suddenly begins projecting in the same manner, we feel that he has succumbed to a blindness from which there is no return, and we are loathe to accompany him to that region. We will continue to praise Sondheim (we tell ourselves) for offering us once again an undeniably clear and talented rendition of his source materials (in this case, Scola's movie and Tarchetti's "epistolary" novella), even if we do not entirely understand (or even reject) its darker implications.

"*Passion* is about how the force of somebody's feelings for you can crack you open," Sondheim said in an interview for the *New York Times* with Michiko Kakutani on the occasion of its Broadway production.[11] Does Fosca's love "crack [Giorgio] open?" Does she offer him "love that, like a knife, / Has cut into a life / [he] wanted left alone" (61)? Undoubtedly. But it is less an outpouring of romantic affection that she extends (or he returns), we want to say, than a death-defying anguish. And if he is cracked open—and it appears that by the end of the play that he is—then it seems to be not because he is persuaded of her love for him (although he may rationalize as much), but rather because his own inevitable childhood wounds have kicked in—and before those wounds he is as helpless as she is before hers. Thus he joins her in a mutually shared depression. Like the young girl who has been enacting or imitating the romantic novels she has been reading, Giorgio finally enacts the script before him: Fosca. Falling to the ground, he *"lets out a high-pitched howl"* (125) in a tantrum reminiscent of his living model.

What Sondheim appears to have offered us, in short, is not "love" but (in Giorgio's words) a "disease that would cripple us all," a poisonous "intoxication," a "great blindness, if you will," the genesis and course of a "medical condition" occasioned by the mimetic appropriation of the kind permeating the great European novels (Cervantes, Stendhal, Flaubert, Dostoyevsky, Proust), and the great English and French dramatists (Shakespeare, Molière) about which critics like René Girard have written so extensively and so persuasively.[12]

But I would like to suggest that Sondheim may in fact do more than that. In another act of "great blindness" (because the critic's intention is to vilify Sondheim), John Lahr articulates a view of the play which ironically extends these insights to realms in which the clue to a deeper strategy on Sondheim's part may be found.

> What we get in this listless *epistolary musical* [John Lahr writes], where the main characters spend much of their time singing love letters to and from each other, is the results of Sondheim's recent experiments with the play's director and librettist, James Lapine: not the big heart, but the dead heart; not the joy of the pleasure dome but the hush of the lecture hall; not dancing but reading.[13] [italics added]

Lahr, of course, is dissatisfied with Sondheim's treatment of his material. He would prefer the "pleasure dome" of Clara's bed to the lecture hall atmosphere of Fosca's tortured imagination. The former context he feels offers the openness, energy, and joy of "the big heart" while the latter offers only the closedness, lethargy, and "hush" of "the dead heart." "Not dancing but reading," Lahr laments. And Lahr links this decision on the part of Sondheim for "reading" to letter writing. This musical, Lahr says, and not without a fair amount of disdain, is "epistolary."

What is an "epistolary" musical? *Passion* is certainly not an "example" of a established genre of musical theater since Sondheim and Lapine are inventing such a genre with this production. The epistolary habits of the characters are borrowed in part at least from the Italian sources of the play in narrative prose. Writing an epistolary novella in the nineteenth century, Tarchetti was already imitating the epistolary structures of earlier narrative prose fiction writers in England and Europe—Richardson in *Clarissa*, Fielding in *Shamela*, Goethe in *Sorrows of Young Werther*, and so forth. The epistolary, literary historians have long argued, was one of the ways in which personal, intimate, and concretely historical experience was conflated with myth and traditional storytelling and bound up at the origin of the prose fictional style that came to be known as the novel or novella.[14]

But there may be a way in which Lahr's appeal to the epistolary, hits its mark despite his interest in deflating Sondheim and Lapine's "recent experiments." The epistolary, I would like to suggest, may describe Sondheim's musical in a manner that exceeds the demands of form, and offers a context in which the strange movements we have been observing make more sense. Sondheim's play, in short, may itself be a kind of letter, one in which Giorgio's relinquishing of his relationship with Clara for one with Fosca spells out a strategic gesture on Sondheim's part within a context that has long been a part of his lyrical, musical, and dramatic work but which has rarely before been addressed or displayed for us so directly.

Reading Sondheim literally, in other words, *à la lettre*, so to speak, we may open for ourselves a richness of understanding that the vilifying Lahr hardly anticipated. To speak more precisely about such "literalism" (or perhaps we should say such "letteralism") in *Passion*, we need to examine its progressive unfolding in more detail.

II

"If only we had more than letters
Holding us together"

Stephen Sondheim's *Passion* is suffused with letters and with letter writing. There are sixteen scenes in the play and only three without a reference to letters in some capacity. In scene 2, for example, Giorgio arrives at the military outpost and exchanges no fewer than six letters with Clara. In scene 3, Giorgio and Fosca stroll in the neighboring garden and Giorgio comments upon their walk in letters to Clara, comments which are interspersed with that walk. In the following scene, Fosca attempts to deliver a letter to Giorgio she has read aloud to us and which he refuses to read. In scene 5, Giorgio is confronted by Fosca when he attempts to leave the barracks and he promises to write her. During the remainder of the scene his words to her (which are intended on his part to conclude their interaction) are interspersed with his loving words to Clara.

In scene 6, Giorgio and Fosca discuss the letter he wrote to her from Milan. In scene 7, at the doctor's request, Giorgio enters Fosca's bedroom and Fosca dictates to Giorgio a "letter" she would have him write to her. In scene 8, Fosca relates to Giorgio in a letter the history of her earlier life. In scene 9, Giorgio retires to a mountainside to read a letter from Clara. Fosca follows him there and they subsequently argue about her insistent pursuit of him.

In scene 11, Clara sends a letter to Giorgio in which she expresses concern about their relationship. In scene 12, Clara discusses with Giorgio her letter to him. In scene 13, at the Colonel's party, no less than three letters are introduced. Giorgio receives one from Clara asking for a definition of their relationship. The Colonel receives one from headquarters transferring Giorgio (presumably on the basis of an earlier letter by the doctor to headquarters). And the Colonel discovers a letter in Fosca's bedroom in Giorgio's hand (the one Fosca dictated to Giorgio) which confirms in the Colonel's mind

Giorgio's implication in his cousin's unhappiness. In scene 14, once again in Fosca's bedroom, Giorgio discusses the letter he has received from Clara from which he deduces that it is over between them. In scene 16, Giorgio is in the hospital and reads two letters: one from the doctor describing events after the duel and his departure from the garrison, and another from Fosca (mentioned in the letter by the doctor) describing her final revelations.

Although the play is far from "listless" as Lahr describes it, Lahr is certainly right to characterize this play as epistolary at a fundamental level. There are, to be sure, at least three scenes in which no letters appear: 1, 10, and 15. In the first, Giorgio and Clara are in bed with each other making love. In scene 10, Giorgio has a fever and his hallucinations are dramatically represented. In the next-to-last scene of the play the Colonel and Giorgio fight a duel. But even in the first two of these scenes, there is the hint of letters and letter writing, at least indirectly if not directly. In scene 1, Giorgio seems already to have received a notification of some kind regarding his assignment to the remote garrison. Giorgio's dream (or nightmare) in scene 10 may be regarded as a kind of letter or communication from the unconscious, one which is hardly very far from the conscious life he is leading, and its enactment on stage before us is certainly a kind of literalism. And if no letters appear in the scene enacting the duel between the Colonel and Giorgio, their absence remains conspicuous. Its exclusion from this one scene only draws our attention to its omnipresence elsewhere.

What is the function of all this letter writing? How does it reflect and in turn determine the play's action? And what in particular is the function of this curious central scene in which Fosca writes a letter which is not a letter, in which Giorgio pens a letter which is not from his hand, in which a drama is described that is not really taking place, and yet upon which the whole play seems curiously to turn?

III

"My cousin loves to read—
It's her only passion, really."

What in the first place is a letter? Avant-guard French literary and critical theorists of the 1960s and 1970s made a great deal of this question. Jacques Lacan and Jacques Derrida, for example, wrote about it extensively.[15] As an invocation of the law, we may say, a letter is an act of social or symbolic communication, an implementation of the realm in which the conventions of language—address, salutation, leave-taking, for example—apply. It is also a vehicle of desire, an attempt by one individual to communicate to another his (or her) observations, evaluations, even desire itself—in short, everything that makes up human thought and feeling.

In this context, much of the letter writing in *Passion* is explainable. Giorgio is notified by letter of his assignment to the garrison. Giorgio and Clara exchange letters sharing their observations about their lives, their separation, their love for each other. In the garden scene, Giorgio comments by letter upon Fosca, and in the scene immediately following Fosca would deliver to Giorgio a letter describing her own feelings for Giorgio. During his trip to Milan, Giorgio writes a letter to Fosca explaining his love for Clara and setting some boundaries to his relationship with Fosca. Later in the play, Fosca writes a letter to Giorgio explaining to him her past history. Clara writes to Giorgio a letter of inquiry and concern. Giorgio receives a second letter from headquarters notifying him of another transfer. And so forth.

There is another kind of letter writing. What we have described so far is what we might call conscious letter writing, an activity that requires social supports for it, and voluntary attempts by individuals to represent and convey their thoughts and desires by means of it. But Freud among others has taught us that there is another place where thought occurs, a place he names the Unconscious ("something thinks there where we think we think" is a common formulation of the Unconscious), and in myriad ways we may receive messages, communications, transmissions from this unconscious realm (dreams, slips of the tongue, or other "accidental" occurrences provide in our lives a conduit for such communications).[16] Freud also taught us, moreover, that the means by which these unconscious communications occur is through a kind of "literalism", that dreams, for example, are a kind of rebus or picture-language in which the thought content is less represented than enacted.[17] Thus in Sondheim's play, the dream sequence in scene 10 may be understood.

But neither a representational account of letters nor a symptomatic account explain scene 7. How are we to understand Fosca's gesture in scene 7? On one hand, her gesture is entirely voluntary and conscious. She dictates to Giorgio a letter she wishes he had written to her, expressing in it the love for her she wishes he felt. On the other hand, since Giorgio has not initiated the expression, since the gesture is only fictively "his" (and only borrows the genre of letter writing, much as a scrivener or copyist borrows the genre he copies), what we understand primarily by Fosca's gesture is Fosca's own desires: here is the desire she would like from him, a desire, we may say, literally, for his desire, a desire for him to give up his former rejection of her love and embrace it unconditionally. That the gesture leads to Giorgio's real appropriation of a desire for Fosca later in the play seems less an ironic confirmation of their interaction than its unexpected extension in a manner that remains to be disclosed.

But let us not get ahead of ourselves. To examine scene 7 in its wider implications, let us turn to the structural context in which it is embedded.

IV

"I read to live"

An analysis of the structure of *Passion* reveals in the first instance that the play is composed of not one narrative sequence but three. Giorgio moves in the first eight or so scenes of the play through eight reorientations. The play opens with Giorgio and Clara in the comfort of Clara's bed, in the midst of their lovemaking. The news of Giorgio's military assignment is announced, and we are quickly relocated to the miliary garrison where Fosca's off-stage screams introduce us to the Colonel's wayward cousin. The captain becomes fascinated with her presence (or absence) and inquires about her with the company doctor on the field of maneuvers. Shortly after their conversation, Giorgio and Fosca meet for the first time. Fosca notes that there are lovely gardens to which they might repair, and in the next scene, with the doctor and the Colonel along, the pair indulge the pleasantness of the surroundings and stroll together in the nearby ruins.

There is a break of some three days and now things begin rather quickly to go sour. Fosca attempts to communicate with Giorgio via a letter she has written to him. He rebuffs her attempts, and her peculiar intensity about the rejection only serves to heighten his disdain. He arranges for a five-day leave and she suddenly confronts him as he is departing. On the point of distraction, she elicits from him a promise to write to her. He does so from Milan, announcing in no uncertain terms the existence and depth of his relationship with Clara. Upon his return to the garrison, Fosca is noticeably cooler to him and they agree to see each other no longer.

The first sequence of the play may be represented in something of the following manner (Figure 12.1).

Were the scene in Fosca's drawing room to end the act, we would have little difficulty understanding the coherence of the sequence. Giorgio is romantically involved with Clara. His departure from her only intensifies his attraction for her (and hers for him). Their frequent exchange of letters both relieves and heightens the obstacles, allowing the lovers to do what many lovers have done (Abelard and Héloïse, for example), although blocking at the same time the interaction those obstacles inspire. The appearance of Fosca serves only to sharpen the contrast with the image of Clara in Giorgio's mind, and the more Fosca (who has also been reading romantic novels) insists upon an interaction, the more odious the prospect of a relationship with her becomes to Giorgio. We might expect that suddenly a new series of events will change things entirely.

Nothing of the kind occurs. What in fact happens now is a repetition of what has already taken place. Three weeks pass and Giorgio notes that his previous difficulties with Fosca appear to have subsided. The doctor sum-

Fig. 12.1

comfort	dislocation	fascination	encounter	indulgence	intensification	distraction	confrontation	resolution
Clara's bedroom	garrison dining room	field	garrison living room	gardens	garrison dining room	doorway interaction	letter sent to Fosca	Fosca's drawing room

mons him and asks him to visit Fosca upon her deathbed. He is startled, but agrees when the doctor presents her as a wounded creature (he has built his reputation in part upon helping those wounded in battle). We are thrust into the bedroom scene which is broken into roughly three parts: a conversation in which Giorgio orients himself to his new surroundings; a period of sleep in which Clara's view of the situation is contrasted with Fosca's; and a sequence in which Fosca asks Giorgio to write a letter for her. As a kind of tag to the scene, Giorgio speaks with the doctor, and in the following scene, as a kind of relaxing of tensions, Fosca writes to Giorgio about her earlier history, a narrative Giorgio also receives orally from the Colonel.

But as before things now once again begin to go sour. Giorgio retreats to a mountainside to read Clara's letters to him. Fosca follows him and a confrontation ensues. A storm breaks, Fosca faints, and Giorgio is forced to carry her back to camp to save her life, an effort which tosses him into a fever and confines him to his bed for three days. The soldiers greet their return cynically. The doctor puts Giorgio on a forty-day rest leave and Fosca (who is now relentless) pursues him onto the train with the intention of accompanying him. He confronts her with the outrageousness of her actions. But in his weakness he is unable to withstand her appeal to duty. He decides to return with her to the garrison, and to give up his plan to go to Milan for forty days. He will go for four days and return to the garrison and Fosca. He relays to Clara this new plan.

We may add this second narrative to the first as follows (Figure 12.2).

Reading the second sequence in this manner—as a repetition of the first—certain features become evident that might not become evident otherwise. His conversation with the doctor is like the bedroom scene: one of comfort from which a new adventure may begin. The bedroom scene with Fosca parallels the three scenes earlier in which Giorgio learned about, became fascinated with, and finally met, Fosca. And the letter writing scene parallels the stroll in the garden.

The souring of his newfound relation to Fosca is also clearer. Fosca interferes with his privacy on the mountainside as she did with his meal previously. His own distraction after carrying her back from the storm parallels her distraction at the doorway—at one point he drags her across the floor as he tries to walk away from her. His confronting of her on the train is like his confrontation of her earlier via the letter. And his conversation afterwards with Clara parallels his earlier agreement with Fosca not to meet again.

But there is a difference. Where before the prospect was romantic love—before which Fosca didn't stand a chance and Clara had no rival, now the situation is one of creaturely compassion and in this regard even Clara has to admit that Fosca's claim is the stronger. It is not, in other words, that Fosca has won Giorgio romantically, but rather that she has at this point won his compassion and the distinction between the two is critical.

Fig. 12.2

comfort	dislocation	fascination	encounter	indulgence	intensification	distraction	confrontation	resolution
Clara's bedroom	garrison dining room	field conversation	garrison living room	gardens	garrison dining room	doorway interaction	letter sent to Fosca	Fosca's drawing room
doctor's room	Fosca's bedroom: talk	Fosca / Clara: dreams	Fosca's bedroom: "letter"	Fosca's / Colonel's story	mountainside interaction	soldiers; fever	train; conversation with doctor	conversation with Clara

On the basis of these first two sequences, then, we might well expect that the third sequence will engender from this dialectical opposition of romantic love and compassion, a new synthesis. Some days pass. It is Christmas eve. The revelry of the season is in full gear. Giorgio has more or less recovered. A song proclaiming peace and rest is sung. Two letters are received at the garrison: one for Giorgio from Clara, another for the Colonel from headquarters. The Colonel reads his own in which he learns that Giorgio has been transferred. The Colonel is outraged and Fosca suddenly declares her love for Giorgio openly. Thinking Giorgio has deceived his cousin and then arranged for his transfer (a move not unlike that of the count about whom the Colonel has informed his young colleague), the Colonel is nonplussed and leaves to inquire further. The scene shifts to an exchange between Giorgio and Clara over the status of their relationship.

Back in the garrison, we learn that the Colonel has discovered in Fosca's bedroom a letter in Giorgio's hand confirming his suspicion that Giorgio has misled his cousin into imagining the possibility of a relationship. Like Othello, who discovers his wife's handkerchief in Michael Cassio's hand, the Colonel acts swiftly. He challenges Giorgio to a duel, and Giorgio strangely accepts. Giorgio solicits the doctor's assistance to see Fosca one last time, and although the latter resists the suggestion, the next scene finds the two together. Giorgio announces to her the end of his relationship with Clara, and he and Fosca make love. The duel takes place the following day. The Colonel is wounded by Giorgio's shot and falls to his knees. Giorgio screams in a manner reminiscent, the notes tell us, of Fosca. In the final scene of the play, Giorgio is in the hospital several months later, recovering from his wounds. He reads a note from the doctor informing him of Fosca's death (three days after their last meeting), and another from Fosca describing her newly transformed state.

Although this final sequence of events contains only four scenes (with the possible addition of Giorgio's exchange with Clara), the movements within these scenes align themselves more or less precisely (albeit in a highly telescoped manner) with the ones to which we have been witness, and the external narrative developments of the play in its structural entirety may be represented in the following fashion (Figure 12.3).

The addition of this third sequence, in other words, both parallels and contrasts with the two earlier sequences. The scene at the party with its supplementary exchange between Giorgio and Clara parallels the scenes in and around the garrison earlier. The scene with Fosca alone parallels the interaction with Fosca alone by the doorway. The duel parallels the letter Giorgio sends Fosca setting the boundaries firmly between them. And the hospital resolution parallels the scene in Fosca's drawing room.

The third sequence also parallels the second. The scene at the party parallels the scene in and around Fosca's bedroom. The scene in Fosca's bed-

Fig. 12.3

comfort	dislocation	fascination	encounter	indulgence	intensification	distraction	confrontation	resolution
Clara's bedroom	garrison dining room	field	garrison living room	gardens	garrison dining room	doorway interaction	letter sent to Fosca	Fosca's drawing room
doctor's room	Fosca's bedroom: talk	Fosca / Clara: dreams	Fosca's bedroom: "letter"	Fosca's / Colonel's story	mountainside interaction	soldiers; fever	train; conversation with doctor	conversation with Clara
Christmas song	party	mail for Colonel and Giorgio; outbursts	Giorgio's conversation with Clara	Colonel's challenge	conversation with doctor	Fosca's bedroom	duel	hospital letters and Fosca's resurrection

room parallels the fever Giorgio feels as he dreams in bed that Fosca is suffocating him. The duel parallels the confrontation on the train and both the conversation with the doctor and the hospital scene parallel the end of the relation in Milan with Clara.

But the forward movement of the third sequence is entirely different. In the earlier sequences, the positive feeling Giorgio offered Fosca in the first half—friendship in the first sequence, compassion in the second—quickly soured in the second half of each. Giorgio's disdain increased as Fosca perceived herself Clara's rival. And his pity quickly turned to anger as her pursuit of him became relentless. In the third sequence, the lighthearted festivity of the party is jolted by the news of Giorgio's transfer, Fosca's outburst, and the Colonel's challenge. The overwhelming and vaguely disturbing happiness of the bedroom scene proceeds unabated. The duel is straightforward, and, except for Giorgio's anguished scream, military. And the hospital scene is expository and oddly tranquil and uplifting.

What are we to make of this structural progression? Let us gather what we have learned. The story line we have said is in fact three story lines, or rather a single story line played out in three distinct registers. The first narrative concerns romantic love between Giorgio and Clara from the point of view of which Fosca's presence is at best a curiosity and at worst a nuisance. The second concerns Giorgio's relationship to Fosca as someone who, in the manner of one of his soldiers, is wounded and may be dying. He feels a sense of duty to or responsibility for Fosca and that sense of obligation is at odds with his sense of romantic love for Clara. He is still willing to marry and run off with Clara (the idea that he is in love with Fosca, he says, is "ludicrous"), but he is also willing to alter his plans vis à vis Clara to tend to Fosca's needs.

In the third sequence of the play, his sense of duty or compassion for the pitiful and wounded creature before him has turned into something else. Something about the unconditionality of Fosca's declared love for him compels him to break off the relationship with Clara entirely, and to free himself to "love" Fosca in an equally unconditional fashion.

Thus the suddenness of Giorgio's shift from one woman to another, which seems to be at the core of interpretive difficulty with the play, needs to be recast. The question the play poses for us seems to be not why does Giorgio give up Clara for Fosca. That question is answerable. He doesn't. His romantic interest remains with Clara. We have to assume that were he to overcome his newfound need to serve Fosca he could return to Clara—and it is not impossible that he will do so after his hospital stay. He has turned his energies for the moment to this deeper issue and that is what compels his interest in Fosca. Even if he declares that he "loves" Fosca and the final scene with her parallels explicitly the opening scene in which he is in bed with Clara (Sondheim notes that he even considered having them sing the same opening song), we have to assume that the two women are not romantic rivals.[18] Giorgio's obsession with

Fosca has simply become all-engrossing. We understand, in other words, how the shift takes place even if we do not as yet understand why.

But a new question now must be asked. Why doesn't this deeper interest lend itself to the same shifts as romantic love and compassion? Why doesn't this new intensity go sour? It is as if the audience and early critical response supplies the souring the play leaves out. Is Sondheim finally suggesting that a shift of context from eros to pathos to agape is one way in which we may understand Giorgio's turn as redemptive? Religious overtones are certainly scattered throughout the third sequence. The Christmas song and holiday talk at the beginning, and the reappearance of Fosca at the end, for example, certainly appear to encourage such an interpretation. Is Sondheim describing a transformation from romantic love and annoyance, to creaturely compassion and passionate obsession, to religious resurrection? Is this Sondheim's "passion play"? Such a rendering may feel artificial and unsatisfying, but if that is the play's internal intention, perhaps we should simply document it as such and read it the way we read disappointing works of other first-rate literary and dramatic artists.

Let us not jump to conclusions. If the play were like *Assassins*, we might argue that it was a deeply cynical account of romantic love as *Assassins* was a deeply cynical account of the American dream, a play in which murderers and would-be murderers alike can sing "Everybody's / Got the right / To their dreams" (7), a kind of mad redoing of the opening scene of Rodgers and Hammerstein's *Carousel.*[19] *Passion*, we might argue, makes a mockery of the conventions of romantic love, much as *Into the Woods* makes a mockery of our seemingly boundless capacity to live our lives according to fairy tale scripts.

But *Passion* is not cynical, finally, I would like to suggest. And there may be a way of taking the redemptive and celebratory ending of *Passion* seriously without either endorsing Fosca's poisonous self-pity as a viable romantic alternative to Clara's light, or crediting Giorgio and Fosca's mutual narcissistic fantasies at the expense of more conventional understandings of psychological maturity and responsibility, and more generally of the distinction between theater and therapy.

To answer the question of why the final narrative sequence of *Passion* is different, we need to examine one other aspect of the play: its internal history.

V

"Why is it that the violets and daisies blossom now?
They mistake Autumn's warmth for April."

One other structure needs to be considered in light of our discussion. The internal narrative described by Fosca in her letter to Giorgio (and by the Colonel in his oral communication with Giorgio) follows curiously the same internal pattern as the three larger movements. Fosca we learn is raised within a comfortable if illusion-based childhood. She is thrust into adulthood when her cousin introduces to her a friend who is strangely attracted to her. She is fascinated by this acquaintance and his worldly charm and drawn into a relationship with him that culminates in marriage.

The marriage not unexpectedly goes bad very quickly. The count is "unavailable" to Fosca, gambles away her money, pursues other women on the side, and turns out not even a "count" after all (as "countless" others have learned). Fosca confronts the scoundrel with this information. He denies none of it. She is devastated. Her parents, who are in poor health anyway, fail, and she is forced to move in with her cousin in the military garrison. The sequence may be plotted in tandem with the others (Figure 12.4).

If we needed any confirmation, in other words, that the structural pattern we have discerned above was the one the play prompted us to consider, here it is. All of the nine steps are there, and the history is presented at once as an oral history and a written one, a conversation and a letter.

Why would Sondheim offer us this internal sequence in such a way that so completely parallels the external narrative movements? For purposes of internal structural consistency? Sondheim rarely offers us structure for the sake of structure alone. The internal sequence certainly helps us to understand the other major sequences in the play. It confirms both their identity and the distinction between them. It records an earlier instance of romantic love gone wrong, a case that is to say, not of love but of betrayal. As the life of Fosca at the garrison is a product of that history, we may understand both the feeling of romantic love she exhibits (which repeats her earlier experience) and the creaturely compassion or pity Giorgio feels in part at least as a response to her betrayal by the count. Fosca's unfortunate past enables Giorgio to feel sympathy for her plight and to make her seem less a romantic rival with Clara (a rivalry she can never win), and more a creature of sympathy. Finding such a creature, one so wounded in the battle of the sexes, how could one not feel a sense of duty, if not of responsibility, toward her?

There is another possibility. The internal story is presented to us as a series of letters or written communications (as well as a series of talks or oral communications). Is it possible that the series of larger sequences of which it is a part may similarly be understood as forms of "letters" or written communications? As Fosca's history prior to her arrival in the garrison may be told as a letter and oral communication, may the entire history of the play, the story of Fosca betrayed and later fulfilled, be told as a similar "letter" and oral communication?

What would it mean to say as much? We can answer that question at least in part. The play as presented registers rather univocally Giorgio's passage from one relationship to another. We have already pointed out that Giorgio has not simply dropped one woman for another, but rather moved from one level of relating to another level of relating—from lush, sexual, erotic, romantic encounters with Clara to more profound, soulful, familial encounters with Fosca. Associating Fosca with dying, he can pretend in that context that

Fig. 12.4

comfort	dislocation	fascination	encounter	indulgence	intensification	distraction	confrontation	resolution
Clara's bedroom	garrison dining room	field conversation	garrison living room	gardens	garrison dining room	doorway interaction	letter sent to Fosca	Fosca's drawing room
doctor's room	Fosca's bedroom: talk	Fosca / Clara: dreams	Fosca's bedroom: "letter"	Fosca's / Colonel's story:	mountainside interaction	soldiers; fever	train; conversation with doctor	conversation with Clara
childhood	*introduction of count*	*flowers*	*dinner*	*marriage*	*gambling; unavailable to Fosca*	*woman informer*	*no denial*	*death of parents and relocation*
Christmas song	party	mail for Colonel and Giorgio; outbursts	Giorgio's conversation with Clara	Colonel's challenge	conversation with doctor	Fosca's bedroom	duel	hospital letters and Fosca's resurrection

he loves her, pretend that he is writing a love-letter to her in her bedroom, really sympathize with her when he learns her history, really rescue her on the bluff, really pity her on the train, feel real duty or obligation toward her when he speaks with the doctor, and finally (if we are to take seriously his words) really love her when he speaks with her in her bedroom in the play's last scenes. He moves from the conditional romantic love of Clara to the unconditional soul-baring love of Fosca.

To say then that the play is itself a "letter" or written communication is to say more specifically that it is like the letter Fosca would have Giorgio write and read to her, a letter which also tells the story of a move from rejection to acceptance, the story of the relationship of Giorgio and Fosca in terms she would find acceptable, namely: "I [wanted to] forget you, / Erase you from my mind . . . [but] now I'm seeing love / Like none I've ever known" (60-1). Giorgio's thoughts of love for Fosca at the end of the play (which summarize his experience for him) are also, we recall, Fosca's thoughts within the play, in the letter she dictates to him in the bedroom in which she expresses her view of their relationship, thoughts about Giorgio, or more specifically, thoughts about Giorgio's thoughts about Fosca. And the terms of that perspective are clear: I would like to forget you, but I cannot do so, and now you will live in me forever. The fact that Giorgio's view at the end of the play is expressed by Fosca's reappearance and singing—with all the confusions that gesture entails—only confirms this external manifestation of this internal plot. The image is a pregnant one. The play at large tells in some measure the story the internal letter describes in miniature.

But only in some measure. Let us grant that the play's overall narrative form reproduces the narrative Fosca recounts in her bedroom at the play's center. A letter is more than a narrative. A letter is a communication, sent to someone, by someone. To whom would such a larger "letter" or series of "letters" be written? And by whom would it be composed?

To probe these questions we need to turn to one final context in which this play may be viewed, a context in which the why of the transformation of Giorgio's affections from romantic love for Clara to soul-stirring passion for Fosca may come somewhat clearer, a context, moreover, in which the sudden compressing and shifting of the structural pattern Sondheim has been pursuing and the adoption of a celebratory and redemptive conclusion may find its explanation.

VI

"What is the cost of a few words . . . "

If we wonder why Sondheim would choose to work through such a seemingly unhealthy and destructive encounter, some remarks he made to

Michiko Kakutani in an interview published in the *New York Times* (March 20, 1994) on the occasion of the mounting of *Passion* (and to which we referred above) begin to acquire a haunting resonance.

"My mother was quite a remarkable character," he said.

> She was going into the hospital to have a pacemaker put in and said many mothers going in for open-heart surgery write their children a letter. I said it's a pacemaker, but she wrote me a letter, hand-delivered because she thought she was going to die and she wanted to make sure I got it. She said, "The night before I undergo open heart surgery,"—underlined three times. Open parenthesis. "My surgeon's term." Close parenthesis. "The only regret I have in life is giving you birth."
>
> "We all think our parents are suffering from misplaced love or possessiveness or whatever," he continues [Kakutani writes], "but she didn't want me on earth. And I realized why: she had a career and she didn't want a child. In a way her letter was a good thing for me. As long as it took the pen to cross the paper, I wrote her a letter saying I finally understand."[20]

Is it really so hard to understand why Sondheim at this moment in his life is attracted to a story about being "cracked" open, of a love which is "like a knife," of an exchange of "letters" involving "misplaced" affections? Is it really outrageous to suggest that this play is Sondheim's attempt, after "years of analysis," to imagine the conditions of his own engendering—in a manner perhaps not unlike that undertaken by Ingmar Bergman, for example, in *The Best Intentions*?

In the middle of *Passion*, in its "centerpiece" as Annette Grant aptly calls it, lies a woman who thinks she is on her deathbed (because her doctor told her so), who writes a "letter" which she "hand-delivers" and which contains the following words:

> I wish I could forget you,
> Erase you from my mind.
> . . . .
> That doesn't mean I love you . . .
> I wish that I could love you . . .
> I know that I've upset you.
> I know I've been unkind.
> I wanted you to vanish from sight,
> . . . .
> And though I cannot love you,
> I wish that I could love you. (60-1)[21]

It is hard to avoid the conclusion that scene 7 of *Passion* is Sondheim's staging, if in a slightly disguised manner, of this earlier primal encounter. What are the implications of drawing such a connection?

Scene 7 is both like and unlike the anecdote Sondheim recounts. It is like it in all the ways we have specified. There are the verbal echoes we have noted ("I wish I could forget you, / Erase you from my mind. . . . I wanted you to vanish from sight," etc.). The situations are similar (she "thought she was going to die"; her doctor's influence is present, etc). Something of the same event occurs in both (she delivers a letter which is not a letter to an individual to whom she feels especially close).

Moreover, the episode in both plays a dominant role in what follows. The hospital scene is presented to us by Sondheim (and others who write about it) as structurative of much that follows in his emotional life.[22] Within the play, it will be on the basis of the discovery later of the letter that the duel between Giorgio and Fosca's cousin will be fought. And we have to assume the scene is especially important for Sondheim and Lapine, since it is one of the few places where their play deviates from both Scola's film and Tarchetti's novella. In the latter two sources it is on other bases that the duel is fought. The centrality of the dictated letter in *Passion* is their invention.

But scene 7 of *Passion* is also unlike the real-life situation (as Sondheim has described it) in some fundamental ways: 1) the real-life scene in Sondheim's life has the effect of driving him away, whereas the fictional scene in *Passion* as experienced by Giorgio is not especially oppressive at the moment and pivotal only later when in the final scene Fosca reappears and repeats the same words; 2) the assumption in the real-life scene (again, as Sondheim presents it to us) is that these are the mother's words, the words of the letter she would send to her son, whereas the presumption at least of scene 7 is that these are the words Fosca *would like* to receive from Giorgio, and failing that, words that she is content to put into his mouth (or more precisely, into his hand); and 3) the words of the real-life "letter" can hardly not have been experienced by their recipient as a rejection (even though they may also be regarded as the expression of an understandable conflict between career and family, as Sondheim points out), whereas the Fosca of scene 7 writes words which revise that position, which speak of it in such a way that reject it as an earlier insufficient perspective.

How are we to account for these differences? I would like to suggest that the fictional scene may be less the staging of the real-life scene than its sympathetic, symptomatic, and prophetic extension. Or rather, and perhaps more precisely, that it is both that scene and not that scene, a letter and not a letter. It is at once the letter his mother "hand-delivers" to him (expressing regrets at giving him birth), and his revision of that letter, the letter he gives in response saying to her, "I understand," or some alternative version of that letter.

Here is the song in its entirety:

I wish I could forget you,
Erase you from my mind.
But ever since I met you,

I find
I cannot leave the thought of you behind.

That doesn't mean I love you . . .
I wish that I could love you . . .

I know that I've upset you.
I know I've been unkind.
I wanted you to vanish from sight,
But now I see you in a different light,
And though I cannot love you,
I wish that I could love you.

For now I'm seeing love
Like none I've ever known,
A love as pure as breath,
As permanent as death,
Implacable as stone.
A love that, like a knife,
Has cut into a life
I wanted left alone.

A love I may regret,
But one I can't forget.

I don't know how I let you
So far inside my mind,
But there you are and there you will stay.
How could I ever wish you away?
I see now I was blind.

And should you die tomorrow,
Another thing I see:
Your love will live in me. (60-1)

In context of the anecdote cited above, in other words, is not the song itself with its conciliatory words an expression of the "letter" Sondheim could
well wish his mother had written to him, one which that is to say takes full
stock of her desire for him to "vanish from sight" and yet which at the same
time renounces that same desire ("How could I ever wish you away? / I see
now I was blind"), one which, in lieu of her capacity to write such a letter expressing such sentiments of regret if not of love (either before or now), he will
undertake to complete for her?
    "I know that I've upset you," his character sings. "I know I've been un-

kind. / I wanted you to vanish from sight, / But now I see you in a different light, / And though I cannot love you, / I wish that I could love you" (61). As the internal letter Fosca wrote rendered the story of Fosca in the garrison a "part 2" to a history for which we now know "part 1" (and which might have led to a very different "part 2"), so the real-life history of the lyricist–composer offered to us via anecdote in the Kakutani interview may be regarded as another "internal history" which renders the play at large a "part 2," one which similarly might indeed have proceeded otherwise. As a moment in the lyricist–composer's real-life history, the play would then tell the story of Foxy/Fosca's real-life rejection, betrayal, and fantasized/desired fulfillment. "Your love will live in me . . . " (131), which are the final words of the play, and sung by both Giorgio and Fosca in echoic fashion, linger after it in a manner that enacts the gestational image it describes.

But if we accept that conclusion, then in writing the letter that is *Passion*, has he not also completed his relationship to her? Has he not turned this song, this "letter," and the play of which it is the "centerpiece" (and which we have suggested is another version of it), into an extraordinary act of "understanding" and forgiveness?

How so?

The key, I suggest, is his granting his mother in *Passion* what she wants.

The logic of this connection needs to be spelled out in some detail. The sentiment expressed in Fosca's letter in scene 7 revises an earlier position in which the narrator wished the other would vanish from sight. That sentiment makes sense in context of Fosca's prior experience (as we will learn momentarily), one in which the "you" might have been the "count," and in context of Fosca's earlier interaction with Giorgio. She could well wish Giorgio had given up his earlier rejection of her, and is perhaps also anticipating a healthier approach to her former marital relationship.

It also makes sense in context of the ending of the play when Fosca expresses (in her second letter to Giorgio) a similar belief. Although Giorgio at times sings them alone, the words are Fosca's.

GIORGIO:
> Now at last
> I see what comes
> From feeling loved.

> Strange, how merely
> Feeling loved,
> You see things clearly.

> Things I feared,
> Like the world itself,
> I now love dearly.

BOTH:
> I want to live.
> Now I want to live,

FOSCA:
> Just from being loved.

> All that pain
> I nursed inside
> For all those years—

GIORGIO:
> All that vain
> And bitter self-concern—

BOTH:
> All those tears
> And all that pride
> Have vanished into air . . .

FOSCA:
> I don't want to leave.

GIORGIO:
> Now that I am loved,

FOSCA:
> I don't want to leave.

BOTH:
> Everywhere I turn,
> You are there.

FOSCA:
> Everywhere I look,
> Things are different.

BOTH:
> Everything seems right,
> Everything seems possible,
> Every moment bursts with feeling.

> Why is love so easy to give
> And so hard to receive?

FOSCA:
> But though I want to live
> I now can leave
> With what I never knew:
> I'm someone to be loved.

GIORGIO:
> I'm someone to be loved.

FOSCA:
> And that I learned from you. (128-30)

The relation of these words to the letter in scene 7 is heightened by her verbatim repetition of the final section of the earlier song (in words which constitute the play's only solo reprise).

I don't know how I let you
So far inside my mind,
But there you are, and there you will stay.
How could I ever wish you away?
I see now I was blind.
And should you die tomorrow,
Another thing I see:
Your love will live in me ... (130-31)

It is as if her earlier words in scene 7 were prophetic. Although offered at the moment, we have to assume, as wishful thinking, they come true—for her and for Giorgio.

And that final repetition is demonstrably derived from the "revelations" that came to Fosca in the days following their lovemaking—from "feeling loved," which in turn derives from her lovemaking with Giorgio and his declaration of love for her (and her consequent "happiness" and fear), which in its turn derives—as we saw—from a process beginning with the writing of the letter in scene 7.

The play as a whole, in other words, grants her her desires: the reciprocated love of the man she has chosen as her love object, a reciprocity that seemed unlikely on the surface given the social and aesthetic parameters involved, and given her prior history—seduced and spurned as she was so cruelly by the "count." Against all odds, a woman who has been spurned and rejected, and who bears all the physical and emotional scars of that rejection, gains the man of her choice.

Is there an analogy in Sondheim's life? In fact, of course, we know that there is. The Kakutani interview details the facts that have already been a part of the several books on Sondheim, and the recent book by Meryle Secrest corroborates this sense extensively: Foxy Sondheim experienced herself (at least from the child's point of view) as a woman spurned and betrayed by her husband, and from all available accounts, she took this traumatic experience out on her single male child.[23]

The situation in Sondheim's life, in other words, parallels almost precisely the earlier situation of Fosca with her husband. With one exception: in the fictional case there is no child.[24] It is as if Sondheim has chosen to represent in *Passion* not the actual situation he lived through, but a fantasized past of it (or a fantasized future of it), one in either case from which he has been subtracted.

Do we understand, then, his strategy? *Passion* as a whole presents us with a woman who has been spurned and betrayed and who gets the object of her desire: the man of her dreams. Viewed against the background of his life, the play does for Sondheim the same. It grants the real-life mother he knew her desire in precisely the terms she has specified: that her son not be born.

And his hope must be that the results obtained are also the same. As the conferring of Fosca's wish upon her transforms her, so we have to assume the play's strategy is that the conferring of Foxy's wish—that her son not be born and that she get her man—will transform her, will enable her to give up, like her fictional counterpart, the poisonous recrimination and self-pity, and that such a relinquishing will engender another release: the child's own.

The play *Passion*, in other words, is situated both before and after the real-life situation it reflects. It is after it historically. It reflects upon a history after the events of that history have occurred, and in fact after one of the principals—Sondheim's mother—is deceased. And it is after it fictionally since the terms it imagines exceed the real-life circumstances (which only parallel Fosca's marital history). It prophetically imagines a fulfillment of what in real-life is only a fervent wish. But it is also before that real-life history insofar as the terms in which it speaks are about the possibility of an alternative beginning: a relationship between his parents (in both the prior and later history of Fosca) in which the child never enters the picture.

Perhaps it is also before the real-life history in another way. Is it outrageous to suggest that the act of imagining a fulfillment of his mother's desire in this fashion brings about real changes in his own? If we assume that the real-life situation for him has been ongoing, then all his life he has been penning the desires of others (to use the word Sondheim employs in the interview). Like Giorgio who is first stalked by Fosca and later feels some pity for her, he pens the desires of the other. He lends them a hand. But what he may discover is that—again, like Giorgio—the act of penning another's desires can sometimes lead to a more profound admission of them—both a confession and a granting of entrance—and that in the end he may join Fosca in her transformed state.

Is the Sondheim, then, who inscribes within his characters the desire for an end to the turmoil of the past, who could well wish his mother had said these words, not, finally, Fosca? Is not Fosca, in other words, Sondheim's "Giorgio," the character, that is to say, by whose hand he is willing to score or inscribe or underscore his own desires, just as through Giorgio she would construct her projected counterpart? Like Fosca who gets the other to say what she wants by dictating her words to him, so Sondheim gets the mother to say what he could well wish she would say on her own by similarly imbuing her desires in Fosca. Although Foxy is no longer alive at the moment Sondheim scores *Passion*, she appears and speaks through it, through the letter it contains and the letter it constitutes, just as Fosca appears and speaks through the letter Giorgio reads (and sings) in the play's final moments, although she too has died some time before.

And so do we not have to assume that the words that Fosca discovers apply to her in fact apply as well to Sondheim?

> For now I'm seeing love
> Like none I've ever known,
> A love as pure as breath,
> As permanent as death,
> Implacable as stone.
> A love that, like a knife,
> Has cut into a life
> I wanted left alone.
>
> A love I may regret,
> But one I can't forget.
>
> I don't know how I let you
> So far inside my mind,
> But there you are and there you will stay.
> How could I ever wish you away?
> I see now I was blind.
>
> And should you die tomorrow,
> Another thing I see:
> Your love will live in me. (61)

Is *Passion*, then, artistic autobiography as well as personal history? Is it the record of Sondheim's move from modalities of being Giorgio to modalities of being Fosca? It is, I have tried to suggest, if we regard it as memory rather than representation. The relation between the two, between the play and the real-life circumstances, is sequential not analogous, diachronic not synchronic, prophetic rather than duplicative. It is important that we not read the play representationally, as simply a copy of Sondheim's real-life conflicts (although it certainly reflects them). Fosca is not simply his mother. Giorgio is not simply either his father or Sondheim himself. The scene in which Fosca and Giorgio are presumed to make love is not a scene of transgression, and it would be a mistake in my view to read it as such.

On the other hand, Sondheim is imagining what might have accrued had he never been born (or perhaps what might have happened in his mother's second marriage after he was effectively out of the picture), namely, the revision of her position with its desired results: the giving up of her prior anguish, the saying of the words Sondheim could well wish his mother had said. If Fosca's gesture toward Giorgio is unexpectedly successful, the play seems to be gambling, may not Sondheim's gesture toward Foxy be similarly successful? And in any event, has Sondheim not chronicled in the attempt the course of his artistic career?

But she did not say them—at least to public knowledge. The conciliatory words of Fosca's song do not occur in the mouth of the "Fosca" with whom he lived in the anecdotes we are considering. Does it matter that the revision (and consequent transformation) that occurs in *Passion* may never have taken place in the real-life drama it reflects? These words may be the ones he could well wish his mother had written (or spoken), but what if she did not write them or speak them?

And what of the fact that Foxy is deceased at the moment of the writing of *Passion*? Is *Passion* itself just wishful thinking? Is it possible that *Passion* is indeed setting itself up as a larger version of scene 7 (as we suggest), but that the corresponding transformation in scene 16 may never in fact take place? Is Sondheim just putting words into her mouth?

The facts of the matter, as Sondheim often reminds us, are always important. But in this particular instance, the psychological process can operate whether the facts reflect its terms or not. It is possible to reconcile ourselves to our parents whether they are dead or alive, although it is admittedly more difficult in the latter case than the former. The completion of a relationship to another does not require the other to be there for the event. Scoring the play *Passion*, Sondheim assumes responsibility for the "character" his mother was (and became even if only fictively), and owns his own identity to her, whether she said the words he wanted or didn't say them, whether she intended them or didn't intend them, whether she was able to say them or incapable of saying them, whether indeed she was deceased at the moment he imagined their utterance or still living. It is a matter for him, finally, as for Giorgio, of "Love unconcerned / with being returned," of "love without cause, / without sense, / without laws" and all else must be reread in that context.[25] Like Shakespeare before him in the sonnet quoted above, Sondheim imaginatively "prays" that his mother will "have [her] *Will*." The "mother's part," like a mother's kisses and a mother's kindness, is gained by giving up the "pursuit" of "that which flies before [your] face" and "turn[ing] back," as Sondheim says in *Into the Woods*, to "calm the child" (135).

And not only in this play. For in context of the completion of the relationship that this play appears to reflect, another Giorgio, who is also an artist, and accused of being cold, intellectual, and remote from a woman who loves him, comes unexpectedly into focus. In fact, the entire history of "Giorgios"—from Milos Gloriosus, Ben Stone, Carl Magnus, and Georges Seurat on—becomes now, in John Lahr's extraordinary slip, subject to "reading."

VII

"The follies one commits before dying"

What if things *had* proceeded otherwise? What if Fosca had lived? What if she recovered sufficiently to marry Giorgio or even just enough to live with him and perhaps bear a child with him? Would Giorgio give up his former ways? Would he, like the hero in Kundera's most famous novel, remain content to live the remainder of his days in the remote Italian countryside reading Rousseau?[26] Or would his ego defenses heal sufficiently so that at some point he would resume his libertine ways, and a chance encounter with another Clara—or even the same one—would once again hurl him into a sensual and anguished romantic triangle?

And if that happened, how would Fosca react? Maturely? Would she take him in and help him to work though the repetition of his earlier life? On what basis would she have gained the necessary skills for such a response? Or rather would she not do what she has always done, what she does best, namely, become the grief-stricken and histrionic individual who long ago learned to manipulate those around her in such fashion? And who, then, is most likely to be the victim of her rage? Giorgio, who, like the "count" of former days, is by now out of reach? Or her young child, who is fully within harm's way and to whom Giorgio remains fatally attached?

The scenario begins to sound like the stuff of Greek tragedy. By a freak of accident (but what, after all, in this context, is accident?) on the obverse of the page on which the Kakutani interview was printed, there was an advertisement for a performance of Euripides' *Medea*, and this accident may suggest something about the choice of Donna Murphy as Fosca rather than another actress. Does Donna Murphy in her fury not look considerably more like Medea as we would like to imagine her, a woman one may expect to find in an ancient Greek tragedy wailing a ritual mourning lament (the figure of Maria Callas comes to mind), than she does like the childlike stick figure playing Fosca in Scola's film, a figure who looks more like a Holocaust survivor than a victim of Greek misfortune, and a figure one critic calls a walking "sight gag"?[27]

Is this play, in other words, excluding Fosca's death, not "act 1" to a drama for which Euripides' ancient play is a possible expression of "act 2"? And does not such a diachronic or prophetic extension of the play's dramatic potentials make sense of other boldly "personal" allusions Sondheim felt moved to include in the same interview? "My mother was a genuinely monstrous woman, and my father whom I liked a lot, left me in the dragon's lair."[28] Is this play not cast in the very terms in which Sondheim has cast his own childhood and especially his experience of his parents' divorce and its aftermath, involving undoubtedly on the part of all concerned profound feelings of rage and the urge to revenge, about which he has written in other plays and to which he also draws our attention here?[29]

Even Oscar Hammerstein finds a role in this family romance—that of King Aegeus who offers assistance to Medea and her children if she gets herself out of the predicament in which she is stuck on her own (which she does, by the way, atop a "dragon") and brings her offspring safely to Athens (New York?) where the good King reigns? " 'It was Oscar and Dorothy's saving my emotional life, combined with his teaching me' that made all the difference," Kakutani quotes Sondheim as saying.[30] "I was able to turn the experience into the desire to make things. Both to emulate him, as a way of making order out of chaos, and turning revenge into something positive."[31] The scenarios of *Sweeney Todd*, as a negative version of this possibility of revenge gone wrong, and of *Sunday*, as an exploration of making order out of chaos, are hardly far removed.

But if we accept such an account—that in representing the dynamics of Giorgio's relation to Fosca, Sondheim is exploring the conditions of his own birth—an unexpected conclusion follows. To identify Giorgio as a simple stand-in for Sondheim, and to read Giorgio's embracing of Fosca, as Sondheim's romantic embracing of "Love without reason, love without mercy, / Love without pride or shame. / Love unconcerned / With being returned— / No wisdom, no judgement, / No caution, no blame" (122) (as a number of critics seem rather facilely to have done), is to distort the drama Sondheim has scored for us in an especially egregious way, whether we in turn hail that embrace as the triumph of romantic surrender, or denounce it as the descent into psychic turmoil and destruction.

Sondheim in this context is neither simply Giorgio nor Fosca, any more than Euripides in his play is either simply Jason or Medea, but the product of their marriage and its consequences, which is to say, of the matrix of alternating psychological and "military" offenses, defenses, and surrenders which issued in his conception, arrival, seduction, betrayal, and abandonment. If Giorgio becomes Fosca at the play's conclusion—and his scream and mental deterioration certainly suggest as much—Sondheim is imagining one possibility among others (the possibility which would have accrued had his mother died and had he never been born), one which, like *Sweeney Todd*, plays out a course which did *not* in fact occur in his life, but which *might* have occurred had the Fosca of his lived experience had her way (at least in the child's imagination), and, in any event, which his mother's "deathbed" letter specifies. The drama of Medea, which was always a family potential (as he apparently once remarked to Nancy Berg) is averted by imagining an alternative conclusion in which Jason gives up Glauce and Creon and returns to Medea, and the children are allowed to grow up. But that drama remains the classical Greek name for such terms of seduction, betrayal, abandonment, and its aftermath.[32]

The play *Passion*, in other words, is his "letter of understanding." Constructed as the elaborate working out of the details of what would have happened had his mother's wish come true—namely, that he was not "on earth"—and its consequences (that Giorgio would have declared his love for her and she would have died happy)—to the dismay of all the critics—the play becomes a prophetic extension of that personal "deathbed" conversation, the "letter" if you will that Sondheim tells us he "wrote her . . . saying I finally understand." From Hamlet's resentful opening words to his father's brother, "A little more than kin, and less than kind" (1.2.65), Sondheim moves to the perspective defined by Cordelia's words to her parent, words that relinquish all blame and judgement: "No cause, no cause" (4.7.75).

VIII

"You have to pay a consequence
For things that you've denied"

The play, in short, is Sondheim's letter in which he completes his relationship to his mother. He does so by giving her what she wants: not sexuality (which he might as a young man have suspected she wanted) but in the language of that other great theme of psychoanalysis that Freud discovered in the 1920s, the possibility of his own death.[33] "The only regret I have in life," she writes to him, "is giving you birth." He responds by imagining her in a comparable situation, a drama in which a woman who has been spurned and betrayed gains the object of her desire against seemingly impossible odds: she gets her man and acquires as a result feelings of fulfillment and completion—even if it means he never gets to be born.

It is an outcome that in the end surprisingly transforms him. Gaining the object of her desire, feeling loved and fulfilled, she finds she can renounce the poisonous self-pity and self-hate she has been "nursing" all these years, and that that renunciation can in turn engender his. Giving up her self-hate (which has been among other things a form of attack against him), she allows him to give up his defense against her. He is thereby freed to love her (and others) on his own (and on their own) merit. It is perhaps not the smallest irony of the play that it is through imagining the cessation of his own existence that he is led to his own rebirth and consequently to freedom and the construction of his own passion. He is suddenly able to live and imaginatively give birth in turn. Beginning as Giorgio who pens her desires without endorsing them, he ends as Fosca who wishfully rewrites or revises the desires of others only to find that the display of such a gesture (as a letter which is not a letter) effects a revision of her own desire, one that now inspires in her, just before her own death, a new desire to live and to love.

The mother knot is undone, in other words, not by cutting it off, nor by denying its existence, but by tracing it to its origins and untying it: by recognizing, as the "Mysterious Man" says at the end of *Into The Woods*, that "every knot was once straight rope" (133).[34] As in Woody Allen's *Oedipus Wrecks*, Albert Brooks' *Mother*, or Harlan Ellison's "Shatterday," the lesson available in *Passion* is that the problem is solved only by giving the mother what she wants, a gesture that strips the woman of her demonic powers and renders her "ordinary" (to use another word from *Into the Woods*), just another individual with assets and liabilities, not unlike the child himself.[35] It is perhaps not coincidental that this insight is purchased in *Passion* at the price of the child's own imagined demise, a demise the denial of which has been perhaps the cornerstone of the child's own earlier perspective (if we are to read Fosca's song as applicable to Sondheim) and the acknowledgement of which signals the possibility of new creative life. Granting his mother her desires grants him his desire, his own passion, which grants him in turn his freedom—to love, to desire without the encumbrance of the mother knot. This is love *à la lettre*, we may say, a dramatistic literalism on Sondheim's part that exceeds the boundaries of conscious or unconscious dream language, and that joins the efforts of other literary writers in a mode we have characterized as prophetic.

And the question with which we opened this discussion of the play— why does Giorgio give up Clara for Fosca—finds an approach in its deconstruction and reformulation. He does not give up Clara for Fosca. He turns to Fosca out of an appeal that exceeds his customary romantic and dutiful affiliations. And if the play is redemptive finally, its celebration derives neither from endorsing nor denouncing (or even neutrally representing) the painful psychological drama it registers but from its prophetic extension of that prior drama that it both symptomatically reenacts and completes. The passage of Giorgio from Clara to Fosca, which is the story of *Passion*, is also, it turns out, the "story" of Stephen Sondheim.

The play is indeed, then, as John Lahr says, about "love," "letters," and "reading"—although Lahr offers the remark as a criticism. It is an "epistolary musical" at a fundamental and autobiographical level and Sondheim's observation in the *New York Times* underlines the relation between *Passion* and his own real-life circumstances, a relation that is at once synchronic and diachronic. Lying on her bed, thinking that "she was going to die" under the heart surgeon's knife, that she would have, in Lahr's words, "not the big heart, but the dead heart," Sondheim's mother (as Sondheim tells it) does what in her view "many mothers going in for open-heart surgery" do, namely, "write their children a letter," one in this case in which she expresses "regret" that the "dead heart" is not the child's. And that child, who has been accused by critics (like Lahr), ironically, of the same "dead heart," scores the play which grants her her fantasy—that he not exist, and that, against all rhyme and reason, the man with whom she falls in love falls in love with her in return and she dies happy. This is an "open-heart surgery" of an entirely different order. "Not dancing but reading," as Lahr puts it so well.

"I'm gonna sit right down and write myself a letter," the popular 1940s American song goes, "And make believe it came from you." Sondheim's dramatization in *Passion* of this milieu from which his own music in part derives draws our attention to social, cultural, and psychological potentials we might not otherwise have suspected, potentials which document in a post war setting the kinds of narcissistic wounds that spawned in turn the kinds of child-rearing practices in which individuals like Stephen Sondheim were raised (and about which psychologists like Alice Miller write so powerfully).[36] It is a tribute to his candor and courage that he is able in this play to confront these one-act dramas his characters have been acting out, and work through them in a manner that is genuinely liberating to all concerned.

IX
"What's love unless it's unconditional?"

The circle is now complete. The process begun in *West Side Story* ("they didn't want to have me," one of the gang members sings, "But somehow I was had"), completes itself in *Passion*. Distinguishing himself from Fosca and Giorgio by identifying himself as their issue, he consequently becomes them. He repeats the gesture first of Giorgio and then of Fosca, and he owns that set of gestures as the course of his artistic life. And becoming them, he completes his relationship to them and gains genuine independence from them. He leaves with regard to them, we may say, "nothing to be desired."

The spell has been broken. The children may leave the tower in which they have been imprisoned. The disclosure has been made. "Wishes are children" (136). They have consequences, and those consequences assume a life of their own. "Wishes come true, / Not free" (136). They also have parents. And those parents are also themselves children struggling with their own progenitors. The company of fairy tale characters (in another of "Sondheim's recent experiments with . . . James Lapine," to quote Lahr again), who have been spending their lives living by definition the scripts of others, now understand all this. The witch is disempowered and has become "ordinary" (76) simply another woman, one who would admittedly sacrifice a child for her own well-being, but nonetheless one who was also a mother with maternal cares of her own ("Children can only grow," she sings, "From something you love / To something you lose" [106]), and as well, a child with her own mother, into whose fury she flies to her death. The father, who disappears and reappears, and who may even be a figment of the son's imagination, acknowledges that "We disappoint, / We leave a mess, / We die but we don't . . ." (124), and the son is then able to admit to him "Like father, like son" (124). A child, whose birth has been alternatively "awaited" and an object of "regret," can now grow up, and another can learn to parent a child of his own.

Despite the controversy surrounding it, Sondheim's most recent musical play, I would suggest, has the feel of a breakthrough, although it may not be the one critics think it is. Is *Passion* "about how the force of somebody's feelings for you can crack you open"? Undoubtedly. But less (if we are to believe what Sondheim tells us) the feelings of Fosca for Giorgio (at least initially), I have tried to suggest, than those of the figures in Sondheim's life from whom his own existence has come and with whom he has endlessly struggled (and of which the relationship between these imagined characters is an extension). "For now I'm seeing love," Sondheim writes, "Like none I've ever known, / A love as pure as breath, / As permanent as death, / Implacable as stone. / A love that, like a knife, / Has cut into a life / I wanted left alone" (61). "I'm happier now personally," Sondheim notes, "than I have ever been."[37]

Love, letters, and reading. "Children may not obey," the Witch sings at the conclusion of *Into the Woods*, "But children will listen. / Children will look to you / For which way to turn, / To learn what to be. . . Careful the tale you tell. / *That* is the spell" (136). In the light of *Passion*, Stephen Sondheim's words from earlier plays concerning emulation or imitative desire and its disclosure begin to read like autobiography. It must be liberating for him at sixty-eight, having survived a heart attack of his own, to be able at last to speak and write so openly and so honestly about such generative and (generational) dynamics, as if, having unburdened himself of years of torment (an unburdening which critics in their inimitable way ironically mistake for the very romantic attitudes he is critically examining) he can finally take some pleasure in his life.

"Our lives aren't scripted," he cautions.[38] That is, of course, a lesson Fosca learns only in her final moments, and one which Sondheim himself attests he learned only "after a struggle," and "a lot of pain."[39] Whether those who read Sondheim as a purveyor of commonplace scripts about American life will finally learn it and free themselves from their passionate and obsessive repetitions of his subject matter remains to be seen. But in the meanwhile, we may celebrate with him whole-heartedly the "richness" and readiness he feels his life has now acquired, the joy he has given all of us who so admire what he's done, and the love which his songs and "one-act dramas" so brilliantly, so plentifully, and now so overtly express.

NOTES

[1] An earlier version of this essay, entitled "The Mother's Part: Stephen Sondheim's *Passion*", was delivered as a talk at an Associated Meeting of the Ars Lyrica Society Modern Language Association Convention in Chicago, December 1995, "Counting in Stephen Sondheim." An abbreviated version of that MLA talk, entitled

"Open Heart Surgery: Commentary on Sondheim's *Passion*," appeared in *Jezebel Magazine* Vol. 1, Issue 1 (October 1996), 13, 29, 37.

[2] Evans 1997, 1869.

[3] Lapine and Sondheim 1994.

[4] I worked on the first issue of *The Sondheim Review*, Vol. I, No. 1 (Summer 1994), as associate editor.

[5] Eric Besner discusses some of those changes in Besner 1994, 5.

[6] *The New York Times*, Sunday May 15, 1994, H 11.

[7] Richards 1994, 19.

[8] Lahr 1994, 89.

[9] Secrest 1998, 382.

[10] A question about the play posed to Sondheim (compiled by Bruce Janiga, a writer for the "Stephen Sondheim Stage" website), seems to misread the play in just such a fashion. In "Side by Side with Sondheim" (http://www.sondheim.com/interview/cyber.html) we read the following: "I saw Passion [sic] in previews and the audience reaction was decidedly mixed. (I saw it on April 20.) It seems that the audience had problems with Fosca's passive-aggressive behavior, and so do I. Isn't her love too obsessive to be held up as something to be lauded as noble (or, worse, as something to be emulated?)? Certainly her love, unrestrained by reason, leads her to insanity and death. Is the audience supposed to find this noble or praiseworthy? Shouldn't love be tempered by some reason?" The following response is attributed to Sondheim. "Obviously, I don't agree with you and what you assume the audience had problems with. I don't think that's what they have problems with so much. But the point is, you say, 'isn't her love too obsessive to be held up as something to be lauded as noble?' When do I call it noble? When do I laud it? I'm writing about it. '. . . as something to be lauded,' you say, 'or worse, as something to be emulated.' Where do I say it should be emulated? You're reading things in. . . .'"

[11] Kakutani 1994, 1.

[12] See Girard 1965 and 1991. The phrase "disease that would cripple us all" occurs in Kakutani. See Kakutani 1994, 30.

[13] Lahr 1994, 89.

[14] The classic study of the origins of the novel in England is Ian Watt's *Rise of the Novel*. See Watt 1957.

[15] See, for example, "The Agency of the Letter in the Unconscious or Reason Since Freud," and "The Purloined Letter" of Lacan (1972 and 1977), and *The Post Card* of Derrida (1987). For a casebook of essays on Lacan's seminar on "The Purloined Letter" and response, see Muller and Richardson 1988.

[16] Freud gives an overall account of psychoanalysis including the use he makes of dreams in the lectures he delivered to Clark University. See Freud 1953.

[17] Freud's theory of dreams is articulated in *The Interpretation of Dreams*. See especially chapter 7. See Freud 1955.

[18] "My original intention, which like most good intentions disappeared quickly, was to open the show with the major love song, the moment of great ecstasy which or-

dinarily would occur later on, and then end the show with the same song, only this time with Fosca and Giorgio in bed" (6). See Sondheim 1995, 3-13.

[19] The posters for the recent revival of *Carousel* at Lincoln Center in 1994, showing a barker holding onto two carousel horses that are rearing out of control, suggested that potentials for rage and violence were already a part of the Rodgers and Hammerstein play.

[20] Kakutani 1994, 30-1. This anecdote is retold in Secrest 1998, 271.

[21] Annette Grant's essay appears in the magazine section of the same edition of the *New York Times* in which the Kakutani interview appears. See Grant 1994, 42-5.

[22] Secrest notes that the rift it occasioned was never resolved during his mother's lifetime. See Secrest 1998, 270.

[23] See Kakutani 1994, 30. See also Secrest 1998, 30-2, 34-6.

[24] On this point as well, Sondheim and Lapine seem to have deviated from their sources. In Tarchetti, Fosca gives birth to a child. See Tarchetti 1994, 112-14.

[25] Kakutani 1994, 30.

[26] See *The Unbearable Lightness of Being* (Kundera 1984).

[27] Scola's Fosca is "virtually a sight gag," Canby writes. See Canby 1994, 5. For a discussion of women's laments in classical Greece, see Holst-Warhaft 1992.

[28] Kakutani 1998, 30.

[29] See Nancy Berg's comment in Secrest 1998, 170.

[30] Kakutani 1994, 31.

[31] Kakutani 1994, 31.

[32] See Secrest 1998, 170.

[33] For a recent biography of Freud, see Gay 1988. *Beyond the Pleasure Principle*, which was first published in 1923, introduces the "death wish." See Freud 1950.

[34] *The Mother Knot* is the title of a book by Jane Lazarre (Lazarre 1997). *A Mother's Kisses* is the title of a book by Bruce Jay Friedman (Friedman 1964).

[35] The Woody Allen movie was the third short film of *New York Stories* (Allen 1989). For the Albert Brooks film, see Brooks 1997. For the Harlan Ellison story, see Ellison 1980.

[36] See, for example, *The Drama of the Gifted Child* (Miller 1981).

[37] Kakutani 1994, 30.

[38] Kakutani 1994, 31.

[39] Kakutani 1994, 30.

Works Cited

Abrams, M. H. "Art-as-Such: The Sociology of Modern Aesthetics." *Bulletin of the American Academy of Arts and Sciences* 38/6 (1985), 8-33.

Abrams, M. H. *Doing Things with Texts: Essays in Criticism and Critical Theory.* New York: W.W. Norton, 1989.

Abrams, M. H. *Natural Supernaturalism.* New York: W.W. Norton, 1971.

Adler, Thomas P. *Mirror on the Stage: The Pulitzer Plays as an Approach to American Drama.* West Lafayette, IN: Purdue UP, 1987.

Adler, Thomas P. "The Musical Dramas of Stephen Sondheim: Some Critical Approaches," *Journal of Popular Culture* 12/3 (Winter 1978), 513-25.

Albee, Edward. *A Delicate Balance.* New York: Pocket Books, 1967.

Allen, Woody, dir. *Oedipus Wrecks.* New York Stories. Videorecording. Hollywood: Touchstone Home Video, 1989.

Altman, Rick, ed. *Genre: The Musical.* New York: Routledge, 1981.

Andrew, Dudley. *Concepts in Film Theory.* Oxford: Oxford UP, 1984.

Aronson, Lisa, and Rich, Frank. *The Theatre Art of Boris Aronson.* New York: Knopf, 1987.

Azenberg, Emanuel. "An Interview: Producing Broadway Musicals," *Yale/Theatre* 4/3 (Summer 1973), 99.

Banfield, Stephen. *Sondheim's Broadway Musicals.* Ann Arbor: University of Michigan Press, 1993.

Barber, C. L. *Shakespeare's Festive Comedy: A Study of Dramatic Form and its Relation to Social Custom.* Princeton: Princeton UP, 1959.

Barnes, Clive, "*Company* Offers a Guide to New York's Marital Jungle. Alvin May Have Hit in a Lean Season," *New York Times* (27 April 1970), reprinted in *New York Theatre Critics' Reviews 1970,* 261-62.

Barnes, Clive, "Stage: Follies' Couples, Years Later, *New York Times* (5 April 1971), 44, 49.

Bennett, Michael, Nicholas Dante, Marvin Hamlisch, James Kirkland, and Edward Kleban, *A Chorus Line*. The Book of the Musical. New York: Applause Books, 1995.

Bentley, Eric. *The Playwright as Thinker*. New York: Meridian Books, 1957.

Bergman, Ingmar. *Smiles of a Summer Night*. In *Four Screenplays of Ingmar Bergman*. Translated by Lars Malmstrom and David Kushner. New York: Simon and Schuster, 1960.

Besner, Eric. "How *Passion* Changed During Those Previews," *The Sondheim Review* 1/1 (Summer 1994), 5.

Bettelheim, Bruno. *The Uses of Enchantment*. *The Meaning and Importance of Fairy Tales*. New York: Random House, 1977.

Bigsby, C. W. E. *Modern American Drama 1945-1990*. Cambridge: Cambridge UP, 1992.

Block, Jane. "Pointillism." In Turner 1996, 78.

Booth, Wayne. *Rhetoric of Fiction*. Chicago: University of Chicago Press, 1983.

Boris Aronson: From His Theatre Work. Exhibition Catalogue. New York Public Library, 1981.

Bowie, Malcolm. *Lacan*. Cambridge, MA: Harvard UP, 1991.

Brecht, Bertolt. "Street Scene. A Basic Model for an Epic Theatre." In Willett 1964, 121-29.

Brook, Peter. *The Empty Space*. New York: Atheneum, 1980.

Brooks, Albert, Dir. *Mother*. Videorecording. Hollywood: Paramount Home Video, 1997.

Canby, Vincent. "Admirers and Fans, Take Note: *Passion* Will Divide You," *New York Times* (15 May 1994), 5, 11, 13.

Carlson, Marvin. *Theories of the Theater: An Historical and Critical Survey from the Greeks to the Present*. Ithaca: Cornell UP, 1993.

Clurman, Harold. "Theater." *Nation* (18 April 1971), NYPL Clipping Folder.

"A Conversation with Stephen Sondheim and James Lapine" with Edwin Newman. PBS Television, 1990.

Derrida, Jacques. *The Post Card: From Socrates to Freud and Beyond*. Chicago: University of Chicago Press, 1987.

Dyer, Richard. "Entertainment and Utopia." In *Only Entertainment*. New York: Routledge, 1992.

Ellison, Harlan. *Shatterday*. Boston: Houghton Mifflin, 1980.

Evans, G. Blakemore, ed. *The Riverside Shakespeare*. Second Edition. Boston: Houghton Mifflin, 1997.

Feuer, Jane. *The Hollywood Musical*. Bloomington: Indiana UP, 1982.

Foucault, Michel. *The Order of Things*. New York: Random House, 1970.

Fowles, John. *The French Lieutenant's Woman*. Boston: Little, Brown, 1969.

Frazer, Sir James George. *The New Golden Bough*. Edited by Theodor H. Gaster. New York: Phillips, 1959.

Freud, Sigmund. *Beyond the Pleasure Principle*. New York: Liveright, 1950.

Freud, Sigmund. *General Introduction to Psychoanalysis*. New York: Pocket Books, 1953.

Freud, Sigmund. *The Interpretation of Dreams*. New York: Basic Books, 1955.

Friedman, Bruce Jay. *A Mother's Kisses*. New York: Simon and Schuster, 1964.

Frye, Northrop. *Anatomy of Criticism*. Princeton: Princeton UP. 1957.

Furth, George, and Stephen Sondheim. *Company*. New York: Random House, 1970.

Furth, George, and Stephen Sondheim. *Merrily We Roll Along*. The New Cast Recording. Varèse Sarabande Records, Inc. VSD-5548. 1994.

Furth, George, and Stephen Sondheim. *Merrily We Roll Along*. Original Broadway Cast Recording. RCA Records. RCD1-5840 (recorded Nov. 29, 1981), 1982.

Gado, Frank. *The Passion of Ingmar Bergman*. Durham: Duke UP, 1986.

Garber, Marjorie B. *Dream in Shakespeare: From Metaphor to Metamorphosis*. New Haven: Yale UP, 1974.

Gay, Peter. *Freud: A Life*. New York: Norton, 1988.

Gershwin, George, and Ira Gershwin. "But Not for Me." *Girl Crazy*. 1930. In *Broadway Musicals Show by Show 1930-39*. Milwaukee, WI: Hal Leonard Publications, 1991.

Gershwin, George, and Ira Gershwin. "But Not for Me." *Vocal Selections from Girl Crazy*. New York: Warner Bros., 1984, 17-20.

Gill, Brendan. "The Theater." *New Yorker* (2 May 1970), 83.

Girard, René. *Deceit, Desire, and the Novel*. Baltimore: Johns Hopkins UP, 1965.

Girard, René. *A Theater of Envy: William Shakespeare*. New York: Oxford UP, 1991.

Goldman, James, and Stephen Sondheim. *Follies: A Musical*. New York: Random House, 1971.

Goldman, James, and Stephen Sondheim. *Follies*. New York: Random House, 1971.

Goodhart, Sandor. "'Happily Ever After': The Criticism of Stephen Sondheim," *Ars Lyrica*, VIII (1994), 43-48.

Goodhart, Sandor. "Open Heart Surgery: Commentary on Sondheim's *Passion*," *Jezebel Magazine* Vol. 1, Issue 1 (October 1996), 13, 29, 37.

Goodhart, Sandor. *Sacrificing Commentary. Reading the End of Literature*. Johns Hopkins UP, 1996.

Goodhart, Sandor. "Sondheim on Campus: A Class for Adults." *The Sondheim Review* 1/1 (June 1994), 17.

Gordon, Joanne. *Art Isn't Easy. The Achievement of Stephen Sondheim*. Carbondale and Edwardsville: Southern Illinois UP, 1990.

Gordon, Joanne. *Art Isn't Easy: The Theater of Stephen Sondheim*. Updated Edition. New York: Da Capo, 1992.

Gordon, Joanne, ed. *Stephen Sondheim: A Casebook*. New York and London: Garland Publishing, Inc. 1997.

Gottfried, Martin. "Flipping Over *Follies*," *New York Times* (25 April 1971), Section 2: 1, 14.

Gottfried, Martin. *Sondheim*. New York: Harry N. Abrams, 1993.

Gottfried, Martin. "Theater. *Follies . . .* 'monumental'," *Women's Wear Daily* (5 April 1971), reprinted in *New York Theatre Critics' Reviews 1971*, 310-11.

Gottfried, Martin. "Theater. *A Little Night Music*," *Women's Wear Daily* (26 February 1973), reprinted in *New York Theatre Critics' Reviews 1973*, 349.

Gottfried, Martin. "The Theater," *Women's Wear Daily* (27 April 1970), reprinted in *New York Theatre Critics' Reviews 1970*, 261.

Gottfried, Martin. "Why is Broadway Music so Bad?" *Yale/Theatre*, 4/3 (Summer 1973), 90.

Grant, Annette. "Line by Line by Sondheim," *New York Times* (20 March 1994), Magazine, 42-45.

Green, Stanley. *The World of Musical Comedy.* London: Tantivy, 1980.

Guernsey, O. L. Jr., ed. *Playwrights, Lyricists, Composers in Theater.* New York, 1974.

Gussow, Mel. "*Company* Anew," *New York Times* (29 July 1970), NYPL Clipping Folder.

Gussow, Mel. "Prince Recalls the Evolution of *Follies*," *New York Times* (9 April 1971), NYPL Clipping Folder.

Gussow, Mel. "Sondheim Scores with *Company* Anew," *New York Times* (28 April 1970), 50.

Haber, Joyce, "Hal Prince: The Brat About Town Makes Good," *LA Times* (30 May 1971), Calendar, 11.

Harris, Leonard. "*Company.*" WCBS TV2 (26 April 1970), reprinted in *New York Theatre Critics' Reviews 1970*, 264.

Harris, Leonard. "*Follies.*" WCBS TV2 (4 April 1971), reprinted in *New York Theatre Critics' Reviews 1971*, 314.

Harris, Leonard. "*A Little Night Music.*" WCBS TV2 (25 February 1973), reprinted in *New York Theatre Critics' Reviews 1973*, 352.

Hewes, Henry. "The Theater," *Saturday Review* (1 May 1971), 16.

Hewes, Henry. "The Theater," *Saturday Review* (9 May 1970), 4.

Highlights from Sweeney Todd. RCA Records, 1979.

Hirsch, Foster. *Harold Prince and the American Musical Theatre.* Cambridge: Cambridge UP, 1989.

Holland, Peter, ed. *A Midsummer Night's Dream.* By William Shakespeare. Oxford: Clarendon, 1994.

Holst-Warhaft, Gail. *Dangerous Voices: Women's Laments and Greek Literature.* New York: Routledge, 1992.

Hunter, G. K. *William Shakespeare: The Later Comedies.* London: Longmans, 1962.

Ilson, Carol. *Harold Prince. From PAJAMA GAME to PHANTOM OF THE OPERA.* Ann Arbor: University Microfilms Inc. Press, 1989.

Jagendorf, Zvi. *The Happy End of Comedy.* London: Associated University Presses, 1984.

Jameson, Frederic. *Marxism and Form.* Princeton: Princeton UP, 1971.

Jenkins, Henry. *What Made Pistachio Nuts? Early Sound Comedy and the Vaudeville Aesthetic.* New York : Columbia UP, 1992.

Kakutani, Michiko. "Sondheim's Passionate *Passion*," *New York Times* (20 March 1994), Arts and Leisure Section: 1, 30-31.

Kalem, T. E., "Floating World," *Time*, Jan., 26, 1976, 46.

Kalem, T. E. "The Theater. Seascape With Frieze of Girls." *Time* (12 April 1971), reprinted in *New York Theatre Critics' Reviews 1971*, 312.

Kalem, T. E. "The Theater. *Valse Triste. A Little Night Music*." *Time* (12 March 1973), reprinted in *New York Theatre Critics' Reviews 1973*, 351.

Kanfer, Stefan, et al. "The Once and Future *Follies*," *Time* (3 May 1971), 70-4.

Kaufman, George S., and Moss Hart. *Merrily We Roll Along*. New York: Random House, 1934.

Kaufmann, Stanley. "*Company*," *New Republic* (23 May 1970), 20.

Kaufmann, Stanley, "Stanley Kaufmann on Theater," *New Republic* (8 May 1971), 24-37.

Kelly, Kevin. "You're in Brilliant *Company*," *Boston Globe* (25 March 1970), NYPL Clipping Folder.

Kerr, Walter. "*Company*: Original and Uncompromising," *Sunday Times* (3 May 1970), reprinted in *New York Theatre Critics' Reviews 1970*, 263-64.

Kerr, Walter, "Yes, Yes Alexis! No, No 'Follies!'," *New York Times* (5 April 1971), 2:1.

Kosinski, Jerzy. *The Painted Bird*. New York: Houghton Mifflin, 1978.

Kroll, Jack. "Backstage in Arcadia," *Newsweek* (12 April 1971), reprinted in *New York Theatre Critics' Reviews 1971*, 311-12.

Kroll, Jack. "Libido Among the Birches," *Newsweek* (12 March 1973), reprinted in *New York Theatre Critics' Reviews 1973*, 350-51.

Kundera, Milan. *The Unbearable Lightness of Being*. New York: Harper and Row, 1984.

Lacan, Jacques. "The Agency of the Letter in the Unconscious or Reason Since Freud," *Ecrits: A Selection*, edited by Alan Sheridan (New York: Norton, 1977), 146-78.

Lacan, Jacques. "The Purloined Letter," *Yale French Studies* 48 (1972), 38-72.

Lacan, Jacques. *The Seminar of Jacques Lacan. Book II*. Translated by Sylvana Tomaselli. New York: W. W. Norton, 1991.

Lahr, John. "Love in Gloom." *New Yorker* (23 May 1994), 89-92.

Lahr, John. "On-Stage," *Village Voice* (7 May 1970), 15.

Lapine, James, and Stephen Sondheim. *Into the Woods: A Musical*. (Original Cast Performance). PBS Television, 1990.

Lapine, James, and Stephen Sondheim. *Into the Woods: A New Musical*. (Original Cast Recording). BMG Music, 1988.

Lapine, James, and Stephen Sondheim. *Into the Woods*. New York: Theater Communications Group, 1987.

Lapine, James, and Stephen Sondheim. *Into the Woods*. New York: Theater Communications Group, 1992.

Lapine, James, and Stephen Sondheim. *Passion: A Musical*. New York: Theatre Communications Group, 1994.

Lapine, James, and Stephen Sondheim. *Sunday in the Park with George. A Musical.* Original Cast Recording. RCA Records (RCDI-5042) Compact Disc Digital Audio, 1984.

Lapine, James, and Stephen Sondheim. *Sunday in the Park with George.* New York: Applause Theatre Books, 1991.

Laroque, François. *Shakespeare's Festive World: Elizabethan Seasonal Entertainment and the Professional Stage.* Trans. Janet Lloyd. Cambridge: Cambridge UP, 1991.

Laurents, Arthur, and Stephen Sondheim. *Anyone Can Whistle.* New York: Random House, 1965.

Laurents, Arthur, Richard Rodgers, and Stephen Sondheim. *Do I Hear a Waltz?* New York: Random House, 1966.

Laurents, Arthur, Stephen Sondheim, Leonard Spigelgass, and Jule Styne. *Gypsy.* In Richards 1973, 331-90.

Lazarre, Jane. *The Mother Knot.* Durham: Duke University Press, 1997.

Lévi-Strauss, Claude. *The Savage Mind.* Chicago: University of Chicago Press, 1960.

Mangan, Michael. *A Preface to Shakespeare's Comedies: 1594-1603.* London: Longman, 1996.

Mankin, Nina. "Contemporary Performance: The Emergence of the Fairy Tale." In *Performing Arts Journal,* 11/1 (1991), 48-53.

McEntee, Ann Marie. "The Funeral of *Follies.* Stephen Sondheim and the Razing of American Musical Theater." *Ars Lyrica,* VIII (1994), 49-62.

McEntee, Ann Marie. "[Review of] *Unsung Sondheim,*" *The Sondheim Review* 1/1 (June 1994), 29.

McMillin, Scott. "Martin Gottfried's *Sondheim,*" *The Sondheim Review* 1/1 (June 1994), 28.

Menton, Allen W. "Maternity, Madness, and Art in the Theater of Stephen Sondheim." *Ars Lyrica,* VIII (1994), 75-92.

Menton, Allen W. "Stephen Banfield's *Sondheim's Broadway Musicals,*" *The Sondheim Review* 1/1 (June 1994), 27.

Michener, Charles, et al. "Words and Music by Sondheim," *Newsweek* (23 April 1973), 55.

Miller, Alice. *The Drama of the Gifted Child.* New York: Basic Books, 1981.

Mollin, Alfred. "Mayhem and Morality in *Sweeney Todd,*" *American Music* (Winter 1991), 405-17.

Mondello, Bob. "Now, not one, but two new CDs for *Merrily,*" *The Sondheim Review* 1/3 (Winter 1995), 27-8.

Muller, John P. and William J. Richardson. *Purloined Poe: Lacan, Derrida, and Psychoanalytic Reading.* Baltimore: Johns Hopkins University Press, 1988.

Newman, Edwin. "*Company.*" NBC 4 TV (26 April 1970), reprinted in *New York Theatre Critics' Reviews 1970,* 264.

O'Conner, John J. "The Theater. *Company,*" *The Wall Street Journal* (28 April 1970), reprinted in *New York Theatre Critics' Reviews 1970,* 262.

O'Neill, Eugene. *Long Day's Journey Into Night.* New Haven: Yale UP, 1956.

Passion: Original Broadway Cast Recording. Capital Cities. Angel Records, 1994.

Popkin, Henry. "The Theater." *The Wall Street Journal* (7 April 1971), reprinted in *New York Theatre Critics' Reviews 1971*, 312-13.

Prince, Harold. *Contradictions: Notes on Twenty-Six Years in the Theater.* New York: Dodd, Mead, & Co., 1974.

Probst, Leonard. "*Follies.*" NBC 4 TV (4 April 1971), reprinted in *New York Theatre Critics' Reviews 1971*, 313.

Probst, Leonard. "*A Little Night Music.*" NBC (25 February 1973), reprinted in *New York Theatre Critics' Reviews 1973*, 352.

Propp, Vladimir. *The Morphology of the Folktale.* Austin: University of Texas, 1958.

Rich, Frank. "A Musical Theater Breakthrough," *The New York Times Magazine* (21 October 1984), 52-4, 58, 60-72.

Richards, David. "Sondheim Explores the Heart's Terrain," *New York Times* (10 May 1994), The Arts, C15, 19.

Richards, Stanley, ed. *Ten Great Musicals of the American Theatre.* Radnor, Pa.: The Chilton Book Co., 1973.

Salinger, Leo. *Shakespeare and the Traditions of Comedy.* Cambridge: Cambridge UP, 1974.

Sartre, Jean Paul. *Huis Clos.* Edited by Jacques Hardré and George B. Daniel. New York: Appleton-Century Crofts, 1962.

Schiff, Stephen. "Deconstructing Sondheim." *New Yorker* (8 March 1993), 76-87.

Schubeck, John. "*Follies.*" WABC TV7 (4 April 1971), reprinted in *New York Theatre Critics' Reviews 1971*, 313.

Scola, Ettore, dir. *Passione d'amore.* 1981. Translated as *Passion of Love.*

Secrest, Meryle. *Stephen Sondheim: A Life.* New York: Alfred A. Knopf, 1998.

Shakespeare, William. *A Midsummer Night's Dream.* 1594-96. *The Complete Signet Classic Shakespeare.* Ed. and intro. by Sylvan Barnet. New York: Harcourt, 1972.

Shakespeare, William. *A Midsummer Night's Dream.* In Evans 1997.

Shakespeare, William. "Sonnet 143." In Evans 1997.

Shakespeare, William. *The Tempest.* In Evans 1997.

Shakespeare, William. *The Winter's Tale.* In Evans 1997.

Shepard, Eugenia. "Flossie's Follies," *New York Post* (30 March 1971), 39.

Shevelove, Burt, and Stephen Sondheim. *The Frogs.* Chicago: The Dramatic Publishing Co., 1975.

Shevelove, Burt, Larry Gelbart, and Stephen Sondheim. *A Funny Thing Happened on the Way to the Forum.* New York: Applause Theatre Book Publishers, 1991.

Side by Side By Sondheim, RCA Victor, 1851-2-RG, 1976.

Simon, John. "*Follies,*" *New York* (19 April 1971), 41.

Sommarnattens Leende. Smiles of a Summer Night. Directed by Ingmar Bergman. Svensk Filmindustri, 1955.

Sondheim, Stephen. "I Never Do Anything Twice." In *Side by Side By Sondheim*, 1976.

Sondheim, Stephen, "Letter," *The Sondheim Review* 1/2 (Fall 1994), 2.

Sondheim, Stephen. "The Musical Theater: A Talk by Stephen Sondheim," *Dramatists Guild Quarterly* 15 (Fall, 1978), 6-29.

Sondheim, Stephen. "Sondheim on *Passion* and Writing for the Musical Theater." *Dramatist Guild Quarterly*, 31/3 (Autumn 1995), 3-13.

Sondheim, Stephen. "Theater Lyrics." In Guernsey 1974, 61-97.

Sondheim, Stephen, and Hugh Wheeler. *A Little Night Music*. Introduction by Jonathan Tunick. New York: Applause, 1991.

Sondheim, Stephen, and Hugh Wheeler. *Sweeney Todd: The Demon Barber of Fleet Street*. New York: Applause Theatre Book Publishers, 1991a.

Sondheim, Stephen, and John Weidman. *Assassins*. New York: Theater Communications Group, 1991.

Sondheim, Stephen, and John Weidman. *Pacific Overtures*. New York: Theater Communications Group, 1991a.

Sondheim, Stephen, and Jule Styne. *Gypsy*. In Richards 1973, 331-90.

Sondheim: A Celebration at Carnegie Hall. RCA Victor (09026-61516-2), 1993.

Sondheim: A Musical Tribute. Original Cast Recording. Warner Brothers Records (2W S2705), 11 March 1973.

Spurgeon, Caroline F. E. *Shakespeare's Imagery and What It Tells Us*. Cambridge: Cambridge UP, 1935.

Staples, Shirley. *Male–Female Comedy Teams in American Vaudeville 1865-1932*. Ann Arbor: UMI Research Press, 1984.

Strutt, Joseph. *The Sports and Pastimes of the People of England*. Edited by William Hone. London: Chatto and Windus, 1876.

Sweeney Todd, The Demon Barber of Fleet Street. RKO Home Video, 1984.

Tarchetti, Iginio Ugo, *Fosca*. 1869. See Venuti 1994.

Tatar, Maria. *Off with Their Heads! Fairytales and the Culture of Childhood*. Princeton, NJ: Princeton University, 1992.

Thomas, Dylan. *Under Milk Wood*. New York: New Directions, 1954.

Thompson, David. "Liner Notes." In *Sondheim: A Celebration* 1993, 5-8.

Time, "A Precious Fancy," March 1973, 58-9.

Tolliver, Melba. "*A Little Night Music*." WABC TV7 (25 February 1973), reprinted in *New York Theatre Critics' Reviews 1973*, 352.

Turner, Jane. *The Dictionary of Art*, XXV. New York: Macmillan Publishers Limited, 1996.

Van Leer, David. "Putting It Together: Sondheim and the Broadway Musical," *Raritan* (1987) 7: 113-128.

Venuti, Lawrence, ed. *Passion: A Novel*. San Francisco: Mercury House, 1994. Translation of Tarchetti 1869.

Watt, Douglas. "*Company* Has Brilliant Fun with Couples in Manhattan," *Daily News* (27 April 1970), reprinted in *New York Theatre Critics' Reviews 1970*, 260.

Watt, Douglas. "*Follies* Is a Stunning Musical About an Eerie Stage Reunion," *Daily News* (5 April 1971), reprinted in *New York Theatre Critics' Reviews 1971*, 310.

Watt, Douglas. "*A Little Night Music*, Operetta That's Exquisite But Fragile," *Daily News* (26 February 1973), reprinted in *New York Theatre Critics' Reviews 1973*, 348.

Watt, Douglas. "Sondheim–Prince Team Scores for Second Time," *New York Daily News* (11 April 1971), S3.

Watt, Ian. *Rise of the Novel*. University of California Press, 1957.

Watts, Richard. "Happy Evening in Sweden," *New York Post* (26 February 1973), reprinted in *New York Theatre Critics' Reviews 1973*, 348-49.

Watts, Richard. "Theater. Lesson From the Married Set," *New York Post* (27 April 1970), reprinted in *New York Theatre Critics' Reviews 1970*, 260.

Watts, Richard. "When Everything Goes Right," *New York Post* (5 April 1971), reprinted in *New York Theatre Critics' Reviews 1971*, 309.

Wellek, René, and Austin Warren. *Theory of Literature*. Harcourt, Brace, and World, 1970.

Welsford, Enid. *The Court Masque: A Study in the Relationship Between Poetry and the Revels*. New York: Russell, 1962.

Willett, John, ed. *Brecht on Theatre. The Development of an Aesthetic*. Translated by John Willett. New York: Hill & Wang, 1964.

Wilson, Edwin. "A Musical Show with Elegance," *The Wall Street Journal* (27 February 1973), reprinted in *New York Theatre Critics' Reviews 1973*, 350.

Wood, Robin. "Art and Ideology: Notes on *Silk Stockings*." In Altman 1981, 57-69.

Wood, Robin. "Art and Ideology: Notes on *Silk Stockings*," *Film Comment* 11/3 (May-June 1975), 28-31.

Young, David. *Something of Great Constancy: The Art of A Midsummer Night's Dream*. New Haven: Yale UP, 1966.

Young, Kay. "'Every Day a Little Death': Sondheim's Un-Musicaling of Marriage," *Ars Lyrica* 8 (1994), 63-74.

Young, Kay. "[Review of] *Putting It Together*." *The Sondheim Review* 1/1 (June 1994), 28-9.

Zadan, Craig. *Sondheim & Co*. Second Edition. New York: Harper & Row, 1986.

Zadan, Craig. *Sondheim & Co*. Second Edition, Updated. New York: Da Capo Press, 1994.

Zadan, Craig. *Sondheim and Co*. London: Pavilion, 1987.

Index